CONEY ISLAND

ALSO BY WILLIAM J. PHALEN
AND FROM MCFARLAND

How the Telegraph Changed the World (2015)

*The Consequences of Cotton
in Antebellum America* (2014)

*American Evangelical Protestantism
and European Immigrants, 1800–1924* (2011)

Coney Island

*150 Years of Rides,
Fires, Floods, the Rich, the Poor
and Finally Robert Moses*

William J. Phalen

McFarland & Company, Inc., Publishers
Jefferson, North Carolina

Maps by Susan A. McDermott

LIBRARY OF CONGRESS CATALOGUING-IN-PUBLICATION DATA

Names: Phalen, William J., 1942– author.
Title: Coney Island : 150 years of rides, fires, floods, the rich, the poor and finally Robert Moses / William J. Phalen.
Description: Jefferson, North Carolina : McFarland & Company, Inc., Publishers, 2016. | Includes bibliographical references and index.
Identifiers: LCCN 2016022319 | ISBN 9780786498161 (softcover : acid free paper) ∞
Subjects: LCSH: Coney Island (New York, N.Y.)—History.
Classification: LCC F129.C75 P47 2016 | DDC 974.7/23—dc23
LC record available at https://lccn.loc.gov/2016022319

BRITISH LIBRARY CATALOGUING DATA ARE AVAILABLE

ISBN (print) 978-0-7864-9816-1
ISBN (ebook) 978-1-4766-2373-3

© 2016 William J. Phalen. All rights reserved

No part of this book may be reproduced or transmitted in any form or by any means, electronic or mechanical, including photocopying or recording, or by any information storage and retrieval system, without permission in writing from the publisher.

Front cover image of photo illustration of George C. Tilyou by Susan A. McDermott

Printed in the United States of America

McFarland & Company, Inc., Publishers
  Box 611, Jefferson, North Carolina 28640
    www.mcfarlandpub.com

For my grandchildren,
Megan, Cassia, and Callan.

Special thanks to Mae Comito
whose knowledge of Coney Island
proves the value of oral history.

Table of Contents

Preface   1

Introduction   3

1. From Sand and Marsh to the Iron Horse   7
2. 19th-Century Players   30
3. The Turn of the 20th Century   59
4. The Parks: Sea Lion Park, Steeplechase Park, and Brighton Beach Park   86
5. Luna Park and Dreamland   110
6. The Nickel Empire   137
7. Decline and Rebirth?   163

Chapter Notes   181
Bibliography   193
Index   197

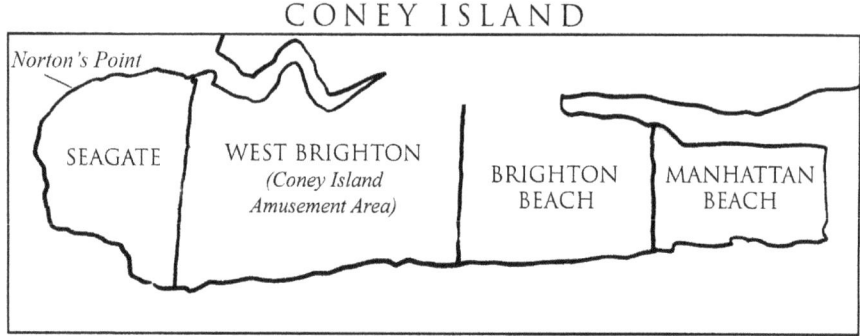

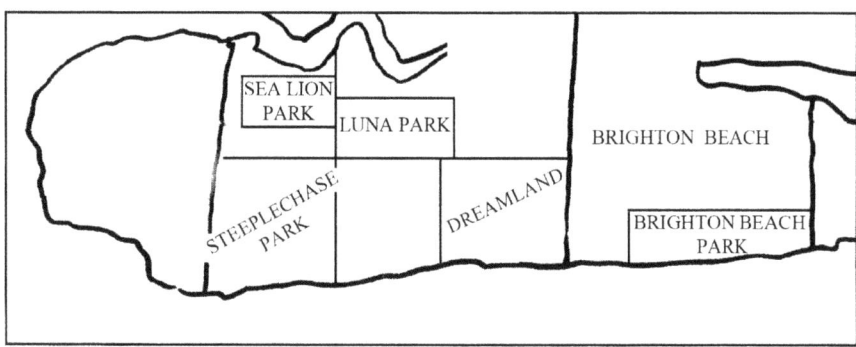

Preface

Amusement parks brought together the legacy of several 19th-century institutions. To quote a park manager of the time, "If anything, the amusement park is the byproduct of the Midway or amusement section of the Exposition or World's Fairs, and virtually the opposite of the Exposition, Circus, County Fair, and Carnival."[1]

As historians Robert Rydell and Rob Kroes put it, "The [1893] Chicago fair with its park-like setting and popular Midway Plaisance ... opened the eyes of several entrepreneurs to the possibility of making their fortunes from perpetuating the legacy of commercialized pleasures found at the fair."[2]

Amusement parks were also descendants of European pleasure gardens, most notably Copenhagen's Tivoli Gardens and London's Vauxhall. For the price of an admission ticket, Vauxhall, opened around 1660, allowed the lower classes access to leisure activities once only enjoyed by the elite. Tivoli, founded in 1843, expanded on the Vauxhall theme, adding cafes, theaters, a merry-go-round, and concerts.

In the United States, a number of parks came into existence before the Civil War. The difference in America was transportation. When the trolley or interurban rail lines reached a park, the rail company bought the land and transformed the park into an industrialized amusement zone. Some charged admission fees, and some did not; the primary goal, however, was to encourage ridership on the rail line, and the parks fulfilled an important economic function by serving as desirable destinations at the ends of traction company lines.[3]

A key factor in the success of an amusement park was the fact that the patron was always in doubt as to whether he was the surveyor or the surveyed. Wandering from attraction to attraction, one was never far from being an object of fascination for others. Historian Kathy Peiss described the situation at Coney Island: "The patrons were whirled through space and knocked off balance, their hats blown off, skirts lifted, senses of humor tried. The patrons themselves became the show, providing interest and hilarity to each other.... Audience participation, the interaction of strangers, and voyeurism were incorporated."[4]

Steeplechase was a prime example of an amusement park that liberated its patrons from Victorian decorum, from rigid codes of social conduct and propriety. Amusement parks thus became important targets for debate about modern urban culture. For some, the amusement park may have symbolized the democratic ideals of a melting pot society. But for others, such as the art critic James Huneker, the opposite was the case: "In a word, it is not a question of restriction but of regulation, decency, good taste. And semi barbarism should not be allowed to go unchecked. Coney Island ... is a disgrace to our civilization. It should be abolished, and something else substituted."[5]

The three major seaside Coney Island parks—Steeplechase, Luna Park, and Dreamland—survived criticism because they combined popular modernity, mass consumption, and a new collective experience while also offering traditional entertainments such as dioramas, firework spectacles, and music and dance halls, as well as freak and girlie shows. As important, the crowds became involved in the partaking of food and drink to excess, social inversion, mockery, and a fascination with the supernatural and abnormal that provided psychological release for people who daily endured the rigors of scarcity, tedium, and the humiliation of authority.[6]

Through the creative use of new technology, these resorts produced new ways of liberating the individual from boredom because of the speed and realism of new rides and spectacles. They offered an exciting encounter with continuous novelty that could fill sometimes lonely and empty lives—if only briefly. And these resorts were incredibly successful. In 1910, Coney Island claimed 20 million visitors, a higher number than Disney theme parks could claim seventy years later.[7]

Introduction

   Coney Island is simply and basically a beach—one that at times was the main attraction and, at other times, a backdrop to whatever was happening on the other parts of this small island at the bottom of Brooklyn, New York.
   In the early 19th century, the beach attracted a few rabbit hunters and swimmers, usually from the neighboring town of Gravesend. As early as 1824, steps were taken to connect the island to the mainland by building a road across the two areas, facilitating carriage traffic from Brooklyn to the beach. As the reputation of the beach increased, it became obvious that horse-drawn carriages were not the ideal mode of transportation to the island, as they were too slow and too expensive. In 1847, steamships from Manhattan and northern Brooklyn began making scheduled trips, docking at the extreme western tip of the island, which became known as Norton's Point. By the Civil War, the beach was still the reason for visitors to make the sometimes arduous trip because the area east of Norton's Point (which would ultimately become West Brighton) had no attractions besides a dozen small hotels with ramshackle bathhouses, some chowder stands, and a few saloons.
   Publicity began to create changes in the area in 1860 when the *New York Times* reported, "There is one cool spot that is healthy and invigorating which New Yorkers can resort to, and that is Coney Island."[1] The first group to visit the island were wealthy individuals possessing the time and funds needed to enjoy the resort. Others came because many physicians prescribed sea bathing as healthy and invigorating, but cautioned bathers to make sure that they had proper attire. For women this meant an outfit roughly the size of a large dress made of wool that weighed fifteen pounds when wet. Despite this encumbrance, many women were seen enjoying the waves with their family or a group of

friends. In 1866, the *New York Times* commented that "the ladies enjoyed this [being tossed by the waves] immensely, as they testify by their laughter and halt-tightened shrieks and their frantic splashings."[2]

With the end of the Civil War, the gentry began to have company enjoying the pleasures of Coney Island. Increased competition lowered the cost of traveling to the island, and continued newspaper stories prompted more and more people to make the journey. The wealthy, however, continued to congregate on the island, but to the east of the lower classes. In 1873, Austin Tobin opened the palatial Manhattan Beach Hotel. A *New York Times* reporter said of the structure, "Yesterday, one of the largest and best appointed appearing hotels in the country uprose out of the salt grass and sand, and so densely populated were its acres of piazzas and dining rooms that locomotion through them was a matter of slow and tedious difficulty."[3] In 1874, the Brighton Beach hotel, another grand structure (although not as grand as the Manhattan Beach Hotel), was erected in an area which became known as Brighton Beach. This area was situated between Manhattan Beach to its east and West Brighton (or Coney Island) to its west. The three areas appealed to three types of patrons—Manhattan Beach to the gentry, Brighton Beach to the merely wealthy, and Coney Island (which included Norton's Point) to the working class.

From the late 1870s to 1920, the entire area was subject to an expansion of transportation lines to the island because of the explosion in the number of visitors who would frequent the area, lured by the opportunity to swim in the ocean. The opportunity existed because leisure time had increased: working people began to have one or one-and-a-half days off each week and Coney Island allowed people from the city to go swimming—in the company of thousands.

Beginning in 1895, with the construction of Sea Lion Park (the area's first amusement park), there would be yet another reason to visit Coney Island in addition to the beach. This park was quickly joined by four others, including the most famous and long lasting, Steeplechase Park. The confluence of better transportation (by 1920, the subway), the amusement parks (and the other rides and games in the amusement area), and the beach would soon attract millions of visitors each summer. Coney now became the "Nickel Empire," five cents for a subway ride, five cents for a hot dog at Nathan's, and five cents for most rides.

Cost became a paramount concern for most patrons, especially

Introduction

the working poor who still wished to journey to Coney to use the beach. They would spend ten cents for the subway ride to Coney and back home, and bring their lunch. The amusement area still did enough business to survive during the Depression and into the post–World War II era, but the last amusement park, Steeplechase, closed in 1964.

With Steeplechase closed, Coney Island lost its bulwark, and the entire area soon became a pawn in the battle between the politicians and the real estate developers. Today there are efforts to revive the old Coney Island, including a new amusement park called Luna. But with all its reversals of fortune, Coney Island still remains, essentially, a beach.

1
From Sand and Marsh to the Iron Horse

> Sodom was not a circumstance to the sin-debauched and crime soaked Coney Island.—*Thomas DeQuincy Tully, Secretary, Law and Order Society*
>
> If this advertising goes on, Coney Island won't be big enough to hold the crowds that want to go there.—*Brooklyn Mayor Frederick Wurster, responding to Tully's statement*[1]

One of the most well known amusement parks in the world began as an island containing marshes and a sandy beach. The land in the early 19th century did have owners, mainly from the town of Gravesend. Coney Island was just to the south of Gravesend, and was separated from it by a narrow creek. The island's owners, however, did not have much to do with it apart from an occasional snipe hunt. The island extends from east to west and is five miles in length, with an average width of less than half a mile. Its western end forms Gravesend Bay; the eastern end has more than two miles of sea front.

In 1814, the writer and traveler David Tallman contacted Gravesend longtime resident and town supervisor John Terhune. "I have been to Coney Island several times this season," he wrote. "If we had money sufficient to build good buildings & a Dock + bridge and get a steam boat to run down from New York in the morning & up towards evening it would exceed any place of resort in this Country." His letter also included an idea for Terhune, a plan to construct "flo[a]ting Baths on the South Shore & establish a race ground on the South Shor[e]s of the Island at low water."[2] The agricultural populace of Gravesend did not initially agree with Tallman. In laying out their town, each of the thirty-nine original Dutch settlers received an equal share of land, both in the town and on the beach. The decedents of these patentees were primarily farmers and, as one gazetteer put it, "With the language, [they] preserve the industry and frugality of their ancestors." And they showed little inclination to profit from the beachfront property. In 1829, the Gravesend and Coney Island Road and Bridge Company was formed as an investment by Terhune with several partners for the purpose of building a toll road across the creek that separated Gravesend from Coney Island, which formerly could only be crossed at low tide. The group sold three hundred shares in the venture at a cost of $20 per share, which sold out quickly. The new road, called the Shell Road,[3] not only crossed the creek but also led to a hotel called the Coney Island House, which the company also constructed. The hotel was built on the western side of the island, near present-day Seagate. In his advertising, Terhune stressed the restorative qualities of the seaside and the safety of the bathing, even for women and children, which supposedly gave "Coney Island advantages which are seldom equaled."[4]

The register of this hotel reveals a mystery. Considering that at this time Coney Island was far removed, geographically, from any metropolis and was basically unknown (unless you count the clammers and local beachcombers), how then can this tome record the names of many famous personages who stayed there? In 1842, there is Washington Irving and his nieces; the next year it was Herman Melville; in July of 1850, Henry Clay and Daniel Webster. Added to these were Sam Houston; William Macready, the English actor; and Fritz-Greene Halleck, the poet. As time passed other names were added, such as Edgar Allan Poe and James Gordon Bennett, publisher of the New York *Herald*, who wrote that he found Coney Island "an objectionable resort ... sandy, clammy and fishy." Jenny Lind, the famed singer known as the Swedish Nightingale, was supposedly at the hotel twice—first on the day of her arrival in America, accompanied by impresario Phineas T. Barnum, then four days later, after her appearance at Castle Garden. Walt Whitman is also on the register, after he resigned from the *Brooklyn Eagle*, describing the island as land with a "long, bare, unfrequented shore, which I had all to myself, and where I loved, after bathing, to race up and down the hard sand, and declaim Homer or Shakespeare to the surf and seagulls by the hour."[5]

Whitman was not the only one to appreciate the lack of development. Until the Civil War, an empty beach littered with the decaying

1. From Sand and Marsh to the Iron Horse

timbers of shipwrecks dominated many island vistas, and landscape artists flocked to Coney to find richly evocative subject matter. Regis Gignoux inaugurated the trend when he presented "A Coney Island Beach" at the National Academy of design in 1844. In John Falconer's "On Coney Island," exhibited at the Brooklyn Art Association in 1864, no sign of the beach's incipient resort status could be ascertained. As at Newport, painters returned again and again to Coney throughout the 1870s and 1880s and stubbornly persisted in painting romantic patches of remote beach and sand hills even as they disappeared under the impact of tourism.[6]

There are other names in the register that cast doubt on the more famous ones. On Thursday, September 12, 1850, Bill Blunderbuss of Shirttail Bend checked in, followed on the next day by Solomon Frizzlepipes, traveling in the company of Judith Snuffs, and the Longsnoot family.

In early September of 1849, Mrs. Boswick and her friend Mrs. Clement signed the book during their stay by the sea, as did the previously mentioned Herman Melville and Edgar Allan Poe. However, according to Melville's biographer, Hershel Parker, "There happens to survive no known record of Melville's even having seen Poe. If, however, the signatures are to be believed, then there is proof that Edgar Allan Poe, Herman Melville, and other literary figures such as Evert Duyckinck, writer Cornelius Mathews, William Gilmore Simms, and Fritz Greene Halleck met at Coney Island on Wednesday September 5, 1849."

Doubt has been cast on the authenticity of these signatures. *The Poe Log*, a meticulously researched day-by day account of Poe's life, locates him around Richmond, Virginia, on this date. A similar book on Melville makes no mention of a trip to Coney Island at this time.[7] Whether or not the signatures in the register are real or an invented ploy to hype interest in Coney Island on behalf of the Gravesend and Coney Island Road and Bridge Company, it was at this time that the island began to attract visitors.

During the early 1840s, John Wyckoff, a Gravesend schoolteacher, opened his own hotel to rival the Coney Island House. This hotel was joined by several others, all having two problems in common. First, many of them burned to the ground within a few years after opening; second, Protestant churchgoers both in Brooklyn and Gravesend objected to the passing through their streets of the gentry in their carriages on their way to the island, especially during church services.

In 1846, two New Yorkers, Eddy and Hart, built a pavilion[8] at Norton's Point, the most westerly part of the island. Commodore Vanderbilt, hoping to capitalize on the island's growing popularity, built the Oceanic Hotel in 1847. When the hotel was destroyed by fire in 1851, he erected another hotel, which also burned to the ground in that same year. Up to this time, the only methods of reaching Coney Island from a distance were a ferry that took half a day to make the journey, a private carriage, or a stagecoach. In 1847, a side-wheeler steamer began regular service to Norton's Point. While the trip from Manhattan was only two hours, the cost was twenty-five cents round trip, which was a high price considering the fact that the average wage at the time was thirty cents a day. An ad in the *New York Times* outlined the service:

FOR CONEY ISLAND AND FORT HAMILTON
- The steamer NORWALK will commence her regular trips as above on FRIDAY, June 1 leaving New-York as follows:
- Pier foot of Amos st. at 9¼ a.m., 12¼ and 3¼ p.m.
- Pier foot of Spring st. at 9½ a.m., 12½ and 3½ p.m.
- Pier No. 3 North River at 10 a.m., 1 and 4 p.m.
- Leaving Coney Island last trip at 6½ p.m. Fare to Coney Island and back to New-York, 25 cents. No half price for children[9]

Harper's New Monthly Magazine described a typical journey:

And then, as the last clang of the bell summons the laggards, a mixed crowd comes pouring over the gang-plank, where [the laggards] are blended with a mass of plain but respectable people, without very noticeable features. As the plank is hauled in, two or three youths, laughing and cheering each other on, leap the widening gulf of foaming water between the boat and pier, and at last we are off. The same scenes are repeated at the wharves on the way down town; and when we at last push off from the Battery, the little steamer is groaning and careening with a multitude twice as great as she has any business to carry.[10]

While the ride along the bay was extremely scenic, the boat itself was a mere shell, small and very dirty, liable to capsize, explode or catch fire.

On Thursday morning last, about 1 o'clock, a fire broke out in the steamboat Trojan (which runs between this city and Coney Island), while lying at the foot of Vestry St., with the officers and ten or twelve hands on board. The fire broke out about amidships in the vicinity of the furnace, and so rapid was the progress of the flames that it was with great difficulty that any of those aboard escaped.[11]

1. From Sand and Marsh to the Iron Horse

When you landed, you merely saw an old dock: sand heaps, shells, and a barn of an inn, with a cheerless looking dining room, and a vile smelling "bar." Once there, if you wished to bathe, you took your chances of losing all your valuables, if not your clothes. The bathhouses were mere shanties, not even filling the demand of decency.[12]

In 1874, looking back on this situation, the *Atlantic Monthly* said of it:

> At the lower end of the island (Norton's Point) there is a wharf to which the steamboats come, and when one of them disgorges its contents, very motley is the crowd that winds its way from it along the rush-laid path that leads to the beach. The women and children usually outnumber the men, and, as is generally the case in New York assemblages that do not rally round the standard of fashion, the German element is largely represented in the throng. Family groups are always a feature here, the thrifty mothers carrying provision baskets, the jars that protrude from which, having probably been emptied during the voyage, are taken by the happy fathers to the bar of some beach hostelry, there to be replenished with lager-beer or something stronger, according to order.[13]

Most of these boats began to journey to Coney Island from lower Manhattan, where the steamship lines employed barkers to lure customers to their boats rather than a competitor's:

> "Will you risk your life madam, on a craft of that character, condemned by the boiler inspectors and without a sound plank in her frame, when the *Leonera* is the only luxurious new water-tight floating palace making unerring connections, and at 20 percent below the regular fare?"
>
> The breeze is somewhat fresh on the sharp forward deck, and is likely to blow your hat off. At the same time it is the more favorable point from which to see how narrowly we escape a row-boat or a maladroit schooner now and then, and to view the crowded water-front of the city, the heights of Hoboken, with a Bremen steamer just gliding into port below them, and further down, the harbor forts and the blue, villa-covered slopes of Staten Island.[14]

The moneyed crowd usually journeyed to Coney Island via stagecoach:

> CONEY ISLAND & BROOKLYN STAGES.–CROPSEY & CARL'S line.—The above line of stages will commence running on Monday, April 15, 1844, from Coney Island to Brooklyn, No. 12 Fulton Street, passing through Flatbush, Flatlands, and Gravesend, every day (Sundays excepted), as follows: Leave Coney Island at 7 o'clock a.m.; leave Brooklyn, 12 Fulton Street, 4½ o'clock p.m.
>
> Coney Island being an old established watering place, situated on Long Island, 10½ miles from New York, bordering on the Atlantic Ocean, directly in front of Sandy Hook, and having a full view of the shipping passing in and out

of the harbor of New York, makes it a very desirable spot in the summer months. For health and sea bathing, and convenience to New York by stage, it cannot be surpassed by any other watering place. Coney Island, April 11, 1844.[15]

The gentry, unfortunately, attracted gamblers who preyed upon them, setting up con games such as thimblerig, a shell game, three card monte, and chuck-a-luck, a dice game. These gamblers, joined by other low-class groups, mainly stayed in the Norton's Point area, while the wealthy frequented hotels that had been erected towards the eastern side of the island.

> Starting from the lower end of the island [Norton's Point], and walking along the beach, one of the first things observable by the visitor is a series of small groups of men, gathered at intervals upon the shelving sand. On approaching one of these circles, the explorer will see in the center of it a man provided with a bit of plank propped upon a crutch or leg stuck into the sand. This fellow is one of the beach gamblers by whom the place is infested during the bathing season, and for whose suppression movements have been made year after year, but hitherto without success. He is manipulating three cards, which he shifts with great rapidity, "pattering" volubly all the time about his game, which he offers to back for any amount the spectators may see fit to "plunk down." He keeps jingling heavy gold pieces to allure the unwary, and his display of greenbacks of all denominations is absolutely profuse.[16]

Those who were not in the gentry could also take advantage of the benefit of a trip to Coney Island:

> SUNDAY EXCURSIONS—The superior steamboat *IOLAS*, *Captain Yates*, will leave Thorne's Dock, near Fulton Ferry, Brooklyn, on Sunday, August 30, at 2 p.m. for Coney Island—returning will leave Coney I at 6½ o'clock-stopping at Fort Hamilton each way. Fare 12½ cents each way.
> There is a regular Ordinary[17] at the island, on the N. York plan—everything 12½ cents a plate; also good stages to take passengers to the upper houses, at 1. Each apply to R.J. Todd, 88 Fulton Street.[18]

Norton's Point was named after Michael Norton, an Irish immigrant who fought on the Union side during the Civil War. After returning from the war, he was elected to the position of Alderman from New York's 3rd District and was a member of the Tweed Ring. He purchased the summer home of William Wheatly, a theatre manager before the turn of the 19th century, erected some wooden shacks around the house and established what he called the Point Comfort Hotel.

Norton's endeavors added to the uneasiness on the part of the Gravesenders, since some of the wealthy beachgoers were shady characters connected to Norton from his position in Manhattan. These characters not only attracted more gamblers to the island, but also prostitution, which had not heretofore been prevalent.

By the late 1850s, the people of Gravesend began to have second thoughts about the increased number of people now coming to Coney Island: an estimated 300, especially on a summer weekend. The revenue from visitors using the toll road and the rent from the hotels and restaurants, however, assuaged their doubts. As an example, Eddy and Hart's pavilion paid $400 yearly rent, an amount that nearly covered the town's annual school bill. Additionally, the rent monies did not go to the individual owners of the Coney Island lots, but rather to the town's general fund. With this in mind, the town of Gravesend replaced the shells on the toll road with planks, making it more permanent.

With the increase in beachgoers to the island, more facilities were erected. John Wyckoff, a Gravesend teacher, built a second hotel. In 1863, in the midst of the Civil War, a Brooklyn harness maker by the name of Peter Ravenhall leased some shore property and constructed a restaurant. And in 1865, Peter Tilyou and his family moved to Coney Island and established the Surf House, a hotel and restaurant whose sign proclaimed that the establishment sold Bavarian Lager for 5 cents per glass and rented bathing suits for 25 cents apiece. Additionally, if you rented a bathing suit, you were given a free bowl of homemade clam chowder. Tilyou reasoned that those who were hungry would spend money at his restaurant. Also, there were signs on the beach warning that bathing without full suits was prohibited by law. To deal with the situation, Tilyou erected bathhouses for those who wished to change from their city attire to a flannel bathing suit.

Flannel was the choice fabric for bathing suits because a noted physician of the day, a Doctor Durant, warned that salt water would leach away the body's salts and that a woolen suit would retain the body's heat, thereby preventing a too rapid evaporation. Also recommended were broad-brimmed hats to fend off the sun and wind and the wearing of shoes to prevent being bitten by crabs. In the mid–19th century, deliberately placing one's body in the surf was not yet a popular pastime. The health implications of such behavior were largely unknown, and all manner of self-appointed experts (such as the aforementioned Doctor Durant) broke into print at the beginning of each summer with frenzied advice about the specialized clothing one should don before entering the water. Even in 1880, a popular Coney Island guidebook offered this advice: "According to Dr. Packard, the material should always be woolen, and flannel is decidedly the best. Those who do not swim will find it more comfortable to protect the skin of the arms and legs from sunburn by having the sleeves come down to the wrist and the trousers to the ankle."[19]

Bathing exemplified genteel recreation at the Brighton and Manhattan beaches. At their antebellum resorts each sex took turns in the ocean according to a fixed time schedule, but these procedures proved impractical when thousands visited the shore. Still, when mixed bathing became necessary, participants followed certain rules of propriety. Newspapers and resort guides warned men never to annoy females by going near them or by dunking them. Such advice left many bathers leery about "devastating shocks" to their nervous system that followed an improper bath.[20] When the *Brooklyn Daily Eagle* advised readers that "few ladies can take a salt water bath ... with advantage to their health," it was a signal that bathing, like other forms of recreation, was to be engaged in cautiously and without undue enthusiasm.[21]

There were, however, pursuits for the elite to engage in other than swimming. The favorite was communing. Secret admirers and dandies used the personal columns of the daily press to evade restrictions on face-to-face meetings. One wrote: "Will stout blond lady, dressed in light suit, who floated while bathing at Manhattan Beach Saturday, communicate with ADMIRER?" Another announcement reflected the comic banter of then-current social conversation: "Brighton Beach 'Smarty' would be pleased to rank as a friend of the 'Large Bodies' moving slowly for the 9:55 train Thursday evening. If the feelings are mutual, address, giving evidence to avoid mistakes." Decried by the *Coney Island Sun* for their carefree attitudes, such ads helped circumvent society's boundaries for public conduct.[22]

"All day Saturday and Sunday," wrote a reporter in 1866, "while thousands of people swelter in our streets, the Coney Island cars from Brooklyn and the little steamer *Naushon*, from the City, were carrying hundreds to the island, where they enjoyed the luxury of a bath in the surf."[23] Happy throngs gobbled down the specialty of roasted clams; ten thousand a day were supposedly consumed at one hotel. An 1868 guidebook listed Coney Island unequivocally as the "best beach on the Atlantic coast," and the *New York Times* noted that Coney Island "has few attractions, but those few are supreme."[24]

1. From Sand and Marsh to the Iron Horse

In addition to the lure of bathing in the surf, Coney Island began to attract pleasure seekers with cruder amusements. As an example the *Brooklyn Daily Eagle* described the activities at Stauch's, a Coney Island dance hall:

> Comedians of the slapstick type used to put on their funny clothes at noon and remain in them till midnight, going through their stunts almost once every half-hour for the entertainment of those who sat at the tables eating their own shoe-box lunches and trying to dodge the importuning waiters who had a special aversion to the customers who tried to make one 5-cent mug of beer last for an hour.
>
> The waiters used to hint strongly of their displeasure by frequent wipings of imaginary "suds" from the table, keeping up a continual drone of "Wot'll youse have, gents? Give your orders!"[25]

In his book, *Mirror for Gotham: New York as Seen by Contemporaries from Dutch Days to the Present*, Bayrd Still writes about Coney Island in the 19th century as

> the American Brighton, [which] grew in popularity as the city increased in size and congestion in the [eighteen] seventies. On a hot Sunday, half a million people ("making a carpet of heads") might crowd its wide stretch of sand in a few hours, a traveler of 1887 reported in the *London Times*:
>> They spread over four miles of sand strip with ... bands of music ... in full blast; countless vehicles moving; all the miniature theatres, minstrel shows, merry-go-rounds, Punch and Judy enterprises, fat women, big snakes, giant, dwarf, and midget exhibitions, circuses, and menageries, swings, flying horses, and fortune telling shops open; and everywhere a dense but good humoured crowd, sightseeing, drinking beer, and swallowing "clam chowder."

Fireworks enlivened the scene at night until time to go home, when "the swelling torrents of humanity," flowing out upon station and pier, emphasized "the vast magnitude of Coney Island Sunday." While the "masses" frequented Coney Island, "classes" were held at such resorts for the wealthy as Long Branch, New Jersey, and Newport, Rhode Island.[26]

By the mid–1880s, Coney Island featured exotic hotels, cafes, boardwalks, carousels, bathing pavilions, racetracks, an aquarium, a huge roller coaster, and musical entertainment. Also featured were reassembled structures from the 1876 Philadelphia Exposition, including an amusement tower that, at three hundred feet, was taller than any existing building in the United States and provided a breathtaking twenty-mile view. At a refreshment kiosk, dairymaids drew iced milk from the mechanical udders of a large metal cow. Sunday crowds on the island reportedly reached 100,000. "Coney Island was simply New

Hoping to escape the heat of the city, a seemingly endless throng of beachgoers traveled to Coney Island to cool off in the late 1800s. Many of these individuals, apparently, did not own a bathing suit, hence the need to rent one (sterilized, thankfully).

York moved down to the sea, men, women and children of all sorts, races, and conditions, mingle in the moving crowds as they would on Broadway, in perfect good order, with entire good nature," as one journalist wrote. Among them, in the words of the *New York Herald*, were many "working men and their families, young clerks and saleswomen—the toiling dwellers in the crowded tenements."[27]

Workers often visited Coney Island in excursions sponsored by unions, businesses, and ethnic, religious, and political organizations. These organizations ranged from the Catholic Knights of America to the Sherman Park Association (real estate), from the Knights of Labor to the Yale Lock Company, from the Odd Fellows to the Turnverein, bringing to Coney excursions of from a few hundred to twenty thousand. The island's expanding commercial amusement businesses depended on luring this type of clientele. Paul Bauer, a leading Coney restaurateur, begged the transportation companies to hold down their

1. From Sand and Marsh to the Iron Horse

A stereopticon slide (circa 1900) depicts a family playing together on the beach at Coney Island.

fares to permit laborers to visit the seaside. When a five-cent railroad rate increase in 1886 threatened the well-being of Coney Island merchants, five hundred hotel keepers, music hall owners, brewery representatives, and local politicians signed a petition asking the railroad to reduce their fares.[28]

The reputation that Coney Island was acquiring, however, was not to everyone's taste. Those with aristocratic tendencies—including one George Templeton Strong—opined that the people who mainly enjoyed the island were the "civic scum" who "ebbed and flowed on Sundays and holidays, infesting Coney Island with gent, snob, black-leg, fast-man, whore, and Bowery girl.... All conveniently accessible hotels and boarding houses are overrun by the vermin that hot weather roasts out of its homes in town."[29] Charles Shanley wrote in the same vein for the *Atlantic Monthly* in 1874, about "the vulgar associations and motley crowd."[30]

By 1879, there began a division between the exclusive resorts on the eastern end of the island located in Brighton and Manhattan Beaches and the area to the west, once West Brighton, now stretching from the western border of Brighton Beach to Norton's Point. In its 1899 Visitor's Guide to the City of New York, the *Brooklyn Daily Eagle* wrote that the "great seaside playground for the people" at Coney Island "was divided equally amongst the rich and the poor," but urged those who stayed in the luxury hotels at the rich end of the island to spend time at "the great resort for the crowds" at the poor end. The Guide marveled,

> There is no sight comparable to it in America. It is a happy-go-lucky place.... Walk through the streets, ascend the tower, see the crowds, the merry-go-rounds, listen to the frankfurter man, see the bathers—and perhaps take a dip yourself—and then go to Manhattan or Brighton Beach [on the rich side] so that you may leave the Island with pleasant, healthful memories.[31]

An elitist by the name of Julian Ralph had this to say to the readers of *Scribner's Magazine* in 1896: "There is not a thing (except the fireworks) in the high priced end of the island that cannot be obtained or witnessed at the cheaper end, but there are scores of attractions at the hurly-burly end that the more exclusive region does not hold forth." He strongly encouraged all visitors to the island, no matter where they stayed, to go to the Bowery to listen to "the oom-pah bands of rusted brass" and "have a luncheon of frankfurters and lager and a dinner of roasted clams and melted butter."[32]

It wasn't simply that the western part of the island became unfashionable because it was not exclusive, but that the eastern end boasted exclusive resorts that began to erect fences separating the resort swimmers from the onlookers. Also, as respectability increased in the East, it simultaneously decreased in the West, evidenced by the large number of establishments catering to "whiskey drinking pugilists and gamblers" whose "inns are the scenes of disorder and debauch."[33] Additionally, the police openly allowed such disorderly activities to occur to the point that, by the mid–1890s, upper-class patronage had dropped to an infinitesimal trickle, leaving the West as an area for middle- and working-class leisure.[34]

At this point, the island's three areas became solidified—Coney Island, Brighton Beach, and Manhattan Beach, reading west to east. More to the point was the dichotomy between two groups inhabiting the three areas—the middle and lower class in Coney Island, and the elite in Brighton and Manhattan Beach. This cleavage can be seen in the choices of spectator sports. In Coney Island it was prizefighting; in the elite areas, horse racing.

Prizefighting appealed not only to urban laborers in the late 19th century, but increasingly to middle-class men. One bout in October 1893 counted doctors, lawyers, bankers, two district attorneys, and a state senator among its spectators.[35] Critics of boxing believed that the sport had implications that stretched far beyond the boxing ring. Because of the association of prizefighting with urban laborers, critics often focused on its potential to infest society with crime. Despite the middle-class spectators, newspaper accounts continually pointed out the most undesirable elements of the crowd, characterizing prizefighting as a sport only enjoyed by saloon keepers, thieves, pickpockets, gamblers, and ruffians. In 1900, the *Brooklyn Daily Eagle* published an article airing its views:

> It is believed in sporting circles that the politicians who control the large "athletic clubs" will be able to prevent the repeal of the Horton boxing law[36]: that if the bill should be repealed they will be able to pass a substitute providing for boxing contests to be supervised by "inspectors." ... The power of this sentiment was notably demonstrated during late Governor Flower's administration. That was when James Corbett and Charley Mitchell were matched to fight at Coney Island. All of our local authorities refused to interfere with the proposed contest. The fight was declared off so far as Coney Island was concerned and was eventually fought in Florida [when the new governor, Theodore Roosevelt] remarked in his homely blunt way that if there was any prizefighting at Coney Island someone would suffer. There can be no reasonable objection to boxing contests where brutality is not permitted and where the contestants do not compete for money. But this is not the sort of athletic sport that the backers of the prizefighting clubs desire to encourage.[37]

Five days before the eventual cancellation of the fight, those who supported an end to prizefighting tied the prospective bout and Coney Island together as examples of things to be scorned. The phrase "Sodom by the Sea" emerged as a characterization of the island. These tactics suggest that much was at stake for individuals opposed to the affair and also implied critical inferences about the nature of leisure, class stratification, and the respectability of Coney Island.

The *New York Times* also became involved in the condemnation of prizefighting and, by extension, Coney Island, in the months before the Corbett-Mitchell fight was called off. The newspaper hired French journalist Raymond De L'Epee to write an exposé on Coney Island and the impending prizefight. In the first part of his article, De L'Epee speaks of two types of people on the island, the respectable citizenry who are basically "pious and civilized" but controlled by the politicians, and people of the "lowest possible dimensions": prizefighters. In his opinion, prizefighting constitutes evidence of the vulgar nature of the lower class. In the second part of the article, De L'Epee portrays the "mad desire" of the patrons of West Coney Island to imbibe alcohol, while a new type of women on Coney Island derives joy from the "moans of the robbed" while plotting to "despoil" strangers with their licentious occupation. De L'Epee expressed discomfort because of the leers of the patrons of Coney Island and compares the area to the "civilized" Brooklyn, where there is justice, the institution of prisons, courts, and law—items that have not reached the island. Finally, De L'Epee's main concern is that those who embraced lower-class entertainments, such as prizefighting, would ensnare members of the middle class, making the moral reform of Coney Island necessary.[38]

Even with the cancellation of the Mitchell-Corbett fight, the calls for the reformation of Coney Island did not cease; Coney Island continued to be seen as a threat to middle-class values. As a result, by 1897 officials believed that halting the middle-class decay of the island required the destruction of the Bowery and the establishment of a park in its place. This reformist zeal carried through into the 20th century as a means of preserving and fostering the values of the middle-class.[39]

The wealthy and fashionable frequenting Brighton and Manhattan Beaches also needed a diversion; in their case, it was horse racing. Before any formal racing was organized, every Sunday there were hundreds of impromptu races along Ocean Parkway which attracted thousands of spectators to watch and to wager on the outcomes.

In early 1879, the Brighton Beach Racing Association was formed and, by June, both the track and a grandstand had been erected. The sandy track caused the races to be slow and sometimes the venue flooded during heavy rains, but the success of the track led to the creation of others.

The area's next track, which opened in 1880, was created by the Coney Island Jockey Club and built in Sheepshead Bay, was a greater success than the one in Brighton Beach because it was supported by such noteworthy figures as: August Belmont, Jr., financier and the founder of Belmont Racetrack; William R. Travers, stockbroker and the builder of the Saratoga Racetrack; Bet-a-Million Gates; Diamond Jim Brady; and railroad baron A. J. Cassatt. These millionaires purchased property on the north side of Sheepshead Bay for their mansions to live and to entertain along with docks for their yachts, and stables for their horses. Additionally, they created three great restaurants: Tappan's, Villepigue's and Lundy's.

1. From Sand and Marsh to the Iron Horse

The third track wasn't built until 1886 by the Brooklyn Jockey Club and was located in the town of Gravesend just off Ocean Parkway. There was even talk of building a fourth racetrack on the west side of Coney Island at Norton's point, however there were no plans to build a railroad to the area, so the idea was scrapped.

The three tracks made Coney Island the racetrack capital of the country. Since their seasons basically overlapped, their supporters could find a race from May through October. The season would begin in the spring with the Brooklyn handicap at Gravesend, move on to the Suburban at Brighton, and then to Sheepshead for the Futurity around Labor Day. During the last fifteen years of Coney's horse-racing dominance, the Preakness became Gravesend's main annual race.

Coney Island's racetracks not only benefitted the elite, but became essential to the development of the island because it drew horse-racing fans from all walks of life. The politicians, easy money men, Wall Street barons, Western railroad men, society leaders, actors and actresses, the parasites of the rich, and large groups of the middle class all visited the island and needed places to sleep, eat, and party. Crowds grew yearly and by the 1905 and 1906 racing seasons, an estimated forty thousand people would attend the Suburban or Futurity races. (The horse-race fans liked novelty in a show as much as speed in a ride. They flocked to the first moving-picture exhibition in the United States, put on by Herman Wacke, circa 1903, at his Trocadero Hotel in Coney Island. This was a rather risqué comedy about French soldiers and their girls entitled *The Wrong Doors*.)[40]

Betting was considered the lifeblood of the sport, and while it was considered illegal, the local officials believed that those who waged knew what they were doing, so any reforms were left up to the Jockey Club. Gambling, however, eventually doomed all three tracks, even though they were financially successful. The first problem was the New York bookmakers who, since they were taking bets on the races, wished to have up-to-date information on the outcomes. To accomplish this, the bookmakers would situate men on poles overlooking the track from the outside; they would then telegraph the race results to them. Since mistakes were costly, other men were planted inside the track to signal the telegraphers. Once race officials were alerted to this practice they put an immediate end to it, forcing the bookmakers to pay them for track information.

The tracks also faced political problems because of the gambling, including legal challenges by Brooklyn reformers and complaints by local preachers. Finally, the public became involved when the crookedness among the racing fraternity became more obvious than ever. In 1908, Charles Evans Hughes was elected governor, and one of his first moves was to call a special session of the legislature to enact laws against betting on horse races. As a result, by 1910 all three tracks had closed.[41]

With the increase in reasons for the public to journey to Coney Island in the 19th century, new means of transportation began to be founded, especially centering around the railroad. The city of Brooklyn inaugurated the Brooklyn City Railroad Company on July 1, 1854, bringing in passengers from New York City. The *Brooklyn Daily Eagle*, commenting on this horse-drawn railway service on its opening day, stated: "Never was any public improvement inaugurated amid a more universal feeling of favor than these railroads."[42] And on July 5, the same paper reported that "the company did a thriving business from early morning until a late hour at night."[43] The journey between Coney Island and Brooklyn was not without its perils, however, as the following item attests.

> One experience [on the railway] would be sufficient to deter many persons from trying it again. Except at very early morning these cars are crowded to excess, and, especially on the way back to the city, roughs of the worst New York type—and what can be worse than that?—not infrequently force their way into these vehicles. The wonder is how little the passengers generally, many of them women of respectable appearance, seem to be incommoded by, or even disgusted at the presence of these pernicious brutes.[44]

The success of this railway coupled with the increasing traffic to Coney Island prompted the erection of a second crossing over Coney Island Creek, called the Coney Island Plank Road, and the chartering of the Coney Island and Brooklyn Railroad on December 10, 1860. The company spent two years constructing tracks from the East River in northern Brooklyn through the city to the new Coney Island Plank Road. The owners of the plank road, however, secured an injunction against the railway claiming that they had no legal right to lay tracks on their road and that "serious, if not irreparable damage would be sustained"[45] if the company were allowed to operate its new railway. The court held that the railroad company could use the plank road and, as a result, a horse-car railway began service to Coney Island on July 4, 1862.

Its service to Coney Island allowed the company to run a newspaper advertisement announcing the route of the new railway: "The public is respectfully informed that the cars of this Company are now running to Coney Island from Fulton and Catherine ferries."[46] Both the Fulton and Catherine ferries connected Manhattan to Brooklyn at different points, allowing passengers to travel from Manhattan to Coney Island. Additionally, the railway entered Coney Island at the section that would later be called Brighton Beach, turned west, running parallel to Coney Island Creek, terminating in West Brighton, an area that would later be called Coney Island.

The Coney Island and Brooklyn Railroad charged riders five cents for the trip between the Brooklyn side of the East River to Park Circle (an area at the start of Coney Island Avenue, just south of Prospect Park) where they would change cars, and an additional twenty cents for the remainder of the trip to Coney Island. Including changing cars, the time for the trip was between an hour-and-a-half and two hours. The day before the new line began operation, the *Brooklyn Daily Eagle* commented: "The opening of this road will be a great accommodation to our citizens; for who does not desire to go to the sea shore in hot weather, and now especially that the opportunity is afforded, at so reasonable a price? And now for Coney Island!"[47]

As Coney Island grew in popularity as a seasonal seaside resort, a great deal of political manipulation, skullduggery, and outright bribery went into the acquisition of railroad franchises, and the competition generated incredible confusion, as railroads changed names, owners, and went in and out of service. Five steam excursion railways were constructed in Brooklyn in the 1860s and 1870s, providing service to and from Coney Island. Also, several kinds of inter-island railways were constructed to link sections of Coney Island together over and above the coverage provided by the horse-drawn Coney Island and Brooklyn Railroad. Until the advent of the subway system, the excursion railways were the primary means of traveling to Coney Island by land.

The Brooklyn, Bath and Coney Island Railroad was the first of the excursion rail lines and remained a horse-drawn means of transportation until approximately 1867, when it was converted to steam power. It was built to serve not only Coney Island, but on the way, Bath Beach. While never the equal of Coney Island, Bath Beach also had a steamboat landing, which attracted enough passengers to make the stop of value to a rail line. This railway originated in the part of Brooklyn near

Greenwood Cemetery where it could be reached by horse-drawn streetcars. Construction of the Brooklyn, Bath and Coney Island Railroad began in 1862, and service began on June 4, 1864. By 1867, the line was extended from Bath Beach to Coney Island and also, by this year, the company switched from horsepower to mechanical motive power generated by steam. The *Brooklyn Daily Eagle* described a typical trip before the advent of the steam engine:

> [The line] carried some venturesome picnickers to Coney, the trains running about once every hour, with many of the sporty passengers making bets as to how long the trip would take. In those days a boy used to ride in front of the engine from the depot out to the city line, waving a red flag as a warning to owners of spirited nags, that the "iron horse" was approaching, so that they might get their pacers and racers out of the danger zone.[48]

The Brooklyn, Bath and Coney Island Railroad enjoyed a monopoly over surface transportation to Coney Island until 1875, when the steam-powered Prospect Park and Coney Island Railroad began service. This line carried passengers from Prospect Park in Brooklyn to Coney Island through Gravesend over the original Shell Road. The location of these lines guaranteed it year-round business because it serviced a more highly populated area than the Brooklyn, Bath and Coney Island line. The railway was supposed to begin operations in early June of 1875, but because its terminus was not ready, the first train reached Coney Island on June 27, 1875. The *Brooklyn Daily Eagle* followed the railway's progress:

> The announcement in the EAGLE of last evening that the Prospect Park and Coney Island Railroad would be open for public travel to Coney Island on and after to-morrow (Sunday), was premature. It appears that a local train for the accommodation of the residents of Gravesend and Parkville is run hourly from Greenwood to Gravesend, and that the company will not run trains through to Coney Island until Friday of next week.[49]

The next excursion railroad was a subsidiary of the Prospect Park and Coney Island Railroad, called the New York and Coney Island Railroad, which again was steam powered and ran from the Prospect Park and Coney Island Railroad's depot in West Brighton westward for a distance of two-and-a-half miles to the steamship landing at Coney Island Point.[50] The benefit to travelers to Coney Island using this line was that they could skip the area around Coney Island Point, which by the 1870s had acquired a reputation of bawdiness and lawlessness and enjoy ocean bathing and a shore dinner in West Brighton. Going further, the new line, in cooperation with the Iron Steamboat Company erected a new steamboat pier in West Brighton, known as the New Iron Pier. "This pier was 1,000 feet long, built on hollow iron piles which will sink by their own weight, the sand and water being pumped up through them from the bottom. They will be embedded in the sand 18 feet. The structure is to be 120 feet wide, and two stories high."[51]

The most unusual of the excursion railways was the steam-powered New York and Manhattan Beach Railroad. The idea was to provide a direct rail link between Manhattan and Coney Island. Since this was not possible in 1877, riders boarded the steamboat *Norwalk* at the foot of Whitehall Street, which then sailed to a railhead in Bay Ridge, Brooklyn. There, they boarded a train whose locomotive bore the name *Manhattan*. The train then traveled south to a section of Coney Island that is now called Manhattan Beach. Another unusual feature of this rail line was that it was built as a "narrow-gauge" railroad. At this time standard-gauge rails measured four feet eight and one-half inches apart, this railroad's tracks were three feet apart, so that cars and locomotives could be manufactured smaller than usual and therefore cheaper.

Speed was the hallmark of the Brooklyn, Flatbush, and Coney Island Railroad that began business on July 2, 1878. This train could make the journey from the southern end of Prospect Park and arrive in Brighton Beach less than fourteen minutes later. The *Brooklyn Daily Eagle* said of the initial trip: "The big engine ... puffed and snorted at the station ... as if impatient to start away on the wings of the wind."[52] Investors in this line believed that since their train would be closer to the commercial and residential parts of Brooklyn (originating at the southeast corner of Prospect Park) than any of the other excursion rail lines, it would be more of a success. Reports from the *Brooklyn Daily Eagle* supported this conclusion:

> The opening of the completed road to the corner of Flatbush and Atlantic avenues considerably increased the traffic over that route, and long into the evening the trains of five or six cars were filled. Passengers were delighted with the trip over the new road and poured blessings on the heads of the projectors of the enterprise, which brought Coney Island almost to their very doors.[53]

Most of the line's cars were the standard passenger cars of the period; however, during the summer, passengers sat on wooden benches in cars without sidewalls that were open to the weather.

The last of the excursion roads was the New York and Sea Beach

Railroad, which opened for business in 1879 and ran from Bay Ridge in Brooklyn to its own terminal called Sea Beach Place in West Brighton. This railroad never achieved any great success from a business standpoint. Competition was a major factor and the line engaged in a series of rate wars with other Brooklyn to Coney Island lines. "The managers of the Manhattan Beach Road did all in their power to prevent the Sea Beach Road from running to Bay Ridge," reported the *Brooklyn Daily Eagle*.[54] Also, the company did not have any steamboat connections to and from Manhattan and therefore had to rely totally on Brooklyn for its passengers.

Before 1878, the only two lines to connect the various areas of Coney Island were the Coney Island and Brooklyn Railroad and the Prospect Park and Coney Island Railroad. In 1880 an asphalt roadway was constructed between Brighton Beach and West Brighton, a distance of about ten city blocks; in 1878, the New York and Manhattan Beach Railroad was extended, first to the east, connecting Manhattan Beach with Point Breeze on the eastern tip of the island, and then to the west, to Brighton Beach. The total distance of the entire line, which was called the Marine Railway, was less than a mile. According to an article in the *New York Times*, this line earned more money in proportion to its length than any other railroad in the nation.[55]

A Brooklyn railroad was first accomplished in 1885 with the construction of the Sea View Railroad that operated for a distance of a mile between Brighton Beach and West Brighton as an elevated railway. One problem that the line had was in crossing over Ocean Parkway because it was believed that the structure would deface the beauty of the parkway. The problem was solved when company officials stated that "in crossing the Boulevard they will use a handsome bridge which will not cost more than $15,000."[56]

The oddest railroad to be used within Coney Island (and later connecting Bay Ridge and Coney Island) was the Boynton Bicycle Railroad. The train only needed one track since all of its wheels were in a line and, to keep it upright, the cars were four feet wide and fourteen feet high; it was double decked and was also connected to a rail above the train. It was constructed in this manner to cut down on friction. The design was also meant to save power lost in rounding curves which would balance the train so that there would be little strain on the top guiding rail and, thus, additional speed would be attained.[57] The inventor, the Hon. M. E. Boyton, claimed that the train could reach one hundred miles per hour, although on its test run in 1888 between Gravesend and Brighton Beach, its top speed was twenty miles per hour. The train was also used between Bay Ridge and Coney Island. The line ceased operations in 1890.

Several other small lines were built or contemplated before 1900 in the Coney Island area. The New York and Brighton Beach line was to have connected Gravesend Bay at a steamer landing with Brighton Beach. Their problem was that, to operate, the line needed to build bridges over competing lines; this proved too costly. The Sea Breeze Avenue Railroad would have linked Brighton Beach with West Brighton if it had been built, but it paralleled the Sea View Railroad and there was not enough traffic for both. A line that *was* constructed was the Coney Island, Sheepshead Bay, and Ocean Avenue Railway, which carried passengers to the Sheepshead Bay racetrack.

While the steam railroads took the place of the horse-drawn lines after 1890, these lines would be replaced by electric powered trains, and after 1900, would be replaced in turn by the city's subway system.[58] In 1906, another type of railroad was contemplated; this was the Behr mono-rail system. The plan fostered by the Rapid Transit Commission was to relieve the congestion on the Brooklyn Bridge by first running a line from Atlantic and Flatbush Avenues through Fort Hamilton to Coney Island. An article in *Scientific American* recounted Behr's proposal to the board:

> This special design of car is capable of accommodating 170 seated and 80 standing passengers and travelling at an average speed of 65 miles per hour including stops. Because of the peculiar construction of the track and cars including the essential fact that the center of gravity of the cars would be below their point of support, it would be possible to travel at speeds of over 100 miles per hour between stops. The railroad is estimated to cost approximately $170,000 per mile, and the estimated cost of the cars, which are of exceptional size, is $45,000 each. The rail is six feet above the roadbed and on account of the low center of gravity referred to, the danger of derailment on curves is eliminated. A mono-rail system of this type is in operation in Germany, and it is believed that the conditions in Brooklyn would be particularly favorable to the successful operation of the road.[59]

Before the board could act on the proposal, another mono-rail was built by the Pelham Park and City Island Railroad in the Bronx, which was involved in a disastrous derailment, dooming the Behr project.

Aside from the Concourse, the city attempted to aid New Yorkers interested in visiting Coney Island by building a road from Brooklyn to the seashore. This was the Frederick Law Olmstead and Calvert Vaux's toll-supported Ocean Parkway. Construction began in 1874 and was completed in 1880. Running from Brooklyn's version of the Arc de Triomphe at Grand Army Plaza to Coney Island's newly created Surf Avenue. Six miles long and two hundred feet wide, it was built at a cost of $1 million. The parkway, claimed its Kings County boosters, represented a work of suburban embellishment without rival—"the finest drive in America"—comparable, even to the Champs-Élysées.[60]

After the rudimentary steamboat service to Coney Island in the 1840s, regular steamboat service was inaugurated the following decade. The two boats that were mainly used were the 303-ton *Norwalk* and the 296-ton *Union*. Both docked at Norton's Point. By the 1870s, because of increased demand, vessels larger than the *Union* and the *Norwalk* were placed in service. First came the 1,752-ton *Plymouth Rock*, and, in 1878, the 1,760-ton *Grand Republic*.

For the most part, during the 19th century, steamboats, unlike the railroads, did not run on a regular schedule. They were owner-operated rather than part of a company; decisions on where to ply their trade were made on an individual basis, usually based on the market, allowing the owners to realize as much profit as possible. Two exceptions were the Sylvan Steamboats and the Iron Steamboat Company.

The Sylvan Steamboats were a fleet of five small side-wheelers that initially were used to ferry passengers between uptown and downtown Manhattan—"the quickest way to get to Harlem."[61] When their service was replaced by the elevated railways, they provided the connection between Manhattan and Brooklyn for the New York and Manhattan Beach Railroad and the New York and Sea Beach Railroad since—with their speed and size—they could make the necessary sailings per day that the excursion lines required.

The Iron Steamboat Company was chartered in September of 1880. It began service with one of the seven vessels that it would eventually have. Although the ships looked like the typical wooden excursion boats of the era, they had iron hulls that were divided into twelve separate watertight compartments. Additionally, the decks were made of iron and the cabins were iron plated. The *New York Times* commented on the boats: "It would be impossible for a fire to make any serious headway even if one should originate."[62] The company's promotional material proclaimed two reasons for the public to sail on them—"They Cannot Burn! They Cannot Sink!" And: "The boats of this company are iron, palatial, first-class sea-going steamers, fitted with every convenience for safety and comfort of passengers, and officered by competent and experienced men."[63]

The boats of the Iron Steamboat Company began regular service to the iron pier during 1881. Its first year was not auspicious financially because of competitive boats that also used the iron pier, diluting the number of passengers for the Iron Steamboat Company. To solve the problem, the company negotiated a contract over the winter of 1881–1882, giving them exclusive use of the pier for transportation from Manhattan. In 1882, the company went further and reached the same agreement with the owners of a second iron pier constructed in Brighton Beach. Because of this agreement, the company began referring to itself as "the only line having exclusive control of all the docks and piers at which it lands passengers, thus preventing annoying changes from boats to cars, laying out in a stream waiting to land, and other vexatious delays."[64] The arrangements were so successful that Iron Steamboat doubled its business in 1882, sending boats from Manhattan to Coney Island every half hour. During the summer, the boats were making fifteen to twenty round trips per day. Finally, Iron Steamboat and the Prospect Park and Coney Island Railroad worked out a joint arrangement to allow passengers to travel between Coney Island and Manhattan in one direction by land, the other by sea.[65]

By 1882, nearly two million people arrived yearly by steamboat at Coney Island, and the piers themselves became major attractions. The newest of the two piers protruded a thousand feet into the ocean and contained a promenade deck, twelve hundred bath lockers, an elegant restaurant, a saloon, two barrooms, an oyster house, and an ice cream parlor. The *New York Times* said of it: "Coney Island's pier advertised itself as first class ... [with all] the conveniences of a hotel."[66]

The massive capital investment needed to sustain huge display piers and steamboat lines implied that Coney Island now had found a mass audience. The new culture of leisure encompassed more Americans as workers earned more money and more free time against declining prices.

2
The 19th-Century Players

In the years between the Civil War and the beginning of the 20th century, a number of men influenced the development of Coney Island as a world-class amusement park.

People familiar with New York history have heard the tales of "Boss" Tweed and Tammany Hall—the corrupt Democratic "machine" that ran and robbed the city in the mid–19th century. Tweed had an indirect effect on Coney Island beginning in 1874 when Michael "Thunderbolt" Norton leased the site of the old pavilion at Coney Island Point and erected the Point Comfort House along with bathing pavilions and a bar and restaurant. With Norton in control, the west end of the island became known as Norton's Point and also became known for its lawlessness. When Boss Tweed escaped from prison in 1875, he sought refuge with Norton at the Point (Norton later became a judge through Tweed's patronage).[1] Tweed's counterpart on Coney Island was known as the "autocrat" of Gravesend"—John Y. McKane, who wielded unprecedented control over the seaside town in the decades before it was annexed by Brooklyn in 1894.

Born in County Antrim, Ireland, on August 10, 1841, McKane moved with his family to Gravesend before he was two years old. His career started out honestly enough—he learned carpentry and became a master builder in the village of Sheepshead Bay. Initially, his main business was building bathing establishments and lager-beer saloons for businessmen looking to profit from the summer tourist trade. He was shrewd in his business dealings and knew when to advance credit. As an example, when people like the Vanderveers wanted to enter the bathhouse business, he built their structures on a speculative basis. They not only paid him back in full, but became his political supporters when he decided to run for office. At the age of twenty-five, with the help of local fishermen, blacksmiths, clam diggers, saloon keepers, and carpenters of the town, he was elected as Gravesend's third constable in 1868.

At this point in his career McKane was an honest citizen who believed that the town was not getting its fair share from leases on the town's common land near the beach in Coney Island. His basic complaint was not that the town's commissioners were dishonest, but that they were farmers, not businessmen, and so did not know the worth of the property. The following year he was elected as one of the town's three commissioners and within a year had doubled the town's rental income to $1,511.50.

As a businessman, after seeing what he could do to help the town, McKane began to looking into ways to make money for himself. He began by making friends of the lease holders and assisting them in obtaining building contracts, realizing that many of these businessmen were sub-leasing their town-owned lots and therefore making a substantial profit.

One of the Coney Island areas that was booming was the beach at Norton's Point because it was close to Manhattan by steamship. Also, the friends and associates of Boss Tweed began to spend their summer weekends at the Point. Even though this area was under McKane's control, he found it prudent to look the other way to gain the friendship of the rulers of Manhattan. As a result, the area became the playground of pickpockets, confidence men, gamblers, strong-arm men, and rowdies who began to mingle with the upper-class citizens who frequented the beach.

In 1873, McKane gained a new and higher lease for Coney Island Point. The previous rent was $400 per year; now it became $600. The lessee was Robert Furey, who had become rich by being the Brooklyn Street Commissioner, a principal stockholder in an asphalt company and a friend of Tammany Hall.

During the next three years, two wealthy businessmen, William Engelmann and Austin Corbin, who were also to become part of the Coney Island story in the 19th century, wished to develop their properties in Brighton Beach and Manhattan Beach respectively Seeing this, McKane began to become involved in the leasing business, buying one next to the Iron Pier, where many of the Coney Island visitors come ashore.

In order to go further in business, McKane needed to gain political control of Gravesend, and this meant becoming a town supervisor, an office that had always been held by the Gravesend elite. While McKane had increased the town revenues, the gentry, sensing his ambitions, wished to get rid of him. In this case the friends that he had cultivated determined the outcome and he was elected to the office in 1876.

The following year he was elected town commissioner and, by 1878, he added the positions of head of the town board of health, supervisor of the water board and, as excise commissioner, was responsible for collecting the town's taxes. In his personal life he was a husband and father (three sons and a daughter), he did not smoke or drink, and became superintendent of the Sheepshead Bay Methodist Episcopal Sunday School. In 1881, his power became complete when he became the chief of police.

The next incident cemented McKane's dealings with Austin Corbin. Corbin wished to purchase the Gravesends' land east of his Manhattan Beach property, which gave McKane an opportunity to tighten his friendship with Corbin. McKane, knowing that the sale could be authorized by a voice vote at the annual town meeting, advised Corbin to pack the meeting with his own people, which Corbin did, bringing with him two hundred of his thugs armed with clubs. The voice vote not only went with Corbin, but even better because since McKane controlled the town appraiser, the land, worth at least $100,000, was sold to Corbin for $1,500. Each time the town gentry attempted to nullify the sale, Corbin's thugs stopped their efforts. While it is not known how much it cost Corbin to buy McKane, they each got what they wanted: Corbin, his land; McKane, the political control of Coney Island.

In 1881, McKane also added control of Coney Island's police force to his political control of the island. Before this time, Coney Island was policed by Brooklyn and the officers were therefore not under the jurisdiction of the town of Gravesend. To give McKane authority over the Coney Island police force, his friends in Albany introduced a bill in the state legislature authorizing the separate force under McKane, who built the island's police station and immediately announced that, when it came to controlling Coney's carnival atmosphere, his attitude was that people went to the seashore to have fun and therefore he saw no reason to expect them to be as straight-laced as they were at home in Manhattan or Brooklyn.

McKane refused to take a salary, relying instead on the income from issuing licenses to support both him and the police force. On the low end, his fees ranged from $50 for guess-your-weight concessions, to $250 for ring-toss boards. All other licenses for such entities as dance and music halls, bathhouses, shooting galleries, saloons, and carousels were higher. Everyone paid tribute to McKane, who increased his fortune by granting licenses to anyone who could pay for them, including those illegitimate businesses that ceased operations when the Tweed Ring was ousted. He gave them licenses to run saloons, gambling houses, carnival concessions, and fleabag hotels. Virtually all of these entities operated primarily in or near the Bowery section of Coney Island.

By the turn of the century, the Bowery was being described by

The Bowery (shown in 1912) is a street and neighborhood in the southern portion of the New York City borough of Manhattan. The area, created by the Tilyous, was a rowdy place, replete with seedy bars, flophouses, and brothels. It was later known as New York City's "Skid Row." Since then, the area has been restored, rising above its once-notorious reputation.

Harper's Magazine as that "wicked half mile of boardwalk."[2] The *Brooklyn Daily Eagle* went further:

> One of the most startling and pathetic things to be seen at Coney Island is the strange attraction it exercises over young girls. The noise, the jingle, the junketing, the music, the flaring pictures, the loud voices of touts proclaiming wonders to be seen for a dime, the boats, the merry-go-rounds, the dancing platforms, the museums, the concert halls, the bathers, and all the thousand and one "attractions" make a Vanity Fair at which young girls swarm open eyed, open mouthed, wondering at everything and taking all the tinsel for gold. To their simple minds the place is a fairyland, and it never dawns upon them that there can be any harm where there can be so much good humor and laughter. The ugly things which lie below the surface of Coney Island are not seen until it is too late to avoid them. The very corruption of the place glitters and the whirlpool of demoralization has them long before they perceive its existence.[3]

The *New York Times* agreed:

> What might have been made a pleasure resort of lasting and increasing attraction—Coney Island and its beach—has been largely turned into a nest of dives, disreputable houses, gambling halls, and cheap and nasty shows. Security of person and property has been seriously impaired, order and decency have been violated with impunity, and respectable people have been steadily repelled.[4]

By 1887, McKane's influence had spread outside of Coney Island. Because of his friendship with Brooklyn boss Hugh McLaughlin, and his control of Coney Island, he had become a force in state politics. His method was the usual—by delivering the votes. He had learned what every 19th-century politician knew: the more votes that there were, the more that could be stolen. As an example, since Grover Cleveland carried New York State by less than twelve hundred votes, there is a good possibility that he would not have become president without McKane.

Commenting on McKane's control, a Gravesend resident complained:

> The town might as well be owned by a closed corporation. For we poor outsiders are denied all knowledge of where our money goes. McKane as Health Commissioner decides that such and such a thing is necessary; as Chairman of the Town Board he orders it done; as Chief Contractor of the town he does it; as Chief of Police he prevents any interference with his work; as Town Auditor he passes his own bills and as Chairman pro tem of the Kings County Board of Supervisors he is careful to see that these bills are paid in full.[5]

2. 19th-Century Players

While McKane was initially allied with Tammany Hall, a machine of the Democratic Party, inside Coney Island he supported both parties, and his preference vacillated. McKane could control whichever ticket he voted for, and everyone followed suit because all of the wards voted in the same building, making it easier for citizens to be intimidated into voting his way. This practice of controlling the Coney Island vote, in addition to supporting the Republicans outside of Coney Island in 1888, may have led to his eventual undoing. In that 1888 presidential election, McKane instructed the Coney Island voters to support Benjamin Harrison, the Republican candidate, even adding the votes of the inhabitants of both Greenwood and Washington cemeteries. Just as McKane had influenced the previous election in favor of Cleveland, in this case, Harrison's win was even closer, and the new president even acknowledged Coney Island's crucial contribution to his victory.

On May 27, 1887, *Harper's Weekly* printed a cartoon showing the completion of the elevated railroad. It is believed that the inspiration for the cartoon came from the New York State Legislature's then-current investigation into corruption charges against McKane. When the judge of the Brooklyn Common Council asked him if he had anything to say in his defense, McKane replied, "I don't know that I can say anything. I have never in my life done anything to harm anybody that I know of. I had nothing to do, directly or indirectly, in the matter with which I am charged.... I say that I am not guilty."[6]

George Tilyou, Peter Tilyou's son was the only one to testify against McKane:

> He named names and places. He had been present when the trustees of the common lands had engaged in flagrant fraud. He told of McKane's police captain and others [who] had frequented gambling joints and how they got kickbacks from sanctioning prostitution. What Tilyou knew of course was all common knowledge, but no one else was brave enough to testify. McKane denied all, but ended up convicting himself anew for dereliction of duty. The committee filed a report with the [New York] State Assembly assailing Coney Island as "a source of corruption and crime, disgraceful ... and dangerous." They stigmatized McKane as "an enemy and not a friend, of the administration of justice." They recommended that he be prosecuted and, when convicted, removed from office. They published their conclusions on May 11, 1887, and to gather public support and pressure the Assembly to act, spread them across the front pages of most New York daily newspapers.[7]

Interestingly, *Harper's Weekly* did not carry the finding of the Commission. McKane's political connections, especially with the Brooklyn

Democratic boss Hugh McLaughlin, halted the investigation once it reached Albany. In addition, the Tilyou family found themselves financially ruined in retribution for George Tilyou's testimony against the Coney Island boss.

Before the election of 1893, McKane received a warning that a group of reformers was going to observe the election in Gravesend, pursuant to a new law passed by the state legislature designed to stop his practice of sitting in the Town Hall where he could eye each voter. On Election Day a group of reformers, armed with an injunction allowing them to enter the Town Hall and observe the election, attempted to enter the polling venue. The *Brooklyn Daily Eagle* described their encounter with McKane:

> [Colonel Bacon] said, "Mr. McKane, I have an injunction from the Supreme Court for you." Mr. McKane cried, "I'll take no papers. Injunctions don't go here!" "You'll have to," I said, at which McKane cried, "Hustle him out of here. Run that party in." He called officers and told them to seize Colonel Bacon and lock him up. The officers did so. Colonel Bacon offered McKane the injunction papers, stating that they were not only from the Supreme Court, but also from Mr. Justice Barnard, but again McKane would not take them, stating, "I don't care a ____ for the injunction of the Supreme Court or Justice Barnard."[8]

McKane was confident that the incident would blow over; however, reform candidates won in the State Supreme Court, the state attorney general's office, and the mayor's office in Brooklyn. Also, newly appointed assistant attorney generals summoned an extraordinary grand jury into session. The only worry McKane had was that he had registered 6,218 voters when there weren't more than 1,500 legitimate voters in all of Gravesend's six districts. Other than that, he believed that his political friends would bail him out of trouble, but it was not to be.

On December 31, the grand jury handed up its indictments against McKane and, on January 23, 1894, trial began in the old Brooklyn Supreme Court House. The testimony that convicted McKane was his own. Allegedly, he attempted to bribe three of the jurors; even if this was true, his lies under oath about not seeing the voter registration lists and paying Coney Island policemen to attack the poll watchers were enough to ensure a guilty verdict. His sentence was six years at hard labor at Sing Sing.

One voice in support of the "chief," was the writer, Walter Creedmoor:

McKane's rule was not a harsh one, as it applied to the people who made their living on the island, and the fallen chief certainly deserves credit for the skillful manner in which he policed the whole place. With a very small force of men under his command he preserved order among the thousands of Sunday visitors, many of whom were of the most lawless class, and preserved such excellent order, too, that serious affrays were almost unknown during his term of office as chief of the local police.[9]

After McKane's departure from Coney Island to the penitentiary, his place as the "Chief" of the island was taken by Kenneth F. Sutherland, recently returned from the same prison to which McKane had been sentenced. Known as the Little Corporal, Sutherland was more involved in politics than McKane, allying himself with the more lawless and reckless wing of the Democratic Party. Perhaps Sutherland's inability to secure as much power as McKane resulted in a series of murders of well-known denizens of Coney Island, including the unfortunate Little Corporal, who was found dead at the Bath Beach station under the wheels of an electric street-railway train.

At the time John McKane was beginning his assent to power in Coney Island, the adjacent area, Brighton Beach, was being developed by William Engeman. Until the late 1860s, Brighton Beach consisted primarily of farms, carved out of sandy hills, and was known as the "Middle Division," a section of Gravesend consisting of thirty-nine lots. Brighton Beach was not only the "Middle Division" geographically, but also in the make-up of its visitors. They were neither the lower-class denizens of the Coney Island midways, nor the elite who frequented Manhattan Beach.

Engeman, an entrepreneur who arrived in Coney Island at the age of twenty-eight in 1868, had an extremely interesting career before reaching Brooklyn. He had been a shipwright in Camden, New Jersey, a river-rat along the Mississippi, a hobo throughout the Midwest, a deckhand, and galley chef on a schooner in the Gulf of Mexico, a smuggler of contraband into Mexico, a bus driver in New Orleans, a mule skinner on the western frontier, and a sutler in Indian territory. Additionally, he escaped capture and execution by both the Union and Confederate armies. He then settled down and began selling horses and mules to the Union Army. In 1865, he retired from this business and moved east.

After settling in Coney Island, Engeman began to look for investments, first opening a restaurant on Washington Street in Brooklyn, which he named after himself, and then, finding the Middle Division, decided to buy there and develop the property. The problem was that the thirty-nine lots comprising the division were owned by hundreds of people. He found a way to purchase the land by befriending William Stillwell, the official surveyor of Gravesend. As a result of this friendship, Engeman was able to purchase several hundred acres of choice ocean front real estate for $20,000.[10]

In 1869, Engeman built a small wooden pier to receive steamboats, and in 1871 he opened the Ocean Hotel. With the completion of Ocean Parkway from Prospect Park to the ocean, carriage traffic brought crowds practically to the door of the hotel. Engeman also benefitted by selling one hundred acres of his Brighton Beach property to the Brooklyn, Flatbush and Coney Island Railroad, created in 1878 in conjunction with the opening of the Brighton Beach Hotel, which was owned by the railroad and brought business to both hotels.

The Brighton Beach Hotel had a frontage on the ocean of 525 feet. The lower ground floor was devoted to "transient" customers, and the meals were served à la carte. As many as six thousand guests were fed at each sitting and as high as 26,500 have dined at the hotel in one day. The upper stories of the hotel were elegantly furnished for permanent guests. There were 168 rooms, and each room had a gas fixture and running water. There were billiard tables and bowling alleys in the basement. In front of the hotel was a bandstand where an orchestra played daily.

Engeman attempted to become involved in the railroad business by building a railway between his Ocean Hotel and the Coney Island and Brooklyn's West Brighton terminus a mile away, but the idea never reached operational status. However, Brighton Beach could be reached by the Brooklyn, Flatbush and Coney Island Railroad. In 1878, Engeman built the two-story Brighton Beach Bathing Pavilion and Ocean Pier, which accommodated twelve hundred bathers. At the end of the summer season in that year, Engeman told a reporter for the *Brooklyn Daily Eagle*:

> We have had a splendid season. Business has been good since we opened on the 16th of last June. We were compelled to open hurriedly, and consequently were unable to complete all our plans this summer. Our bathing facilities, while they are not so perfect but that they can be improved upon, will, I think, compare favorably with any in the United States. The number of people who have bathed here within [the past] two months will probably exceed 100,000.

2. 19th-Century Players

In a single day we have had 3,800. Trade has been best on Sundays. We have also done well on Saturdays. Bathing at night has been popularized by the introduction of our electric and calcium lights. The restaurant has turned out to be an agreeable adjunct of the house. People seem to regard it as an attraction rather than otherwise. As soon as the season closes we shall at once enlarge the pavilion by the addition of several hundred feet. It will be improved in every particular. The bridge, by which the bathers pass from their bathing rooms to the sea, is to be extended to [the] low water mark, so that all publicity will be avoided. An arch or tunnel will be under the bridge where vehicles may pass without interruption. Improvements of a very extended kind are in preparation.[11]

To compete with Coney Island, Brighton Beach began to bring in entertainment. In 1883, William "Buffalo Bill" Cody rode into town with a spectacular Wild West Show before moving on to play Madison Square Garden, and then Europe.

In addition to the Brighton Beach Baths, Engeman formed the Brighton Beach Racing Association and built the first racetrack in Coney Island, at a cost of $80,000. Over five hundred men worked day and night and completed the course in six weeks, from start to finish,

A rare 1880 rendering of Steeplechase's Jockey Club site. In 1886, the club opened the first turf racecourse in the United States.

in time for opening day in June 1879. The course was a mile long with a two-and-a-half-mile steeplechase course inside it. Two grandstands, the larger one made of Georgia pine to match the nearby Hotel Brighton, could hold thirteen thousand spectators, at an admission price of fifty cents each. There was also a smaller stand, the charge being a quarter. The track was so successful that it had six meets, which extended the season until September 17. Engeman's experiment had turned into a fixture which prompted the creation of the area's other two tracks.

Two years before Engeman died, in 1884, he had testified before the Senate Committee on Villages, which was engaged in investigating his method of acquiring Coney Island property. The *New York Times* covered the hearing. The following is their account of Engeman's testimony:

> [Engeman] began purchasing property in 1868, and has been confirming his titles by purchasing those held by heirs under the original patents ever since. For these he has paid from $5 each up to as high as $300. For the strip of land he owned, and on which, at the present time, the Brighton Beach [Hotel], Ocean Hotel, and other buildings devoted to various enterprises are situated, he paid from $20,000 to $30,000. He sold to the Brighton Beach people the land on which their hotel stands, with 400 feet [of] water front, for $5,000, and another piece in the rear for $21,000. Then he organized the Coney Island and Rockaway Railway Company and sold it to the tract between the Brighton Beach and Manhattan Beach Hotel[s] for $210,000. He claimed he had been robbed by the State and by Kings County when they took 30 acres of his land for the proposed park and Concourse and paid him only $8,000 under condemnation, though with improvements he had made it cost him $21,000. Kings County also took from the town for the same purpose 40 acres, for which they paid $10,000. To prevent the condemnation of his racetrack property he organized the Kings County Railroad Company of which he was the principal owner, and sold the land to the company for a nominal consideration.[12]

In his will, the "Pioneer of Coney Island" did not forget the man who had aided him in acquiring his Coney Island property:

> In case of a sale of my real estate at any time I give and bequeath to my friend, William Stillwell, and direct my executors and the trustees of this, my last will, to pay him, the said William Stillwell the sum of $10,000, to him and his heirs assignees forever.[13]

The development of Brighton Beach helped justify Brooklyn's status as a great city. Brooklyn measured her own worth by the excellence of her churches and homes, by her unimpeded growth in population and, now by her ocean resorts. After the establishment of the new

Brooklyn, Flatbush and Coney Island Railroad connecting Prospect Park and Brighton, Brooklyn's Corporation Counsel, William C. DeWitt, argued that Brighton Beach's presence on the city's southern border would inspire residential growth:

> No sensible man will house himself on the tongue of land that constitutes the City of New York when he can live on the commanding heights of the City of Brooklyn in the daytime and spend his evenings by the roaring billows of the ocean at Coney Island. In thirty years Brooklyn will be the largest city on the American continent.[14]

This booster spirit was not unfounded. Brighton Beach appealed primarily to Brooklyn businessmen and their families who sought a quiet vacation by the sea. An 1881 editorial in the *Brighton Beach Daily Music Programme* in aptly summarized the resort's lure to these people:

> What can be more enjoyable to the city merchant or clerk who lives convenient to the network of lines that feed the Brighton Beach Railway than a jaunt at evenfall to Brighton? Leaving a crowded heated city quickly behind him, he passes through a picturesque section of the country, fanned by cooling breezes, to be treated to a musical feast rarely equaled, returning at a reasonable hour, prepared for refreshing sleep and pleasant dreams.[15]

With Engeman's investments, Coney Island was now divided into three separate zones: West Brighton for the working or poorer classes; Brighton Beach for the middle class; and, with the arrival of Austin Corbin, the creation of the upper-class enclave, Manhattan Beach. Corbin, a wealthy New York banker heeding the advice of his physician to give his ailing child the benefits of salt air, brought his family to Coney Island, lodging at Engeman's Ocean Hotel. While there, Corbin had time to explore the eastern end of the island, called the Sedge Bank by the locals. Realizing the potential of this desolate plot of sand flats, little hills, and marshland, and by investigating the matter more closely, Corbin discovered that the eastern end of the island possessed decided advantages over the West end—a finer beach for example, which was washed on both sides by the sea—a beach which afforded still water as well as surf bathing—in addition allowing for boating and fishing. His greatest discovery, however, was that the water at this beach did not have an undertow, that dangerous out-to-sea current which forms the bête noire of most seaside resorts. The reason was that the ocean currents and the currents running through the Narrows met at the eastern edge of the island and, in effect, canceled each other out, resulting in water that came to a comparative standstill. In 1873, Corbin began working to acquire the entire eastern end of the island. It took him two years and a bit of chicanery, but he eventually assembled more than five hundred acres, which he named Manhattan Beach. There, he proposed to build a "resort for the wealthy and refined multitude" of New York.[16]

However distasteful Gravesend residents might have found these maneuverings, public pressure compelled them to comply in the name of progress. In 1874, the local county newspaper scolded those recalcitrant citizens who had yet to sell their land to Corbin:

> Unless a spirit of sordid selfishness actuates the holders of the few lots yet unpurchased, to an extent which will compel the abandoning of the entire undertaking, this enterprise ... will do more to enhance the value of real estate in the Town of Gravesend than all the other causes which have operated in that direction for the last century and will culminate in the establishment of a watering place far surpassing in the adornments, both of nature and art, even Long Branch itself.[17]

Corbin's main project was his Manhattan Beach Hotel, built on the far eastern shore of Coney Island. The architect, J. Pickering Putnam, designed a structure with covered verandas and manicured lawns facing the sea. The hotel contained 258 rooms, restaurants, shops, and a ballroom. It had a frontage of 669 feet and was situated 150 yards from the ocean.

The dining capacity of the hotel was four thousand in the various dining rooms, at its maximum; to accommodate the guests, 32,000 people had to be fed within a twenty-four hour period. The hotel had 1,100 employees. Though chiefly for transient guests, it contained 238 handsomely furnished rooms for permanent guests. In addition to the dining rooms in the hotel proper, there was a Grand Pavilion near the hotel that could accommodate fifteen hundred people at dinner. Also one-half of the space was reserved for families and parties, allowing these groups to bring their lunches with them. This was unusual for this type of establishment, especially when tables, chairs, and waiters were supplied free of charge.

The Queen Anne–styled Manhattan Beach Hotel struck many observers as an odd building. Resort architecture in America had traditionally been rather plain, but the Manhattan Beach was topped by turreted roofs and pinnacles, which led one acerbic visitor to claim that it "looked like a village after an upheaval by an earthquake with a barn or two thrown on top of the mass." The *Brooklyn Union and Argus* quickly rushed to the hotel's defense, ridiculing the observer's ignorance of "modern composite architecture." Despite such disparaging remarks, Corbin's hotel enjoyed immediate popularity.[18]

With the completion of Corbin's and Engeman's hotels, *Century Magazine* noted,

> Within the memory of many of us, a complete change of residence during the hot months was a luxury confined to the comparatively few. Now the case is changed past recognition. Social conditions seem to be ordered to meet a general summer exodus. Summer hotels are everywhere.[19]
>
> Corbin's bathing-houses were built at the cost $125,000. There are 2,700 separate rooms and the fee was 25 cents which included a bathing suit which was of the finest quality and kept scrupulously clean by the attached steam laundry. The bathing-house also had electric lighting so that bathing could be done at night.
>
> In addition, Corbin constructed an amphitheater adjacent to the bathing-house which featured band music. Admission was free for the bathers, all others paid 10 cents. One of his more spectacular attractions was the Captive Balloon, capable of carrying fifteen people to a height of 1000 feet. The view was said to be worth more than the five dollars charged for the ride. Finally, at the East end of Manhattan Beach there was a Fishing Pavilion, where a Rhode Island clambake was served daily. The Pavilion had rowboats, sailing vessels, and fishing yachts for hire and was connected to the hotel by the Marine Railway which ran along the surf—the fare was five cents.[20]

In order to ensure the success of his Coney Island enterprises, Corbin began the purchasing of railroads that could be used to service Manhattan Beach. In 1876, he bought the New York, Bay Ridge and Jamaica Railroad Company, renaming it the New York and Manhattan Beach Railway Company and changing its main purpose to carrying passengers rather than freight. His purpose was to draw riders from both Bay Ridge and eastern Manhattan to Manhattan Beach. He also purchased the Glendale and East River Railroad, which began in northern Brooklyn, and connected it to the Manhattan Beach Railway Company in Bay Ridge. Finally, Corbin purchased the entire Long Island Railroad, which, by 1883, allowed rail transportation to Manhattan Beach from Brooklyn, Manhattan, and Long Island—all on Corbin's railroads.

The following is the text of one of the newspaper ads run by Corbin:

> MANHATTAN BEACH!
> THE NEW WATERING PLACE!
> AN IMMENSE SUCCESS!
> TAKE YOUR FAMILIES WEEDKDAY MORNINGS AND AVOID THE CROWDS
> FINEST BATHING BEACH AND SEASHORE HOTEL IN AMERICA
> Two miles and a half of rolling surf in one stretch, belonging to the MANHATTAN Beach Railway company!
> Unquestionably the safest, most pleasant beach for bathing and finest bathing houses on the coast! An average of 400 ladies bathe daily at MANHATTAN BEACH!
> GRAFULLA'S FAMOUS SEVENTH REGIMENT BAND (twenty-five pieces) give GRAND FREE CONCERTS, of the choicest music, EVERY AFTERNOON AND EVENING, with strictly Sacred Concerts on Sundays.
> Take Broadway and Fulton st. horse cars for East New York, or
> Take steam cars for East New York at Atlantic avenue depot of Long Island Railroad.
> FARE. ROUND TRIP, ONLY 40 CENTS.[21]

To ensure a respectable class of travelers, Corbin retained total command over public access routes to both the Manhattan Beach Hotel and his newly erected Oriental Hotel, completed in 1880. He eliminated pedestrian traffic by building a high fence around his grounds and hired Pinkerton detectives to filter out the undesirables arriving on his trains. The captain of the private Manhattan Beach police force justified this policy as a means of keeping order:

> The purpose of having this property enclosed is to enable us to see everybody that comes here. No person can get to Manhattan Beach now except by trains, and our men watch every trainload that comes. No pickpockets or roughs are allowed on the premises. Even the orderly crooks are banned.

This ban also extended to cheap amusements. When "peddlers, jugglers, or the dozen and one caught penny annoyances, all were banned at Manhattan Beach. The *Brooklyn Union* commented: "The grounds of the property [are] as exclusive and free from plebeian intrusion as can well be desired, even by the most fastidious."[22] Both hotels were also separated from West Brighton by an unimproved expanse of sand, and according to the promotional material, the company possessed sole proprietorship of the land, enabling "it to control the character of its visitors; consequently, at no watering-place is the representation of the best social classes larger than at Manhattan Beach."[23]

In 1879, a rumor began to circulate in New York concerning Austin Corbin and the Jews of the city. A journalist with the *New York Herald*,

Stanley McKenna called Corbin at his office to inquire about the rumor that he had taken a stand against admitting Jews to his beach or hotel. According to McKenna, Corbin stated:

> You see, I don't want to speak too strongly, as it might be mistaken for something entirely different from its intended sense. Personally I am opposed to Jews. They are a pretentious class, who expect three times as much for their money as other people. They give us more trouble on our road and in our hotel than we can stand. Another thing is, they are driving away the class of people who are beginning to make Coney Island the most fashionable and magnificent watering place in the world.... The Jews drive off the people whose places are filled by a less particular class. The latter are not rich enough to have any preference in the matter. Even they, in my opinion, bear with them only because they can't help it. It is not the Jews' religion I object to; it is the offensiveness which they possess as a sect or nationality. I would not oppose any man because of his creed.... They are not wanted at the Beach and that settles it.[24]

While the reaction of the Jewish community to Corbin's opinion of them was, of course, one of outrage, the majority sided with Adolph L. Sanger, the first vice-president of the Union of Hebrew Congregations:

> Talk is cheap, but let Mr. Corbin or any of his associates commit an overt act—that is to say, prove by deeds what he says—and I dare him and defy him to turn a single Hebrew out of his premises or his grounds simply because [that individual] is a Hebrew. This is a country of laws, as Mr. Corbin will find out if he attempts to enforce his ideas. The first attempt he makes to turn one of our co-religionists away from his public place he will not only be arrested, but imprisoned, as the law dictates.... He may prate about the capitalists who are backing him in his Coney Island venture, but I can assure you that, should he commit an overt act [of discrimination], at least $1,000,000 can be raised, and that too, in less than twenty-four hours, to convince Mr. Corbin that the Jews mean to vindicate their rights.[25]

While there is no evidence that Corbin did not serve Jews at his Coney Island complex, the newspapers had their say. The *New York Tribune*:

> The great race problem which is now exercising hotel keepers and others can be safely left to public opinion, which will find means of giving itself an authoritative expression at last, so that nobody's inalienable rights will be seriously impaired. But the current discussion is not without general interest, especially as the unrestrained deliverances of some talkative proprietors of "resorts" furnish instructive revelations of the mode of thought and feeling in regard to their so-called guests.[26]

The *New York Commercial Advertiser*:

The sudden and gratuitous attack made upon the Jews by Mr. Austin Corbin has raised a storm, but a great deal too much has been made of it. Mr. Corbin chose to go out of his way to abuse a large class of people who are no better and no worse than any other class or race, and by doing so he has made a spectacle of himself. If he should try to exclude Jews from his hotel, he could not succeed any better than if he had made war upon the Irish, the German, the Scot, or any other people who might have happened to arouse his spleen or touch his prejudices.[27]

The *New York Evening Post*:

If we may exclude a class of persons from one public place on class grounds, we may exclude them from another public place; we may exclude them from all public places; we may exclude them from the United States. We do not suppose that Mr. Corbin, who, with or without the consent of his fellow managers, has just fulminated a decree against the Jews, intended or desired to begin a movement which would drive all our Hebrew citizens out of the country. But if Mr. Corbin had a little more of the logical faculty than he seems to possess, he would see that his exclusive policy pushed to its legitimate conclusion, will crowd the Jew out of every inn in the land, out of every railroad car, out of every theatre, out of every open and public business, for the same reason that he is crowded out of Manhattan Beach, and will at last crowd him off the beach of the whole country into the sea. Is Mr. Corbin ready for that? Certainly public opinion is not ready.[28]

The *New York Evening Mail*:

The experience of two years since proved that it was easy to get up an explosion on the subject of conceding or denying to our Hebrew fellow citizens the freedom of our best hotels. All that was needed was to have some prominent hotel proprietor, with decided views, denounce this class as unworthy of the privileges of first-class hotels. Mr. Corbin was the man for that amiable and enterprising design. The hotel which he controls receives thousands of classes of New Yorkers daily, although its regular patrons are somewhat exclusive.... Perhaps after it is all over, the Jewish race, as such, will gain in recognition of its great and historic qualities, while those whose manners and habits have brought odium on a people whose representatives are among the most honored and powerful of our time, may be driven by "the bright sunlight of publicity" into more retired places for their manifestations, and held in check by the better classes of their own people.[29]

The *Philadelphia Ledger*:

When the ordinary vulgarian obtrudes himself in offensive display, or the everyday ruffian disturbs the peace of a pleasure party, or the grasping and aggressive man or woman insists on better places and in having more for their money than other people get, no one stops to ask whether the offender is Baptist, Methodist, Episcopalian, or Catholic. He, she, and they are set down simply as coarse, vulgar, ruffian and offensive people, without any thought of their national origin or denominational surroundings. Much less thought would there be of denouncing or ostracizing the entire national bodies or ecclesiastical communities to which they are thought to belong. This would be accounted in the highest degree unchristian and unjust. Why, then, apply such rule to the Jewish people because of the offending behavior of a few who claim to be of that race or religion, but who are no more true Israelites than the others are true Christians.[30]

Jews were not the only group having a problem in Coney Island; blacks also had had difficulties. Most American beaches had Jim Crow sections and special bathhouses for African Americans. Even in an age that deified success, wealth alone did not guarantee security or respect. Race served as an identifying tool because it remained one of the last characteristics identifiable at a glance. African Americans at Coney Island were subjected to an unofficial color line, made more rigid in the enclosed amusement parks, and were discouraged from bathing on certain sections of the beach. Hostility against blacks also took on a symbolic form. At Coney Island, any national prejudice could be gratified by knocking over Turks, Frenchmen, or Prussians in the shooting galleries and rifle ranges, but the most popular aggressive amusement was the various "Kill the Coon" (or "African Dodger") ball-throwing games. A black man (or a white man in blackface) thrust his head through an opening in a canvas screen while the public tried to hit him with baseballs, three throws for ten cents.[31]

The Prospect Park and Coney Island Railroad was created by Andrew Culver; it began service on June 19, 1875, between Prospect Park Gravesend. During the same year, the line was extended to the West Brighton section of Coney Island, ending at Culver Terminal. In 1879, Culver leased the New York and Coney Island Railroad, running it between his terminal and Norton's Point to connect to the steamboat traffic from Manhattan. Culver aggressively promoted West Brighton as a travel destination of choice, and the railroad produced immediate profits, carrying one million passengers the first year, two million the second, and almost four million by 1879. The line culminated in a broad, grassy piazza planted with flowers, perfect for promenading, where Culver erected a hotel known as Cables.

In June of 1878, Culver announced that he was selling his railroad because he "had been beset by Brooklyn politicians on all sides, but that he did not propose to "bleed like a martyr,"[32] and they had thought to compel him to do so. The politician's latest move was to enforce payment of his rolling stock at par value. Because of this type of harassment,

Culver decided to sell his railroad. On June 25, 1878, Culver put the line up at a price of 50 percent of its value. Since he could not get a single buyer at that price, he decided not to lower the price any more, and withdrew the sale.

Shortly afterwards, Culver, possibly because of his problems with the elected officials, reduced his round-trip fare to Coney Island from forty to twenty-five cents. His new low fare was widely celebrated; consider the following high-spirited poem:

> Oh, isn't it delightful
> To leave the dusty street
> And have the cooling billows
> Come dashing at our feet,
> To view the sea by moonlight,
> And walk old ocean's shore,
> Inhale the bracing breezes
> And hear the breakers roar
> All this for a quarter
> Let all Brooklyn sing
> For Culver and Coney Island
> Let the wide welkin ring.[33]

Possibly because of this battle with the Brooklyn politicians, when the decision was made to extend Surf Avenue, the extension would have gone through Culver's property. To prevent this from happening, Culver had a clause inserted in a bill before the governor which, if signed, would have prevented extension of the avenue across ground that had been condemned for railroad purposes. This was the ground used for the New York and Coney Island Railroad.

The *Brooklyn Eagle* came out strongly against Culver:

> If the *Eagle* was Mr. Culver it would go to Albany and either urge the Governor to veto the bill or have it recalled by the Legislature and the obnoxious clause stricken out. It comes with the worst possible grace for him to be in this kind of business, and, beside[s], it won't pay. Surf Avenue must be opened, if not this year, certainly in the not remote future. If this [is] not done, the Island will suffer; people will tire of [an] irregular conglomeration of hotels and hostelries, and when they do, Mr. Culver's little beach railroad will profit him nothing.[34]

In June of 1880, Culver capitulated and opened Surf Avenue, probably because of the involvement of John McKane, whom the *Eagle* said, "handled the scheme and overcame all resistance."[35]

Culver again had a problem in 1881 when he attempted to lease part of his land to the Brighton Pier and Navigation Company for the purpose of erecting an iron pier stretching one thousand feet into the Atlantic. The trustees of the town of Gravesend, to which the land belonged before the railroad company acquired it, claimed that the latter did not own the land in fee,[36] but only as an easement which could be used exclusively for railroad purposes. This could have been another attack on Culver because the pier company was composed, in great part, by the owners of the railroad company. This time, Culver was the victor when the Gravesend trustees sought an injunction to stop work on the pier. The Supreme Court of New York State modified the injunction, allowing the work on the pier to continue.[37]

At the end of 1881, Culver was again embroiled in a controversy involving his railroad. The Brooklyn Bridge was being constructed, and Culver wished to connect a railroad from the Brooklyn side to Coney Island by the shortest possible route. This railroad was called the East River Bridge, and Coney Island Steam Transit Company and its tracks would be elevated because the route would travel through heavily populated areas. At the same time another railroad, the Brooklyn Elevated Railway Company, better known as the Bruff enterprise,[38] also petitioned the city to be allowed to erect an elevated railway over some principal streets in Brooklyn. Both of these railway companies petitioned the Aldermanic Committee on Railroads of the City of New York for permission to build elevated lines in Brooklyn.

Because of the impact of the proposed lines on property owners and businessmen, there became a growing opposition to the new railroads, especially when it was rumored that as much as $100,000 was made available to the aldermen who voted for the resolutions. When the mayor's decision was announced, only Culver's company was allowed to proceed, albeit with the proviso that all legal obstacles be removed.

Culver was interviewed by the *Brooklyn Daily Eagle* about his part in the elevated railroad situation. His reply to the reporter was that everything that was done was legal and that he did not, in fact, get all that he wanted:

> In the first place, I desire to speak in reply to the complaints that have been made that the property owners have not been heard. As you know, our matter has been pending to the Board of Aldermen for months past, and at various meetings of the Railroad Committee of that body the property owners were fully represented. There was originally great opposition made to building on Debevoise [P]lace and also on Baltic [S]treet. That opposition carried us up to

Albany, and we were deprived of Debevoise [P]lace by an act of the Legislature. We were obliged to take Hudson [A]venue much to our injury and inconvenience because of a sharp curve and bad connecting. Still we agreed to take. The Supreme Court Committee took away our South Brooklyn route, which we regarded as valuable as it would connect with the elevated railway system of New York.... The company also produced a petition signed by 14,000 residents and owners of property along the line in favor of building the road. Therefore, I think that the criticisms about hasty action are unfair.

There is one thing certain and that is that the company I represent neither expects nor intends to attempt to build any railroad in the streets of the City of Brooklyn until all those questions shall have been fairly met and disposed of, even if we should be fortunate enough to get the legal right to build on the route under our charter.[39]

In the end, however, Brooklyn Elevated, not Culver, was given the franchise. Culver then adroitly rerouted his Prospect Park & Coney Island Railroad to connect with Brooklyn Elevated at the new Union Depot at 36th Street and Fifth Avenue. This connection permanently altered the very nature of the original excursion lines to Coney Island and began the transformation into the coming subway system. In 1885, Culver joined his railroad with the railroad of Austin Corbin. The new line connected to the ferry terminal at Whitehall Street. Both owners claimed that they could reduce the travel time from Whitehall Street to Coney Island from one hour to forty-five minutes and also proposed to make the trip as pleasant as possible.

In 1887, both Culver and Corbin were asked about the possibility of lowering their rates for train trips to Coney Island:

President Corbin of the Manhattan Railroad—"We mean to keep our fares up and think them cheap enough. Excursions over English roads cost twice as much and they are not run with any system. Our railroads alone do not pay us and we are under $40,000 every season for music.... We pay for the best of everything and the people get [it]. No sir, we will not reduce fares, first because we cannot afford it and secondly because if we did there would come down [to Coney Island] the class of people we do not want."[40]

President Andrew Culver of the Prospect Park and Coney Island Railroad— "No committee has yet called on me in relation to lowering the fares to Coney Island, but I can say most emphatically that there will be no reduction on the roads with which I am connected.... Cheap fares were tried for two seasons by the Sea Beach Railroad and it was found they precipitated upon Coney Island the very worst class in the two cities."[41]

In addition to his Coney Island railroad holdings, Austin Corbin was the owner of the Long Island Railroad. In 1891, he purchased the Prospect Park & Coney Island Railroad from Andrew Culver, making him the single-most dominant factor in Coney Island transportation matters.

Andrew Culver's most lasting contribution was probably the erection of the Sawyer Observatory, which he reassembled after bringing it to the island in 1878. In an age before skyscrapers, this forerunner to the Eiffel Tower seemed of truly stupendous height. Two steam elevators hoisted spectators three hundred feet over Coney Island (higher than any building in the United States) to witness a twenty-mile view. Immigrants arriving from Europe saw the electrically lighted amusement tower before they ever glimpsed the Statue of Liberty, until the tower burned in the great Dreamland fire of 1911.[42]

In the late 1860s, Charles Feltman, a German emigrant, arrived in New York City. In two years he had established his own bakery, and used a pie wagon to deliver baked goods to his Brooklyn customers, which included the hotels and restaurants in Coney Island where there was a demand for his prepared foods. Looking to enhance his market, Feltman created what was, in effect, a sausage sandwich. In order to keep the food warn, he customized his pie wagon to include a small charcoal stove and a tin-lined chest to keep the rolls fresh. He began selling his hot sausages on a bun—called the Coney Island Red Hots— a forerunner of the American hot dog.

In his first year in business, Feltman sold nearly 3,700 sausage sandwiches, with the number increasing each year to the point that, in 1871, he opened his own stand in Coney Island, on a small plot that he subleased. By 1874 he was so successful that he purchased his own lot for $7,500 and erected his own restaurant, the Ocean Pavilion. All of this came because of his invention in an area where, formerly, the clam was king. Clams were easily raked up from the shores of Sheepshead Bay and were very cheap—even the biggest restaurants only charged a penny a clam—whereas Feltman charged a dime for a Red Hot.

Feltman's culinary invention was copied by competitors in Coney Island. Rumors began to circulate that the sausages were made of dog meat, and the local politicians alleged that they found a rendering plant making sausages for Coney Island vendors out of horse meat. John McKane's take on the issue was that "nobody knows what [is] inside those sausages." Seeing a way to make money out of the situation, McKane put an excise tax on every sausage stand. "We cannot dictate to a man what he must sell, but we can make it hard for him to carry on his business," he said. Fortunately for Feltman and the other vendors, the rumors subsided and the Red Hots (or, more popularly, hot dogs) were back in vogue. Interestingly, when Feltman's lease price became too high, he began leasing a plot from McKane.

The Ocean Pavilion was situated on a shore front plot of land whose area increased yearly as the ocean piled more and more sand upon it. Feltman was not content to erect merely a restaurant. The building contained a series of dining rooms, a beer garden, and a ballroom. Additionally, he installed a carrousel in the beer garden and his sons added a roller coaster, the Ziz. The Ocean Pavilion, however, was a success not for the rides but the food. While the Red Hot was not forgotten, the restaurant featured planked steaks and shore dinners at reasonable prices.

Feltman's became a favorite of the racetrack crowd during Coney Island's racing heyday. Under a huge maple tree in the beer garden, the trainers, jockeys, and gamblers sat in chairs with their names etched on brass plates. In the 1880s, Feltman served an estimated 200,000 patrons; in the 1890s, 370,000; in the first decade of the 20th century, 900,000; and, in the second decade, over two million. The multiple dining rooms were geared to serve eight thousand at a time, justifying Feltman's slogan, "Caterers to the Millions."[43]

Feltman was also enough of a power in Coney Island to evade the law. When Oliver Cotter, an agent for the Society for the Prevention of Vice, went to Coney Island on a Sunday in the summer of 1877, he found Feltman's bars operating at full capacity, despite previous warnings. As a result, he charged Feltman with keeping a disorderly house where drinking and dancing were permitted on the Sabbath. A Coney Island jury immediately found him not guilty. Less than two weeks later, an enraged Cotter brought Feltman up on charges for selling liquor on Sunday. Again the charges did not stick, although "no effort was made by the defense to contradict the evidence offered by the prosecution that beer and whisky were sold at Feltman's without any attempt at concealment."[44] The Temperance Brotherhood brought charges against Feltman in August of the same year, and again the jury found in favor of the defendant. The *New York Times* reported that "several witnesses swore that they had purchased and drank lager in Feltman's house on Sunday, the 24th, and no testimony was offered for the defense, but not withstanding this fact the jury brought in a verdict of not guilty.[45]

2. 19th-Century Players

William Vanderveer settled in Coney Island in 1873. He had a professional background as a plasterer and bricklayer, but because of his political connections was appointed to the position of sewer inspector. During this tenure, he befriended John McKane, whom he hired to build bathhouses for his wife on two shore-front lots that she leased. In addition to the 287 bathhouses that were erected, McKane also built a three-story hotel on the combined lots.

By 1885, Vanderveer's wife, Lucy, began a civil action suit against her husband, with McKane claiming that the lease on the two lots had been assigned to her brother, who had then assigned it to her. Also,

> Supervisor McKane came to her and demanded that she assign to William Vanderveer the hotel, the lands, the barns, the sheds, hotel furniture and fixtures, reserving for herself four or five suites of furniture. On her refusal McKane threatened that if she refused to assign her interest to her husband he would have nothing more to do with her and she could not get her land.[46]

Lucy Vanderveer prevailed, keeping both the pavilion and the hotel. According to the *History of the Town of Gravesend, New York*:

> Mrs. Vanderveer naturally recalls with pleasurable pride her early struggles in the erection and equipment of this pavilion; which, when furnished, her sons painted for her, and which her daughters assist in caring for. Not less is she proud of her excellent hotel, 100' × 40' in size, and with three stories, containing 86 guest rooms, parlors, a large bar and restaurant; and having attached a livery of twenty horses, etc.
>
> All this, as a result of thirteen years of a woman's hard labor and industry, is a record which cannot be despised; and overlooked by the veracious chronicler.[47]

One of the three opulent hotels—The West Brighton Beach (or Brighton Beach) Hotel. The others were the Manhattan Beach Hotel, and The Oriental Hotel was built by Paul Bauer, a German emigrant who fought in the American Civil War, entering as a private and leaving as a captain. After the war he held various positions in the hotel and restaurant business in New York City. On a visit to Coney Island, when his carriage was almost overturned in the sand, his wife remarked, "This is the worst place I ever saw." To which he replied, "It can be made the best."

With this thought in mind, Bauer leased twelve acres of beach front property and in less than a year erected the Brighton Beach Hotel. The hotel was an immense structure capable of comfortably seating six thousand diners. It contained the largest and most tastefully decorated

Erected in 1874, the Brighton Beach Hotel (photographed in 1902) had a frontage on the Atlantic Ocean of 525 feet. Its immense restaurant comfortably seated 6,000 guests.

dining room in Coney Island. As with other hotels on the island, it also had an attached bathing pavilion.

In 1885, the *New York Times* rated the hotel highly:

> It is easily accessible by all lines of railway and steamboats, and a more popular place of resort on the whole of West Brighton Beach cannot be imagined.... Mr. Bauer's management of his hotel has elicited encomiums from all classes of the public.[48] He always strives to excel and lead far in the van in any enterprise in which he may engage.[49]

The hotel's biggest claim to fame, however, came in 1888, when it was threatened by the erosion of sand in front of the hotel. While Charles Feltman's Ocean Hotel gained ground because of the tides, the Brighton Beach Hotel lost it. The *New York Times* supplied an answer to this dilemma:

> One of the most moving spectacles that has presented itself in the eyes of New Yorkers and the inhabitants of the neighboring islands since the 1st of May last was seen yesterday at Brighton Beach, Coney Island. Not only was it

moving; it was astonishing. Indeed it will astonish many people even to read to-day that "The Brighton," the great hotel, 460' × 130', on whose shady piazzas so many have sat in summer and listened to the music of Cappa and Neptune, was taken up bodily and moved by 117½ feet from its former foundation. Nevertheless, such is the fact, as may be proved by a crowd of witnesses who stood amazed at the sight and dug holes in the sand to keep themselves warm.

... Large crowds of people were brought down to see the hotel move, the trains on the Brooklyn, Flatbush and Coney Island Railroad running half hourly during the afternoon. To-day the move will be continued. Many of the 3,000 people who were at the beach placed pennies or dimes on the rails over which the building was drawn, and kept as mementoes the crushed coins after the building passed over them.[50]

Bauer ran the Brighton Beach Hotel until he was committed to an insane asylum, where he died in 1893. The hotel was then run by his wife.

The first railroad to reach the island was the Brooklyn, Bath and Coney Island Railroad, called the Dummy Road because of its very slow progress in the journey from Brooklyn. The rule at the time was that until the train crossed the Brooklyn line, it had to be preceded by a man on horseback waving a red signal flag. (The local joke was that the horse was needed to pull it.) The terminus of this railroad in Coney Island was where Peter Tilyou built his hotel and restaurant, the Surf House, in 1865, which catered to the family trade. Tilyou was known as the innkeeper who fired off a small cannon, nicknamed Molly, when the fancy took him, usually when a ship passed, or, perhaps, when the Dummy Road brought a new batch of customers. Peter Tilyou was also the father of George C. Tilyou, who, in the 20th century, would greatly affect Coney Island and the amusement industry as a whole.

Inadvertently, both Tilyous caused problems for themselves with John McKane. Their struggles with him paint a picture of the Coney Island legal system in the latter years of the 19th century. In addition to the Surf House, Peter Tilyou built the Surf Theater. In order to direct patrons to the theater, in 1882 he constructed a street paved with planks. He named it Ocean View Walk, but it was soon commonly known as the Bowery. The Surf Theater prospered for a time, but the competition became too great when McKane began issuing licenses to other venues, especially the dance palaces and concert halls erected by Anson Stratton in 1884.

The battle between the Tilyous and McKane began in early 1884, when Peter Tilyou accused McKane of being crooked. At issue was the sale of Coney Island land whose proceeds, Tilyou argued, would be stolen by McKane. To make his case, Tilyou created and passed out a circular attacking McKane:

> Down with Corruption!
> To the Voters of the Town of Gravesend—
> Reasons Why You Vote Against the Sale of Coney Island—
> 1. Your Supervisor[51] and trustees are buying themselves lands which you own as electors of the town.
> 2. They are selling at utterly inadequate and ruinous prices the best lands in the town, in order that they may get the money and squander it.
> 3. They can't steal the common lands, but they can and they will steal the money.
> 4. The town of Hempstead sold its common lands a few years ago for a large sum of money; but the money has made its way out of the town treasury into the pockets of the trustees.
> 5. Those voters who sympathize with the Land League movement in Ireland must vote against this sale. Why? Because it is selling lands over the tenant's head, and robbing them of their improvements, and it is to prevent this that the Land League exists.
> 6. Why was this sale concocted in secrecy? Because it is a fraud, and every honest man should vote against the fraud.
>
> Supervisor McKane states that he wants to vindicate himself as regards the meaning of the words and "they will steal," which, he claims, virtually stamp him as a thief.[52]

McKane claimed that the words of the circular formed a "malicious libel" and therefore arrested Tilyou. A grand jury was then formed to investigate McKane's charges and, on March 11, 1884, declined to indict Tilyou. Tilyou's argument was that part of the land to be sold was leased by him and that not only had he made $32,000 in improvements to the land, but it was sold for $7,000, even though his lease had eight more years to run.

In 1887, George Tilyou was arrested on the charge that he did not have a license to operate two of the games he owned—the flying boats and the slide for life. On the advice of his attorney, he refused to pay the fifty-dollar fine on the grounds that the commissioner of police had no right to impose the fine. Tilyou made the following comment to a *Brooklyn Daily Eagle* reporter:

> I was called upon some weeks ago in regard to taking out a license for my machines, but I refused to do it. At first the Commissioners wanted $75. I kicked, and they offered to let me run them, if I paid $30. When I was arrested to-day they wanted me to give up $60. Justice Warring told me if I would pay up he would make a good reduction. I refused to give them anything and will

persist in refusing until my lawyer informs me to do so. My trial has been set down for Wednesday, and it is more than probable at that time [that] I will furnish some very interesting matter to the public. I don't propose to be bulldozed by anyone on Coney Island.[53]

The charges were eventually dropped, possibly because of a *Brooklyn Daily Eagle* editorial, which stated:

> Vendors, showmen and other persons at the Summer resorts in this vicinity are being subjected to extortion which partakes closely of the nature of blackmail. That the charges for the license are excessive is as certain as that they are imposed without reference to law or orderly methods of procedure.[54]

The next confrontation between the two men concerned charges against Justices MacMahon and Waring and Paul Bauer, owner of the Brighton Beach Hotel for violations of town gambling laws. These charges stemmed from the actions of the Bacon Investigating Committee, a group formed by the State of New York to look into official corruption. Bauer had pled guilty and was sentenced to jail. However, Justice Waring claimed that he knew nothing about any gambling. One of the witnesses against him was George Tilyou, who testified that Waring had become involved in gambling on horses entered in races by Assemblyman Newton, an associate of McKane. Also that Tilyou

> swears that McKane's assistant health officer told him that he feared McKane's testimony in March before the committee would break up a weekly tariff of $2 levied for the "combine" through the Health Board doctors on each inmate of the bagnios,[55] ostensibly for medical service! By Mr. Tilyou's evidence—a lifelong resident and observer there—authority blackmails every form of vice and amusement in the place. Names, dates, and amounts are precisely given with the admissions of the wretches themselves.[56]

From this point on, it was the Tilyous vs. McKane, until the latter was sentenced to Sing Sing.

McKane struck back in June of 1887, when Peter Tilyou applied for a permit to operate a roller coaster—or, as it was termed then, a jolly-go-round—on Coney Island. The Town Board refused to grant the license on the grounds that the apparatus was "too dangerous to life and limb."[57]

Justice Waring also had an opportunity to strike back at the Tilyous for testifying against him during the Bacon Investigating Committee hearings when George Tilyou was brought before him on a charge of grand larceny. The case involved a lease that George Tilyou had given to an Ira P. George on land that supposedly Tilyou did not own. Justice

Waring then gave the case to the grand jury, who decided to indict Tilyou. A warrant for his arrest was issued, but McKane's police could not find him. The police *did* find Peter Tilyou, who when asked where his son was; his reply was "Go and look for him." The constable then arrested Peter Tilyou for breach of the peace. He was taken to a rear room at police headquarters with his thirteen-year-old daughter clinging to his arm. "Never mind, child, don't cry," said Mr. Tilyou. "Many a tear this family has shed on account of this persecution!"[58]

In July of 1887, George Tilyou applied for an injunction against John McKane and the Board of Police Commissioners of the town of Gravesend to restrain the commissioners from interfering in his operation of a roller coaster. Tilyou's argument was that he had a circular, rather than a straight, roller coaster and that the police board refused to grant him a license because it was believed that this type of coaster was "too dangerous to life and limb," without proving that contention; therefore, he should be allowed to pay the $50 and operate his roller coaster. On July 19, 1887, Judge Cullen handed down a decision denying Tilyou's application for an injunction.

Peter Tilyou made out better than his son. First, he was going to be tried for disturbing the public peace before Justice Waring, but made application to Justice Cullen to have his case go directly to the grand jury on the grounds that he could not receive a fair trial in Coney Island. The application was granted. Secondly, the grand jury did not hand down an indictment.

In January of 1888, McKane gained the upper hand when he had the Town Board of Gravesend open West 15th Street so that it would run from Gravesend through to Coney Island and through Peter Tilyou's Surf House Hotel. Tilyou claimed that the line of the street was purposely changed to drive him from Coney Island. He lost this case, his property was condemned, and the street was lengthened. This was the last confrontation between the Tilyou family and McKane, ending a significant part of Coney Island history.

3

The Turn of the 20th Century

By the end of the 19th century, most of those men who had shaped Coney Island had either died or were no longer a factor in controlling the direction the island would take in the new century. As an example, Austin Corbin died after falling from his carriage in 1896. John McKane returned to Coney Island in 1898 from prison and began selling insurance, dying in the same year. Peter Tilyou survived into the next century, but was never again a player after McKane destroyed his business. The *Brooklyn Daily Eagle* described their encounter as McKane was beginning his journey to prison:

> Peter Tilyou looked at McKane at the depot. The two men are very much alike in appearance. Years ago Tilyou was ruined by McKane who ran a street through his hotel, because Tilyou was opposed to the boss of Gravesend. Tilyou would have done better not to have put himself in evidence to McKane, when the latter was going to prison; but the dramatic character of the event is unquestionable. Tilyou must have opened McKane's memory to many another ghost, for the number of those bankrupted by bossism at Gravesend is large.[1]

The island itself began to change completely. *Harper's New Monthly Magazine* saw the changes coming in 1878:

> The worst of the matter is, it is getting fashionable. Perverse encroachment of the great ones of the earth, who can't rest content with their own delicate fare, but yearn for a sup of their neighbor's black broth so soon as they see him smack his lips over it! A year or two ago Coney Island was *sui generis*, racy with a flavor of its own—the people's watering place, in the fullest sense. But it was *too* good. Since Manhattan Beach and respectability have come in, it needs no Cassandra vision to foretell the transformation of the picturesque resort of old times. And before all the picturesqueness is gone we will hurry for our share.[2]

This development began in 1875 and transformed the island, as if by magic, leading to comparisons with western mining towns. By any quantifiable standard, the changes were dramatic. In 1878, bathers found 3,500 bathhouses for their convenience, and almost 100,000 visitors could dine at Coney restaurants at one sitting. Whereas investors staked barely $100,000 on the island prior to 1874, by 1880 buildings, piers, improvements, and transportation represented revenue somewhere between $10 and $20 million. Almost five thousand jobs existed where barely one hundred people found employment in 1874. One visitor commented, "Surely watering place enterprise has reached its climax in Coney Island."[3] The island was developing entertainment options of a public character, and bathing constituted but a minor part of an experience that included promenading along boardwalks, gazing at views, gulping salt air, and collecting things. Even before the enclosed parks were constructed, Coney Island in the Gilded Age offered encounters with everything odd, different, new, spectacular, and strange. One poet promised "sights you never saw before you'll see on Coney Island's shore." As a city of play, it was a place for bending social norms and relaxing the rigidities of life promulgated by the etiquette books. Like fairs, expositions, beer gardens, and other watering places, Coney functioned at the edge of conduct officially acceptable to mainstream society.[4]

At one time its amusement area stretched from Norton's Point on the western side to Manhattan Beach on the east. In 1892 a lawyer by the name of Alrick Man began to develop the Norton's Point area. The land had sold to Michael Norton by John McKane, who did not record the passing of title allowing Man to begin his project as the Norton's Point Land Company. By the turn of the century, there were about fifty cottages on the property and five years later, one 150, three or four boarding houses and a hotel.

Among the early settlers were the Morgan, Dodge, and Vanderbilt families, perhaps lured to Norton's Point, which was now called Seagate by the relocation of the Atlantic Yacht Club, for many years one of the largest and most prestigious yacht clubs in the New York City area.

The idea of a communal government for Sea Gate came to be in 1890 with the formation of the Sea Gate Association. Since the property was at the extreme end of the point and therefore bordered on three sides by water, and one on land, there would be no purpose for any

3. The Turn of the 20th-Century

An unidentified man and woman take in the view from atop the 85-foot Coney Island Light. The lighthouse was originally established in 1890; the current tower was first lit in 1920 and remains in operation today.

government to need a right of way, with the exception of servicing the lighthouse located on the point.

In 1901, the Norton's Point Land Company deeded to the Sea Gate Association the land required for streets and other public purposes. The association then restricted the sale of Sea Gate land to a minimum of three lots, giving a sixty-foot frontage for each house and restricting commercial enterprises. In order to eliminate the tawdriness that was endemic in Norton's Point, each property owner had to join the association and be subject to its regulations. Also, every member could sit in on an association meeting and voice his opinion on any subject—effectively emulating a New England town meeting.

The colony also had its own police department dressed as New York City policemen but receiving their orders from the Sea Gate Association. Unlike the police in the rest of Coney Island, crime was so low in Sea Gate that a daily police duty was to visit every house on a daily basis to see if any careless servant may have left pots or pails of water standing around to become breeding grounds for mosquito larvae.

The only commercial enterprises in Sea Gate were a municipal boat service to Manhattan and a municipal livery stable that was leased out as a franchise. By 1906, the last remaining lots were acquired by the association, so that the community became completely self-governing.[5]

When a fire destroyed a large part of the Bowery in 1899, including Feltman's Ocean Pavilion, reformers urged that the entire section be decimated and replaced with a seaside park extending from the Concourse on Surf Avenue to Sea Gate. The journalist Walter Creedmoor disagreed:

> The masses love Coney Island as it is, and although they will probably bear with dumb resignation any attempt to transform it into a region of asphalt walks and patches of "keep off the grass" sward, they will certainly turn their backs upon it in its new form and seek their recreation elsewhere.[6]

The city's chief health officer, Doctor Black, looked upon the fire as a means of cleaning up the Bowery:

> The city should not be any longer disgraced as it is by the Bowery at Coney Island, a perennial seat of vice and crime which can never be cleaned out until the city condemns the whole stretch and turns it into a public park. I speak for myself only in protesting the regeneration of this part of the Island, but it seems to me the turning of it into a public park would be a great benefit to the entire city and one of the most wholesome improvements that can be thought of for Brooklyn.
>
>   Coney Island has been a constant disgrace and menace to this city for the past twenty-five years. It is the seat of vice and crime and a source of pollution to the morals of the great mass of the population of this city.[7]

Whether or not the park should have been built became a moot point when the Bowery was quickly rebuilt.

3. The Turn of the 20th-Century

This morning however, found the people very busy and although portions of the ruins of the fire are still sending forth sheets of flame, a number of businessmen have already made plans for the erection of new places. The roads leading to the island, as early as noon yesterday were crowded with lumber trucks, heavily laden, and Surf [A]venue, on the side toward the ocean, is piled up with lumber. Even the trolley cars carried down some lumber this morning and along the line where the board walks used to be there was some great activity displayed by the tenants of the burned buildings.[8]

In 1906, however, fire struck the Bowery again, the blaze of which made an incredible spectacle. Seventy thousand spectators gathered on Surf Avenue to watch the conflagration, creating a dangerous situation that became worse for those watching from the beach as they became trapped between the advancing flames and the ocean. The police had to lead many of the gawkers to safety, while other fled in rowboats. While this fire gutted the Bowery, it only tamped down the island's vices.

The reformers believed that politics would control Coney Island. Within two months of John McKane's removal from power in 1894, the city of Brooklyn annexed the town of Gravesend. The *Brooklyn Daily Eagle* believed that this action would be the turning point in the battle against Coney Island's vice and corruption: "The people of Gravesend have been rescued from barbarism. Civilization has been extended to that town." A month later, the paper editorialized: "Now that Coney Island is part of the city, it will be cleaned out." In the end, however, these new developments had little effect on Coney's vices, which reflected the social desires of an age and not the work of a local boss or machine. When Brooklyn merged with Manhattan in 1898, the island's political decline was complete. In five years, the island went from being the major concern of the town of Gravesend (population: 5,000) to just another neighborhood in the bureaucratic maze of a city of 3.5 million. As the new century dawned, the *Eagle* acknowledged the status quo in banner headlines: "Vice Is Supreme at Coney Island: The West End More Degraded To-Day Than Ever in History." John McKane's ouster simply meant that outsiders would control the patronage and rule virtually all of Coney Island.[9]

In 1906, Robert Wilson Neal, writing in *The World Today*, added:

> It is to this product and survival of criminal days [Coney Island] that New York flees for amusement when the first hot breath of summer, caught in the gorge of tenement and skyscraper, begins sirocco-like to choke the city. No

other one place of recreation and diversion attracts so many New Yorkers. Enthusiastic press-agents give estimates of attendance that deal in combinations of scores and myriads and of hundreds and thousands. The attendance of a "good" day is said to be one hundred thousand, one hundred and fifty thousand, even two hundred thousand. It no doubt reaches the highest of these elements, for toward the littler Rome of Coney Island, the railroad, elevated, and trolley lines carry there in a day more people than live in Bridgeport, Connecticut, or Oakland, California. A fleet of boats exists solely for this passenger traffic, and its vessels ply hourly back and forth to Coney's piers, carrying at every trip as many people as would populate a rural city.

According to Neal, amusement is one reason for the success of Coney Island; another is its contribution to democracy:

> Coney Island is not only a notable example of democracy but also a manifestation of the steady improvement that democracy always works. I do not refer to the proximity to it of other communities settled by other classes of people, to the fact that alongside Coney Island, the resort, there stands, at the western end of the poor little strip of sea-locked land likewise so called, a colony of America's moneyed elite, nor that on the same poor strip of sand are Manhattan and Brighton Beaches, the one place frequented by New York's good and in part fast livers, the other a place across which all the virtues and dullness of Brooklyn have decorously made a way for themselves down to the sea.... The democracy of Coney Island is a more vital one, a mingling of individuals, not a proximity of villages, a democracy that throws people of all ranks and classes together and brings forth new conditions as a consequence.[10]

In 1905, Richard Le Gallienne wrote an article in *Cosmopolitan* about Coney Island at the turn of the 20th century from the viewpoint of *need*, simply because of what the island had to offer.

> All the wonders, I say, and I use the plural advisedly: for, have you noticed how men and women flock to wonders—but how little they know, or care, of Wonder? That, of all things, most struck me in Coney Island—man's voracity for wonders, and his ignorance of Wonder.

As an example he makes a rather esoteric comparison: "Sword-swallowing is scarcely so arduous as brick laying, and, though one is as essentially interesting as the other, the humble brick layer draws but small audiences for his exhibitions of skill." So it is not only the wonder, but also the place itself—Coney Island.

The sense of wonder also needs a suspension of one's usual sense of reality. As he elaborates:

> If you are too superior to have your fortune told by some peasant woman who knows nothing about it, and knows that you know that she doesn't—don't go to Coney Island. The great charm about Coney Island is just there. It not only

knows itself a fake, but, so to speak, it makes so little bones about the matter. It knows that you know, and it expects you to pretend to be taken in, as it pretends to think that it is taking you in.[11]

Channeling the braying voice of the carnival barker, Le Gallienne goes on to illustrate the grotesque entertainments on display for the island's visitors:

> Frrrreaks, wonders, and curiosities! A panorama of the strange, the weird, the odd, the bizarre, the macabre, and the unusual. Ladies and gentlemen, on the inside, everything that's pictured, painted, and advertised out here you will definitely, positively, see on the inside. Frrrreaks, wonders, and curiosities! And put away the fifty-cent ticket. Don't sell any.... But if you go right now, for two minutes, by my watch, as long as there's a line going in, I shan't raise the price: It's a quarter. Twenty-five cents. Frrrreaks! Fat Alice from Dallas![12]

By 1900, freaks were a more profitable draw than Coney Island's landscape. Visiting the resort in 1881, Jose Marti remarked on the "fifty-cent museums where human monsters, freakish fish, bearded ladies, melancholy dwarfs, and rickety elephants, ballyhooed as the biggest elephants in the world, are shown."[13] The journalist Djuna Barnes wrote of Coney Island's "sideshow with its fat lady and its human enigma." She described an exhibit of Somali Islanders as "chocolate-colored savages ... whooping and dancing.[14]

John Kasson wrote of the Coney Island sideshow,

> As in traditional carnivals and fairs the grotesque was prominently represented, symbolizing the exaggerated and excessive character of Coney Island as a whole. Midgets, giants, fat ladies, and ape-men were both stigmatized and honored as freaks. They fascinated spectators in the way they displayed themselves openly as exceptions to the rules of the conventional world. Their grotesque presences heightened the visitors' sense that they had penetrated a marvelous stream of transformation, subject to laws all its own. The popular distorting mirrors furnished the illusion that the spectators themselves had become freaks. Thus Coney Island seemed charged with a magical power to transmute customary appearances into fluid new possibilities.[15]

The quintessential type of sideshow, known as the *ten-in-one*, was created at the Canadian National Exhibition in 1904. Until then, midway attractions were individual exhibits. These shows belonged in two categories, pit shows and platform shows. Pit shows were "typically viewed from above by climbing stairs and filing past a plywood enclosure or small room visible only to the paying patron." Platform shows utilized elevated staging.[16]

The term *ten-in-one* refers to the number of acts or exhibits that are featured, although there were frequently more than ten attractions. Ten-in-one is an insider term, never appearing in the show's billing, and a show would not fail to open for lack of an act or two. "As few as four performers sometimes make up the 'ten' Side Show acts—the Rubber Girl doubling up (so to speak) as the Electric Girl and maybe even as the target for the Knife Thrower!"[17]

Whether the ten-in-one is of the platform or pit variety, the show was conducted by an "inside talker" or "lecturer."[18] It is he who introduces each of the features, either moving along the platform from one exhibit to the next or working as sort of a ringmaster in the pit. Frequently, the attractions—especially the freaks (or human oddities)—do their own lectures, perhaps talking briefly about their deformities and life histories. "Theatrical license" is freely utilized and the presentations typically made use of one of two major types of exaggerations: the exotic, whereby the exhibit is represented as being from some distant land (e.g., Borneo rather than Coney Island), or the aggrandized, in which the oddity is endowed with some status-boosting characteristic, such as having appeared before royalty, possessing some talent or ability, or coming from a prototypically normal American family.[19]

The individual who, more than anyone else, was responsible for the side shows at Coney Island was Samuel Gumpertz. Gumpertz was born in Washington, D.C., in 1868 and had a remarkable upbringing. He worked as a child acrobat at age nine, performed as a member of the Congress of Rough Riders in Buffalo Bill's Wild West Show, worked as a theatrical producer and as a publicist who advanced the career of Harry Houdini, and managed four Midwestern amusement parks before coming to Coney Island in 1904.

Gumpertz's approach to the amusement business was straight forward: "Novelty, that's the answer," he declared. "None of these amusements is lasting. Few people try one more than a half dozen times in a visit and almost nobody wants the same thing the next season. The only way to make an old show go is to hang out a new sign—and that won't work more than one time with the audience." To secure novel attractions for his shows, Gumpertz circled the globe six times to bring back "wild men" from Borneo, Berbers from Africa, Somali warriors, "plate-tipped" Ubangi women from the Congo, and "giraffe-necked" women from Burma. During twenty-eight years as a Coney Island showman, he established himself as the amusement industry's premier exhibitor of indigenous peoples as sideshow attractions, while at the same time displaying an attitude of paternalism that was typical in his day toward those he exhibited. "The primitive tribes and savage peoples have a fascination for me—we are in sympathy, as the Latins say."

Gumpertz's organization was called the Dreamland Circus Sideshow, which was the venue for his Congress of Curious People and Living Wonders of the World. For many sideshow performers who traveled during the winter months, it became a summer residence. Gradually, however, the resort became a second home for many of the performers. Abnormality loves company, and the sideshow folk enjoyed a community life of their own at Coney Island.

Amanda Siebert, known as Jolly Irene, the hypothyroided fat woman who weighed 689 pounds, clung to the beach as a residence because of an insulting offer from Ringling Brothers circus. Since her bulk would not pass through the entrance to regular railroad cars, the show people asked her to travel in the baggage car. Another Coney Island favorite was Jane Darnell, who had a longer career as a sideshow performer than any other American woman; she first appeared on a platform at the age of four and was still in demand as a curiosity at seventy. She turned down an attractive offer from the New York World's Fair because she believed that the salt air at Coney helped her asthma. However, she did make a number of circus tours throughout the nation, billed as either Princess Olga, Madame Olga, or Lady Olga, the woman with the thirteen-inch beard.

> Probably the most memorable event in Coney Island sideshow history was the parade down Surf Avenue during the First World War. The Strong Man, the Tattooed Man, and the Lion Faced Boy among other freaks were to go off to the military, and so they marched to martial music and the waving of flags, while the freaks who could not go cheered and wept with the rest of the people who were being left behind.[20]

The sideshow was not always inhabited by human beings. In 1915, Gumpertz took possession of the Eden Musee in Manhattan and brought its celebrated wax figures to Coney Island. The Eden Musee was renowned for its lifelike wax tableaux and its famous Chamber of Horrors. When the museum went bankrupt, Gumpertz was able to buy several of the pieces at auction such as "Too Late for the Opera" and "The Electrocution of the Four Gunmen." More importantly, he secured exclusive use of the name Eden Musee. Later, Gumpertz added an annex called Underground Chinatown, complete with an opium den and a wax tableaux called "Killing the Missionaries by Chinese Boxers." In 1928, the entire collection was destroyed by fire. A reporter for the *New York Herald Tribune* wrote about what he saw during the inferno:

> Marat slumped in his bathtub and Charlotte Corday, dropping her knife, [which] melted at his feet. Ex-President Taft dwindled within his clothes and ran out over his shoe tops. The sprucely erect policeman caved in at his knees, buckled at the waist and collapsed within his blue uniform. Leopold and Loeb mingled in common wax with Gerald Chapman, the garrote murderer, and the rest of the Chamber of Horrors ran out through a crack in the floor.[21]

Animal exhibits were also part of the sideshows. When promoter Frank Bostock arrived in Coney Island from England in 1893, he brought with him "a queer mess of show stuff." He had "a small but gaudy animal show known as 'Noah's Ark,' [featuring] a boxing kangaroo, Jolly the elephant, Wallace the untamable lion, [and] a tattooed yak. Some performing lions and 'whatnots' were [also] exhibited."[22]

Despite minor deceptions, by the early 20th century, games such as three-card monte and the shell game were considerably less crooked. According to lion tamer George Conklin, "The roughest show on the road to-day would not dare countenance the least of the methods by which great sums of money were regularly taken from the public by swindlers in the late [eighteen-] 'sixties and early 'seventies."[23]

Coney Island had basically three categories of games: *games of skill* (which depend on the players own ability), *games of chance* (in which the player has no control over the outcome, thus constituting gambling), and *flat games* (in which the player cannot win and is "flat out" swindled). But sometimes a purported game of skill is actually not. Such a game is called an *alibi store*, because the operator is ready with a pat explanation for why the player did not win—"You threw too hard," for example.[24]

Coney had two aquariums, the Sea-side aquarium, a branch of the New York Aquarium built in 1878, and Brandenburg's Aquarium, which included a museum erected in 1902, and another museum, Bunnell's, built in 1907. But the rides—especially the roller coasters—were the big attractions.

The origins of roller coasters can be traced back to Russian Ice Slides, which first appeared in the 1700s. A slide consisted of a steep drop made entirely of ice. The rider sat on a sled that was made either of wood or ice and attached to runners. These slides were potentially dangerous, requiring agility on the part of the rider, so skilled guides made their services available to novice riders for a fee.

The idea was adopted by the French, but was not as successful because France's climate did not allow the ice to stay frozen. An enterprising French businessman covered the slope with wood, which he waxed, and then put rollers onto the wooden sleds. This new recreational attraction debuted at a public garden in the Ternes quarter of Paris in 1804, and in keeping with its eastern European heritage, it was named the Russian Mountains. As in Russia, however, skill was needed to drive the sled, and accidents were common. Strangely, the more accidents there were, the more people were drawn to them. The next step was to create a track structured so that each rider would go down the hill in a straight line on their own track, avoiding collisions. The ride proved even more popular when tracks were set up side-by-side since it encouraged wagering on who would finish first. The French also made the first attempt at a loop-the-loop, which they called the Centrifuge Railway. The French government halted the ride after the first accident; this occurred because centrifugal force was the only thing holding the car to the track and the rider to the car.

In the United States, the idea for a coaster was devised not as a pleasure ride, but as a transportation system for the mining industry. In the 1840s, mine owners built a railway from the top of the mine to the port in Mauch Chunk, Pennsylvania. The rail cars were filled with coal, allowing gravity to take them down the mountain. Someone got the bright idea of creating a ride by loading the mine cars with people and pushing them down the hill (possibly based on the Russian and French experience). Since the ride lasted for eighteen miles, it became an instant success. As a result, the cars hauled coal by day and people by night. A steam engine was added to take the riders up the hill at the cost of one dollar. By 1870, the railway was being used exclusively for pleasure rides.

At the same time that the Mauch Chunk Railway became exclusively a pleasure ride, a derivation of the French coaster began in Haverhill, Massachusetts. In this version, the riders were all placed in a sled that was hoisted to the top of a building by means of an elevator. The riders pushed themselves out of the elevator and onto a series of rollers that sent the sled down the side of the building in a figure-eight configuration until landing next to the elevator. Each rider was charged five cents.

As the various ideas for coasters engendered improvements and different methods of construction on other rides, the Mauch Chunk Railway was the inspiration for L. A. Thompson to create the first authentic American roller coaster in Coney Island in 1884. The ride was called the Switchback Railway. The structure, made entirely out of wood, stood fifty feet tall and was six hundred feet in length. Riders climbed a flight of stairs to board the coaster car, which was then pushed out of the station, gravity taking it along a track to the other end. The riders would then exit the car and climb a stairway to the second level, where workers would have hoisted the car; the passengers would then reboard and ride back to the starting point. The cars traveled at the leisurely speed of ten miles per hour, which allowed the riders, seated in benches facing out sideway, to enjoy sightseeing.

The next improvement was the Serpentine Railway, invented in 1885 by Charles Alcoke, which was another gravity-driven coaster, although this one traversed along an oval-shaped track, making it possible for passengers to remain in their cars until the ride's conclusion. Described in *Frank Leslie's Weekly* as "a contrivance designed to give passengers, for the insignificant expenditure of five cents, all the sensation of being carried away by a cyclone."[25] Also In 1885, Philip Hinckle began the roller coaster speed race by using a power-operated chain elevator to carry the cars to a far higher height than ever before, thereby increasing the speed on the downhill run and also placing the seats facing forward, so that the ride became more important than the scenery.

The next improvement in Coney Island roller coasters came in 1895—the "Loop the Loop," a variation on the French ride, manufactured in the United States by Lina Beecher. This version was the last coaster to use a truly circular loop in which the riders were inverted. The thirty-foot-high vertical ellipse formed the central part of the roller coaster track circuit. A car accommodating four passengers was pulled by a chain to the apex of the structure and then allowed to zoom down a steep incline leading into the loop. There, the car gradually turned upside down until it emerged right side up on a moderate incline that checked the car's speed before the track led the car to the starting point.

The loop probably ranks as the outstanding thrill ride of all time at Coney Island. Scientifically it was flawless. The centrifugal force

3. The Turn of the 20th-Century

Loop the Loop, the second looping roller coaster built on Coney Island, was based on the principle of centrifugal force, demonstrated in this photograph by an upside-down bicyclist.

developed by the ride exceeded the passenger's weight—even a glass of water carried on an experimental trip failed to spill a drop. However, the Loop posed the fundamental paradox of all roller coaster rides; the customers had to be convinced that it was (a) desperately dangerous, and (b) perfectly safe. The Loop was advertised as the "Safest and the Greatest Attraction—No Danger Whatsoever," but the customers didn't believe it. Straps were no protection against the fool who decided to stand up, or the drunk who lurched at the wrong moment. Together, these two factors caused four-fifths of all roller coaster casualties. After watching a while, the crowd decided the ride was too dangerous. That doomed the Loop, even if had not also revealed another fundamental disadvantage: limited capacity. The number of persons who could be carried at one time determined the ceiling of possible profit, and in the case of the Loop, the ceiling simply wasn't high enough.[26]

By 1906 Thompson created a new type of coaster that, while it was still one in which scenery was a major part of the ride, fell into the "screaming category." They were the Pike's Peak Scenic Railway and the

Oriental Scenic Railway. Pike's Peak, among Thompson's most imposing creations, had a track that ran over a mile, winding its way over the streets of Coney Island and ascending to a height of 138 feet. The ride was 258 feet in diameter at its base and incorporated a water ride called the Whirlpool. Each of Thompson's scenic railways had architecturally distinctive terminals equipped with beer gardens, dance halls, and soda fountains made to resemble doll houses and souvenir kiosks. "Many of the evils of society, much of the vice and crime which we deplore," he once said, "come from the degrading nature of amusements entered into. To inveigh against them, avails little, but to substitute something better, something clean and wholesome, and persuade men to choose it, is worthy of all endeavor."[27]

American humorist Guy Wetmore Carryl used poetry as a way to described a ride on Thompson's creation:

> You plunge into the entrance of the Screaming Scenic Railway,
> > Newly joisted, and are hoisted in a car up the incline:
> And surveying all that frail way in a palpitating, pale way
> > Go lunging down and plunging down each giddier incline
> > Shrilly squealing, with a feeling like a fly upon a ceiling
> You are grateful when you're through it, and you're wiser if you do it
> > (That's unless you want to rue it) half an hour before you dine.[28]

The roller coasters at Coney continuously evolved because of permanence. Coney Island was not a midway or a sideshow, nor was it simply an amusement park. Between 1897 and 1904, it was transformed into a technologically sophisticated mass-entertainment center, attracting patrons from all socioeconomic levels. It contained environments composed of mechanical, exotic settings, and flamboyant architecture, which provided pleasure seekers with collective stimulation and constant activity.[29]

Roller coasters provide an instructive, if not altogether typical, example of how designers strove to reconcile consumer demands for thrills, safety, and novelty on one hand, and the economic and operational concerns of ride operators on the other. In the 1910s, giant wooden roller coasters became the most prestigious area of design. While coasters were not new, improvements in safety devices made it possible to build very large, very fast coasters that were predictable and reasonably safe.

Various kinds of rides based on the idea of the railroad persisted

3. The Turn of the 20th-Century

into the 20th century. The scenic railroads, based on L. A. Thompson's Switchback Railroad, were the most common. Many scenic railroads were thematic—they offered thrills partly through the opportunity to travel to some exotic place. The brochure of the Edward C. Boyce Company described their version as "2,500 feet of bewilderment ... passengers find themselves being dashed along down sharp inclines and up again ... through caves of darkness and tunnels containing beautiful scenery, and lighted by many colored electric lights."[30] Other companies built versions that featured scenes from the Bible or a trip around Pike's Peak or some other tourist locale.

On September 4, 1911, the *New York Times* reported that May Kalligan and Alice Provost had been killed in an accident on the Giant Racer roller coaster at Coney Island.

> The shrill scream of a woman, followed by the screech of metal against metal and of splinted wood, brought everyone within earshot running yesterday afternoon to the Giant Racer, a scenic ride on the southeast corner of Surf Avenue and West Tenth Street Coney Island. Spectators saw that the rear car was tilted outward at an angle of 45 degrees, and from it hung the limp forms of the two women. Two other women and a man, the former screaming, were struggling to hold their places in the side of the damaged car."[31]

Much to the chagrin of early 20th-century amusement park operators, such accidents often made front-page news. The reason was that those who ventured to Coney Island did so in the hope that they would be involved in the type of risk that would be thrilling, not injurious. They would be subject to the experience of being in danger, without the possibility of real physical consequences. They assumed that if they paid the cost of admission, they would be guaranteed both thrills *and* safety.

Guy Wetmore Carryl described the thrills of riding a roller coaster in one of his humorous columns:

> Whether one patronizes the Scenic Railway or any of those cousins of hers which resemble her so closely, or prefers the water chute, which is dignified by greater age, it seems to be absolutely necessary to scream loudly and continuously from start to finish and to embrace one's nearest neighbor with such varying degrees of ardor as the particular circumstances of age, sex, and length of acquaintanceship may dictate. These conditions are sine quibus non.[32] Why, there is no knowing. Coney Island has a code of conduct which is all her own, and it is not only proper, but essential, to conform thereto, as it is proper to have one's tintype taken and to eat crimson sausages, green corn on the ear, and retrospective soft shell crabs.[33]

This situation showed the downside of permanency, first because it put pressure on the operators to come up with attractions that would draw in returning customers. They were forced constantly to weigh the potential attraction of novelty against the cost of installing new rides. Permanency also enforced the accountability for the safety of patrons. Bad news could rapidly spoil box-office receipts or even bankrupt ride owners with inadequate insurance against lawsuits. Alice Provost's husband, for instance, sued the owners of the Giant Coaster for $30,000—a substantial sum in 1911.[34] Secondly, there was the conglomeration of enterprises that resulted from a variety of entrepreneurs who set up shop. A visitor to Coney Island in 1906 described the curious mix that resulted: "Here and there we find a modest little haberdasher or trimming-store tucked away between the gaudy entrance to a scenic railway or a Johnstown flood."[35] Potential social danger, as these entrepreneurs quickly realized, was far more threatening to prospective customers, particularly women, than the physical risks of the rides. Open midways soon obtained an unsavory reputation for drunkenness, prostitution, and crime.[36]

This permanence allowed for the staging of elaborate spectacles. As early as 1884, Henry James Paine staged fireworks shows over Manhattan and Brighton Beaches. Paine's most famous spectacle was the eruption of Mount Vesuvius, which "spewed out a colored fire" as spectators saw the city of Pompeii disappear "beneath torrents of blazing magnesium powder."[37] This success engendered a host of topical disaster spectacles, such as the aforementioned reenactment of the Johnstown Flood of May 30, 1889, when a rainstorm caused a dam to collapse. The resulting flood destroyed the Pennsylvania town and killed an estimated 2,200 people. According to the Coney Island souvenir program, "The Johnstown Flood [exhibit] appeals to all, young and old, and should be seen by every visitor to the island."[38] Coney Island also had a re-creation of the 1890 Galveston flood, heralded as a "stupendous reproduction" of the great Texas tidal wave that killed some seven thousand people.[39] War was also a subject for a re-enactment. The Boer War had no sooner ended in 1902 when Piet Cronje, the commander of the Boer army, staged a depiction in a Coney Island area approximately the size of a football field; the surrounding grandstand accommodated upwards of twelve hundred spectators, Cronje employed a thousand actors and soldiers, in addition to hiring "real" Africans, who were paid four dollars a week in order to add "authenticity to his production."[40]

As John Kasson has noted, part of Coney Island's importance was the challenge that it presented in those genteel times. Victorian culture was rigid and formal in defining people's roles. It emphasized restraint, self-improvement, sobriety, moderation, and self-control. The cultural standard setters were puritanical regarding sex. These cultural tastemakers rightly perceived their values and hegemony to be under assault in the late 19th and early 20th century. They viewed with great concern social and cultural trends and feared the emerging commercial mass culture. Kasson accurately described amusement parks as "laboratories of the new mass culture."[41] Coney Island and its amusement parks represented one especially important battleground in the struggle between mass culture and the hegemony of older Victorian values.[42]

As the average workweek declined and workers' expendable monies increased slightly, the issue of leisure became more prominent. Reformers and proponents of a civilized culture saw leisure as both a problem and an opportunity. Play should ideally be put into the service of moral uplift. It should build character and encourage traits of discipline, fortitude, and self-control. Organized play in the workplace should encourage employee loyalty and help employers identify natural leaders who might be promoted to supervisory positions.[43] Furthermore, time dedicated to regulated, uplifting recreation and exercise, was time unavailable for the dissipation of the poolroom, beer hall, movie house, dance hall, or worse.

It is hard to overstate both the allure of Coney Island during this era and the challenge that it posed to Victorian values. In 1909, for example, over twenty million people visited Coney Island. Adjusting for population increases, the number of visitors in 1909 exceeded by approximately 20 percent the total number of visitors to Disneyland and Disney World combined in 1989.[44] Articles about Coney Island and other amusement parks appeared in countless popular magazines, including *American Mercury, Atlantic Monthly, Harper's Weekly, Frank Leslie's Illustrated Weekly, Munsey's Magazine, New Republic, North American Review, Popular Mechanics, and Saturday Review*. From 1905 through 1910, *Scientific American* published a series of stories on various Coney Island rides, focusing primarily on their mechanics. Aldous

Huxley and Maxim Gorky both weighed in with their views of Coney Island, neither of which was favorable.[45]

Popular culture took note of Coney Island in another way—the movies. As an example, the 1927 Paramount romantic comedy *It*, starring Clara Bow, is the story of a pert salesgirl who becomes the object of desire for the owner of a department store. The wealthy gentleman—played by Latin heartthrob Antonio Moreno—takes his employee on a nighttime date to Coney Island, where they take in the sights and enjoy the rides in Luna Park; at one point Clara briefly loses her sense of modesty when a wind-blowing grate causes her short skirt to billow upward, exposing her lingerie. The following year (1928) another Paramount star, Harold Lloyd, took his film crew to New York to shoot his newest comedy, *Speedy*, directed by Ted Wilde. As in the Clara Bow film, Harold and his fiancée (Ann Christy) have a rollicking date in Luna Park. In one scene, Harold is seen mugging outrageously at his distorted image in the Hall of Mirrors; he is also the last survivor on the Human Roulette Wheel—before an errant land crab's pinch makes him forfeit his position as "King of the Mountain." (For more information on this unique ride, see Chapter 4.) The last major silent feature to employ location shots in Coney Island was *The Crowd*, a stark drama directed by King Vidor for Metro-Goldwyn-Mayer in 1928. The film's downtrodden couple (played by James Murray and Eleanor Boardman) goes on a double date to Coney's amusement park to escape their workaday lives. This was likely a similar scenario for many real-life couples.

One of the areas of Coney Island that added to its less-than-stellar reputation was The Gut, situated in the approximate center of Coney, was comprised of a ramshackle group of wooden shanties and cottages that served as bars, cabarets, fleabag hotels, and houses of ill repute. The area was partially hidden in a culvert in the sand, in a part of Coney that was formerly under water. The Gut became popular with the construction of Coney Island's racetracks, which brought them an influx of touts, jockeys, rubbers, stable boys, hangers-on and their women. They came there to live for weeks at a time during the spring and fall racing seasons.

Gutters (the nickname for residents of the Gut) thought little of giving knockout drops to outsiders. Laudanum, morphine, and snuff were used occasionally, but the orthodox dose consisted of a teaspoon

(30–40 grams) of hydrate of chloral to a tumbler of liquid. In most cases the drug slowed the heartbeat of the unwitting customer, although in other instances—especially concerning those who had been drinking heavily—heart failure could be the result. Such a fate was considered an intrinsic risk of visiting this den of iniquity.

"I don't suppose there was a wickeder place on the globe then the Gut in its palmy days," John McKane said. McKane took action to tame the Gut, and what he couldn't accomplish, fires and the closing of the racetracks did, and these establishments moved out of the immediate area. These honky-tonks, however, proved to be tops in New York nightlife. Song publishers started scrambling for the ear of Surf Avenue, where the hits of the United States started.[46]

Many of the nation's most famous entertainers began their careers in show business at this time on Coney Island. The comedian known as "Schnozzola," Jimmy Durante, was only fourteen when he was making $25 a week playing piano from early evening to 6 a.m. at the College Inn on Surf Avenue. He learned a lot of things quickly, but chiefly this: "Keep your nose out of other people's business. If you follow this advice, you'll never have to alibi a black eye." Orchestra leader Vincent Lopez worked in a five-man band at Perry's Café on West 15th Street in the Bowery. Eddie Cantor, a song and dance man called "Banjo Eyes," was only a skinny teenager when he started singing at Carey Walsh's, earning three dollars a night. When he learned that he could make more as a singing waiter, he became one. Legendary songwriter Irving Berlin worked in Coney Island as a singer at Stauch's and a singing waiter at Perry's. Many of the more notorious cabarets fell to police raids due to changing ideas of public morality. The entertainers never worried though, as Durante said: "You couldn't build a Sunday school out of those night spots. People knew they were tough joints, and if they gave 'em a play, had nobody but themselves to kick if they lost their shirts."[47]

During the mid–1890s, with their original resort builders, Austin Corbin and William Engeman, out of the picture, Manhattan and Brighton Beaches acceded to the growing commercialization of leisure and the spread of heretofore lower-class tastes throughout society by booking vaudeville and circus performers. To house these acts, Manhattan Beach erected a 2,300-seat theater in 1894, a 12,000-seat bicycle oval in 1895, and an arena to seat 10,000. Brighton Beach opened a 1,800-seat music hall in 1879.[48]

In an approving assessment of John Philip Sousa's arrival at Manhattan Beach in 1892, the *Brooklyn Daily Eagle* credited him for "recognizing that Manhattan Beach is not a conservatory of music where taste is to be cultivated and people to be educated, but a pleasure resort where they come to be entertained." In 1899, Manhattan Beach presented its first minstrel show and the *Brooklyn Daily Eagle* exclaimed, "Judging from the enthusiasm with which the performance was received, it will not be the last one." The same year, the Brooklyn Rapid Transit Company (which by that date owned or leased nearly all of Brooklyn's surface and elevated rail lines) purchased the Hotel Brighton and began running electrified trains to the resort, which allowed for faster and more frequent service to the island.

The construction of the Brighton Beach Amusement Park in 1906 represented the east end's final concession to popular tastes. The decline of Manhattan and Brighton Beaches was due in large part to the heavily capitalized amusement parks, such as Steeplechase, Luna Park, and Dreamland. Two other factors were the spreading suburbanization of Brooklyn and the closing of Coney Island's racetracks in 1910. As the entertainment gap between the areas of Coney Island narrowed, wealthier visitors fled to still more exclusive resorts and those of more modest incomes found their tastes satisfied and their respectability honored at the New Coney Island.[49]

The growing acceptance of summer vacations among broad segments of the American populace after the Civil War stemmed in large part from the increase in disposable income. Between 1880 and 1890, the national consumer price index showed a steady decline. Moreover, within New York City and Brooklyn, retail prices of dry goods and groceries remained stable or declined slightly. Additionally, Brooklyn's population increased by 42 percent between the years 1880 and 1890.

Working men and women could visit Coney Island on an impulse, without planning or saving money for the journey. Saturday half-holidays and reductions in daily hours enabled industrial production workers to spend much of their free time at seaside resorts. With few exceptions, people expected to return to Brooklyn or Manhattan at night. Since this was the case, there was little financial incentive to build the enormous hotels of the type constructed in the 19th century. Small boarding houses sprang up to accommodate overnight stays.

Beginning in the mid–1880s, the summer Saturday half-holiday movement became widespread across Brooklyn and New York and were promoted for commercial and moral reasons. Steamboat and railroad companies organized excursions to picnic groves and seaside resorts. Advocates of the half-holiday were not entirely altruistic. The New York Chamber of Commerce, for instance, argued that the holiday would prevent the growing secularization of the Sabbath. Backed by a variety of supporters, the Saturday half-holiday movement contributed much to the leisure aspirations of working people.[50]

Actions by progressive organizations had an effect on Coney Island. Finding a direct link between sanitation and good health, they demanded clean housing for the poor and encouraged workers to visit the shore. Middle-class reformers encouraged employers and charities to help city dwellers escape disease-ridden areas. Only recently exposed to the benefits of a summer vacation themselves, the civic-minded bourgeoisie enthusiastically supported the notion that a few days in the open air would compensate for an environment that "ghoul-like, suck the life blood of its inhabitants." For them, a yearly rest had become a reward for hard and successful labor; now, they sought to extend the benefits to the poor.[51]

Middle-class moralists and factory managers supported weekend visits by the working class to Coney Island. They believed that such trips provided a healthy alternative to the neighborhood bars, theaters, and pleasure gardens that bred vice and an overall sense of disrespect for labor. Factory managers undoubtedly preferred a regulated work week and a Sunday of recreation at the shore to a pattern of casual labor and St. Monday observances.[52]

Reformers did not have to justify Coney Island's position as a haven for mothers and children. The *Brooklyn Union and Argus* hoped that the shore could undo the negative influences that had accumulated during the week:

> To the mother who reaches Saturday night wearied and worn with household chores, to the children cooped in 7' by 9' rooms whose only experience of air is that which comes up from heated pavements laden with the fragrance of the gutter and the sewer, the cheap Sunday excursion is the renewal of the lease on life.[53]

Similarly, the *Brooklyn Daily Eagle* explained that the drop in infant mortality owed much to clean air and water. It was no coincidence that "the gain [in infants' health] was most visible when Coney Island was crowded with mothers and their little ones. It is not a question of luxury with parents; it is a question of life and death to their children.[54]

The *New York Times* completed the journalistic joy in having Coney Island available, "When that terrible scourge, cholera infantum, rages in New York and Brooklyn, it will be to Coney Island that mothers will carry their little ones, [because] the tonic influences of untainted salt air will revive the suffering children."[55]

The New York immigrant population was also involved in Coney Island, although the behavior of German and Irish Catholics occasionally aggravated the still puritan sensibility. Fearful of the increasing influence of immigrants, the *Illustrated Christian Weekly*, a leading New York–based Protestant newspaper, denounced the 60,000 persons who frolicked at the shore on one Sunday in 1878. "It is a sad thought that so many thousands in one resort are desecrating God's day," the paper lamented. "We know it is very largely our foreign population that forms the bulk of the crowd on Sundays, but we wish they would learn lessons from us, instead of becoming our teachers."[56]

Defending the right to be different, the *Catholic Mirror* criticized those Catholics "who have got[ten] so Protestantized that they are horrified if they see other Catholics indulge their propensities for innocent amusement on the Sabbath." Instead, it argued, "once having complied with his religious duties on Sunday ... the Catholic is free to enjoy himself in all innocent amusements—just as free as any other day."[57] Coney Island's special appeal extended to Catholic prelates, as one priest explained to a reporter who asked why so many of his brethren visited Coney Island. "Because we find here a healthful and convenient resort. We cannot take the long vacations so liberally accorded our Protestant friends."[58]

The South Brooklyn Turaverein and the North German Brothers celebrated their ethnic heritage in Coney Island at such places as Feltman's by singing songs like the one printed on the back of a West Brighton Beach Hotel Concert program:

> In time of peace, in time of strife,
> For old and young it brings new life,
> The Flowing Bowl that makes us free
> In Unity-Fraternity
> Drink, brethren, drink
> With hearts of joyous harmony
> Drink, brethren, drink
> While rings the melody

German culture also flowed at the Sea Beach Palace during the 1885 National Saengerfest when more than two thousand singers performed selections by Schumann and Wagner.[59]

German groups visiting Coney Island elicited frequent praise from the *Brooklyn Daily Eagle*. Following an outing by the Hanover Society, which contained "as large a percentage of prosperous citizens as any such society can lay claim to," the paper exclaimed that "a more desirable class of people has never taken possession of a West Brighton ballroom."[60] When the Retail Grocers Association met at Feltman's in 1888, its participants were described as "jolly German shopkeepers." The contrast between Americans and German immigrants at West Brighton appeared greatest after an exuberant outing by the Saengerbund. Criticizing the American mentality towards pleasure, the *Brooklyn Daily Eagle* noted:

> The trouble with Americans is that they are too much afraid of what people may think of them. They dress, walk, ride, and act in public entirely to suit the folks who will be looking at them ... making themselves and those about them very stiff and uncomfortable.... A German spends 25 cents, gets $10 worth of fun out of it and goes home happy as a king.... Really, we are carrying too much dignity and the sooner we become Germans the better.[61]

Coney Island's most popular beverage was unquestionably beer, and its chief commercial enterprise, the saloon, was ubiquitous. In 1878, the *Irish-American* counted seventy-two liquor enterprises that paid taxes at Coney—many more outlets evaded this license. An 1887 business directory listed seventy-seven liquor stores, seven brewers, and six bottlers. In 1886, the *Brooklyn Daily Eagle* recounted how ten years earlier only German and Central European immigrants drank beer in the United States. "The American was utterly unfamiliar with it ... and if mentioned at all by the non-German population was spoken of in a disparaging way." By 1885, however, more than 21 percent of the malt liquor sold in the United States was consumed in New York and Brooklyn and "no bar room or place of public entertainment, from the first class hotel to the lowest dive, is without it."[62]

Coney Island's development as a popular playground for the working class disturbed those influential clergymen, lawyers, politicians, and newspaper editors who believed that the increasing commercialization of leisure time activities had sabotaged their own efforts to provide purposeful recreation. At the turn of the 20th century, Coney Island scarcely resembled the idealized environment that might invigorate tired and sickly industrial workers. Instead, it sold a mindless escape through drink, gambling, and mechanical rides. Men and women who spent Sundays racing around on roller coasters rather than improving their minds apparently lessened their opportunities for advancement.[63]

According to the reformers of the day, Coney Island was not getting better, and worse, a sense of malaise was spreading. Other resort areas, such as Rockaway Beach, South Beach, Staten Island, Revere Beach, Atlantic City, and Long Branch were now offering cheap food, dance-hall shows, and thrill rides in order in increase patronage. And at Coney Island itself, the gambling dens and brothels were moving from the shadows to relocate along the Bowery and Surf Avenue, the resort's major arteries. Additionally, the once-tonier areas of Brighton Beach and Manhattan Beach had begun to resemble Coney Island due to their economic problems, which made them bring in circus acts and vaudeville shows.

The answer, to the reformers and those with real estate interests, was to create public parks in Coney and to turn it into a middle-class residential community. This effort was led by General James Jourdan, a Civil War officer. After the war, as part of the Internal Revenue Service, he led raids on moonshiners in Brooklyn; he was also a Brooklyn police commissioner and president of Brooklyn Union Gas. As a politician, he was one of the "three graces."[64]

As John Kasson noted:

> Public parks and gymnasiums would replace city streets as the playgrounds of the poor and, by instilling habits of discipline and cooperation, help to eradicate poverty itself. Community centers would supplant poolrooms and saloons as agents in the acculturation of recent immigrants. Recreation programs for factory workers and their families would make employees more content and productive. In such ways, reformers wished to supersede amusement parks and other commercial recreations with more orderly and highly regulated amusements, designed to discipline instincts and institutionalize them.[65]

Walter Creedmoor, a writer for *Munsey's Magazine*, rebutted the reformers:

> Just now a good many of these reformers and humanitarians and representatives of what they themselves usually term the "Better Element" are crying aloud to have the most picturesque and popular summer resort on the continent turned into a public park. The enthusiasm with which this proposition has been seconded and approved by everybody who does not know anything

about the subject whatever leads me to fear that our municipal authorities, who are notoriously prone to lend an ear to the clamor of ignorance, may succeed in establishing these parks on sites where nothing higher than a currant bush will grow, and I therefore venture to raise my voice in mild protest. The fact of the matter is that Coney Island has had parks for twenty-five years and no one will visit them because they are barren and dreary spots that are in no way comparable with the great region of merry-go-rounds, chowder pots, variety shows, lung testers, and cane boards, in which the human heart finds recreation and relief on hot afternoons.[66]

Some Coney Island businessmen also objected to the direction in which the island was headed. Paul Bauer, owner of the West Brighton Hotel, objected to the "loud, weird noises" of the carousel organs and street bands. "They produce a dire and a clatter," he complained, "which is very offensive and detrimental to the health of a numerous body of people who visit the ocean for its restorative health giving atmosphere, instead of which they encounter a Babel of noises which distract their senses and drives them away to other more congenial hygiene resorts, where public decency has not been so outrageously insulted as at Coney Island."[67]

Bauer's comments were seconded by Alrick H. Man, the founder of Kew Gardens and director of the Sea Beach Railroad, who also owned land in Coney Island that contained more cheap games and dance halls than any other area of the island. Man, told the *Kings County Rural and Brighton Gazette*, however, that he intended to remove all the carousels, hot dog vendors, and saloons from his property and build a park where respectable families could "wander amid acres of trees and flowers, eat ices, look at fireworks, listen to band concerts, and experience many novel seaside delights. A most determined effort," he concluded, "will be made to overcome the bad elements which now control West Brighton."[68]

The clergy also became involved in the activities at Coney Island. Their objection primarily to the racetracks with its attendant gambling. The Rev. T. DeWitt Talmage, the nationally known leader of the Presbyterian Tabernacle in Brooklyn, organized a protest meeting at the Brooklyn Academy of Music to rally support against the Ives Pool Bill, which would allow thirty days of betting at each racetrack per year. In his scathing denunciation of the bill, the Reverend stated:

> It means the damnation of public morals. It means the subjection of a hundred thousand boys and young men to a temptation which many of them are

not strong enough to resist. It means the boring of a hole in the money drawers of merchants from which the dollars shall be filched for the purchase of pool tickets. It means an invitation to the bad people of other cities to come here with their scoundrelism and their harlotry and their beastliness and make Brooklyn a Saratoga, the capital of an earthly pandemonium.[69]

Brooklyn's annexation of Gravesend in 1894 had little effect on Coney Island's vices. During the 1890s, New Yorkers traveled to Coney to see Little Egypt and scantily clad Turkish dancers much as they visited neighborhood vaudeville shows. According to its severest critics, West Brighton had become "New York's Vast Training School of Vice and Vulgarity." Admitting that Coney Island's reputation as "the friskiest, wickedest place in the world" had been largely a myth, the *New York World* nevertheless proclaimed that "the island's current atmosphere of dancehalls, brothels, dives, fakes, frauds, and vulgarities was truly supercharged with poison."[70]

The *New York Times* did not agree with the *Eagle* and the *World*. In 1877, it stated: "Coney Island is the true republic of watering places, the magnificent exclusiveness of Newport ... does not affront your comparative poverty."[71] Another reporter for the same newspaper viewed Coney as an egalitarian utopia:

> Toward sunset, all along the shore, on a Midsummer's day, myriads of people of all ages and both sexes may be seen tumbling among the breakers ... salt sea bathing, especially at Coney Island, makes you see the companion of strange beings sometimes. Old Ocean is a grand old Democrat, and levels all petty distinctions. He buffets the rich and the poor alike, who clad for bath, present very much the same appearance.[72]

Although this rhetoric belonged to the long tradition of describing Coney Island as an inherently democratic locale, the image had some justification. The anonymity of the beach and midway allowed people to believe that the seaside experience abolished boundaries of class identity, diminished economic tensions, and brought people together. Slumming fashionables who did not respond to Coney Island's "frank assumption of equality" were assumed to be either hardened aristocrats or bigoted aesthetes. Strollers from various stations of life mingled on the beach, pier, Bowery, or Surf Avenue, cloaked by the crowd. In 1878, *Harper's Weekly* declared Coney Island supreme among America's seaside resorts, a place which "offers her sunny expanse of wave washed sand as a playground where rich and poor alike may take their pleasure."[73] An 1899 visitor's guide to the city of New York urged those with money at the Manhattan Beach and Oriental Hotels to consciously spend some time at "the great resort of the crowds."[74]

Coney Island in the Gilded Age differed mainly from Newport or Saratoga in that it was easily accessible, highly affordable, and only an hour in travel time from two of the nation's largest cities, New York and Brooklyn. In 1890, the *Brooklyn Daily Eagle* listed Coney's attractions:

> The noise, the jingle, the junketing, the music, the flaring pictures, the loud voices of the touts proclaiming the wonders to be seen for a dime, the boats, the merry-go-rounds, the dancing platforms, the museums, the concert halls, the bathers and the thousand and one attractions make up a Vanity Fair at which young girls swarm, open-eyed, open-mouthed, wondering at everything and taking all the tinsel for gold. To their simple minds, the place is a fairyland, and it never dawns upon them that there can be harm where there is so much good humor and laughter.[75]

The reformers, however, did not give up. To them, Coney Island joined dance halls and movie theaters as corrupting aspects of urban life. Reformers worried about the effect on the family of amusements that catered to groups of young people. They decried the free and easy sexuality in a setting where so many young people had escaped the supervision by their parents. They also brought to bear on commercial amusements the same skepticism they had toward other unregulated commercial activity.

The reformers responded to the challenge of these urban commercial amusement parks (Coney Island being a prime example) in a variety of ways. As had earlier critics, they importuned would-be indulgers (especially young women) to avoid the temptations of such places and cautioned their parents to keep their children from a path that led to dissipation. Robert Harland, one of the most notable of the Progressive Era reformers, urged parents with daughters: "Teach her that it is not the White Slave Traffic she must dread alone. Teach her that it is the place of amusement that seems innocent, the drinking of pleasant drinks, the association with characterless men."[76]

4
The Parks: Sea Lion Park, Steeplechase Park, and Brighton Beach Park

The first modern amusement park, Sea Lion Park, was created in 1895; the second, Steeplechase Park, in 1897; they were joined by Brighton Beach Park in 1905, and all were in Coney Island. With these three parks, the practice of selling leisure as a commodity was initiated. They were joined by two more parks—Luna Park and Dreamland—before 1910.[1] (These will be be the subject of the next chapter.)

In the 1890s, a number of social, economic, and political forces converged at Coney Island, causing dramatic changes in the organization of its recreational and amusement activities. These changes included the passing from the scene of major hotel builders such as Austin Corbin and William Engeman, but also the end of two problems endemic to Coney Island. The first was the death of John McKane, which ended his stranglehold on the island's judicial and financial affairs. The second was a series of accidental fires on the West Brighton side of Coney Island, where the amusements and the midway were situated. These conflagrations consumed many of the more objectionable properties (e. g., gambling dens, brothels, fakir booths, and girlie shows) so that now-vacant land was available for more public-spirited recreation.[2]

The essence of Coney Island was not, however, completely changed. When the writer Stephen Crane walked on Surf Avenue on a blustery September day, he passed the clangorous crowds on the Bowery, the endless music halls, beer gardens, sideshows, shooting galleries, roller coasters, and preposterous architectural curiosities. For Crane, the

4. The Parks

autumn detritus of Coney seemed to symbolize insatiable longings and appetites for pleasure and release:

> The mammoth empty buildings, planned by extraordinarily optimistic architects, remind me in an unpleasant manner of my youthful dreams.... There is a mighty pathos in these gaunt and hollow buildings, impassively and stolidly suffering from an enormous hunger for the public. It was 1894; there was not an amusement park yet in existence.[3]

Two changes that allowed for Coney Island's tremendous growth were, first, advances in transportation. Joining the traditional modes of transportation, such as streetcars, railway lines, and steamboat routes, were excursion boats, ferry boats, elevated trains, electric trolleys, hackney carriages, and bicycles. Additionally there were municipal investments in new bridges and tunnels connecting the city's boroughs. Because of these improvements, Coney Island was flooded with visitors, not only from the other parts of the city, but also from Long Island.

Although the means of transportation varied by accessibility, and the time required for the journey varied by the means of transportation, the cost was consistently low. In the early 1890s, the cheapest fare ranged from forty to fifty cents. By 1895, improvements in rapid transit—beginning with the nickel trolley—forced prices to drop, which brought the trip within the means of the great masses.[4] Suddenly, the exclusive seaside resort became a popular playground for a diverse crowd, reflecting a wide range of immigrant working-class and native middle-class residents.

The second advancement had to do with the ability to supply power to the rides. The Columbian Exposition in Chicago in 1893 inspired the use of electricity to illuminate the parks and power the rides at Coney Island. However, the entrepreneurs of Coney Island surpassed the White City in creating an environment conducive to whimsical amusement. Electrical engineers worked to keep up with modern advances in amusement advances in order to create an inviting fantasy escape. An excerpt from an article in the *New York Times* describes their success:

> Yawning on the dingy old pleasure thoroughfare was a monster arch, covering half a city block. The interior of this arch was a solid mass of electric lights and rising many feet into the air were four monster monoliths, traced in electric lights and surmounted by great balls of fire.[5]

Electricity made twenty-four hour entertainment possible—it lit the midway and powered the rides at Coney Island. It was also the force behind one of the most famous expositions on the island—the electrocution of Topsy the Elephant.

Topsy was a three-ton female Asian elephant that gave rides to customers and performed in circus-like attractions. She was also was said to have a bad temper, and killed three of her handlers. As a consequence, her owners decided that she had to be put down. Believing that electrocution would be the most efficient means of doing so, they enlisted the aid of Thomas Edison, who seized on the opportunity to show everyone just how deadly the effects of alternating current could be. The park's publicity-hungry owners, Frederic Thompson and Elmer Skip Dundy, hoped to gain financially by turning this atrocity into a public spectacle, but were stopped by the American Society of Prevention of Cruelty to Animals. The event, which took place on January 3, 1903, was opened only to invited guests and members of the press. Among the small crowd of spectators was a crew from the Edison Manufacturing Company movie studio. The resulting short film, *The Electrocution of an Elephant*, was later released to be shown in Edison's coin-operated Kinetescope viewing machines.

Efforts to reform Coney Island, together with late 19th-century trends in society, led directly to the invention of the modern amusement park. The advances in technology changed the structure and pace of leisure, and nowhere was this more apparent than at Coney Island. In a relatively short period of time, the languid seaside resort was transformed into a frenetic amusement center featuring exotic hotels, cafés, boardwalks, carousels, bathing pavilions, racetracks, an aquarium, a huge roller coaster, and musical entertainment. Reassembled structures from the 1876 Philadelphia Exposition were used, including an amusement tower that, at three hundred feet, was taller than any existing building in the United States and provided a breathtaking twenty-mile view. Two wonders that were constructed at Coney Island during this period were the Elephant Hotel and the Captive Balloon.

While the original idea was to construct a hotel in the shape of an elephant, the architect J. Mason Kirby added to the idea and constructed the interior with the purpose of also using it as an auditorium for concerts. To enter, visitors climbed a stairwell in a rear leg to reach the reception desk in the abdomen. From there, for the cost of a penny,

4. The Parks

they could get an elevated elephant's eye view of the ocean. For the price of a full night's stay, a guest could sleep in the Shoulder Room, the Throat Room, the Stomach Room, or any of the other twenty-seven bedrooms; there was also a howdah (a carriage which is positioned on the back of an elephant), on top, located eighty-eight feet from the ground, which was used as an observation platform. The elephant was constructed of wood throughout and covered with sheet tin. The legs were eighteen feet in diameter, and the two hind legs contained circular stairways leading to and from the rooms above. *Scientific American* quoted the architect regarding the statistics of the structure:

> The colossus, he informs us, weighs about 100,000 tons. It contains 1,500,000 square feet of timber, and 700 kegs of nails were consumed in its construction. In addition to this, 7 tons of bolts were disposed of, and it required 35,000 square feet of tin to cover its surface. In size it compares favorably with many of the large hotels and other structures in its neighborhood, and some idea of its magnitude may be had by comparing it with Jumbo [the first international animal superstar, and the first African elephant to reach modern Europe alive], which is drawn in scale by its side, and which would find plenty of room for a promenade within one of the legs of the colossus.[6]

Financially, the hotel was a disaster. Within a few years, the owner, James Lafferty, was forced to sell his poisonous white pachyderm of a public house to a Philadelphia syndicate. The new owners switched to a different business model. The Elephant Hotel was converted into a bordello. With its numerous crooks and crannies, "seeing the elephant" acquired an entirely new meaning.

Vice flourished to such an extent in Coney Island that prostitutes, con artists, gamblers, and petty crooks all flocked there, and their patrons and marks eagerly followed. The *New York Times* lamented in 1887:

> What might have been made a pleasure resort of lasting and increasing attraction—Coney Island and its beach—has been largely turned into a nest of dives, disreputable houses, gambling halls, and cheap and nasty shows. Security of person and property has been seriously impaired, order and decency have been violated with impunity, and respectable people have been steadily repelled.[7]

Public association of Coney Island with prostitution was so strong that when a New York newspaper mistakenly described a women as a "concert hall singer and dancer at Coney Island," the New York Court of Appeals held that the news item constituted libel per se.[8] The plaintiff, Ida Gates, alleged in her complaint that a Coney Island concert hall is a place of evil report, and a resort for disorderly and disreputable persons of both sexes; that the female singers and dancers therein are generally depraved and abandoned women, or are so regarded and understood to be, and as such are shunned and avoided by orderly and respectable people.[9]

The Court explained that had the newspaper reported that she sang in Manhattan or Brighton Beach, it would have done nothing to tarnish her reputation. But to place her in a Coney Island concert hall was tantamount to calling her a "women of the pave," and a member of "one of the lowest classes of the great army of fallen women."[10]

In addition to the Elephant Hotel, Coney Island also had another wonder in the Captive Balloon, an observation craft that ascended to a height of seven hundred feet, carrying a wicker-work car which could be comfortably occupied by ten to twelve passengers.

> At this height the view was pronounced magnificent by the small party making the first venture. All the ocean approaches of New York harbor were at their feet for a radius of thirty miles, and inland they could see the numerous towns and cities about the bay of New York City. Along the sound to Flushing, up the Hudson River as far as Tarrytown, and the Orange Valley, and other parts of New Jersey as far as Patterson, Perth Amboy, and Long Branch.[11]

These rides and attractions, along with two double-decked steel piers with shops and restaurants, outnumbered and outclassed amusements at any other location. The increased population in New York City, improvements in rail and water transportation, and people's desire for more participatory and fast-paced forms of recreation, were all changes that produced crowds of thousands at Coney each summer day. A number of local entrepreneurs and showmen, eager to capitalize on the American worker's increased leisure time and spending power, were largely responsible for forging the mass market for consumption of amusement products. By fencing in hitherto-independent rides, side shows, and games, excluding gambling and prostitution, charging admission, and employing guards to keep the riffraff out, these Coney Island businessmen, with one stroke, were able to satisfy the demands of the reformers and reap huge profits. The new parks, catering to a primarily middle-class clientele, enjoyed great popularity and contributed to the island's moral and cultural renaissance.[12]

Amusement entrepreneurs appealed directly to the mass market through extensive daily advertising. They enticed people with fantastic visions of make-believe worlds and spectacular displays from around the globe. A visit to Coney Island was like no other experience. Luna

Park, Dreamland, and Steeplechase treated entertainment as a commodity and carefully packaged it to reach the widest audience.

Coney Island became the quintessential North American urban resort. At Coney, anyone could "vacation" because time and distance from the metropolis had been eliminated. A lack of wealth no longer prevented one from emulating social superiors at play. Moreover, class distinctions tended to disappear in a crowd of people wearing bathing suits.[13]

The first of these amusement parks was Sea Lion Park, built in 1895 by Paul Boyton. Boyton had achieved worldwide fame for exhibiting his invention of a rubber suit designed as a life-saving device for steamship passengers. In addition, before opening his park in Coney Island, Boyton operated a traveling aquatic circus in the United States. This sixteen-acre attraction, called Sea Lion Park, was enclosed by a fence in an area behind the Elephant Hotel, and was the first park to charge a single admission at the gate, entitling those entering to use any ride as many times as they wished. He could do this because he personally owned all the attractions as opposed to leasing space to concessionaires.

The park's rides included the Flip Flap Roller Coaster, an innovative ride for its time since it was the first to flip passengers upside down while traveling through a twenty-five-foot diameter loop. Riders stayed in their seats because the G-forces were stronger than gravity:

> A representative of the *Scientific American* who rode in the car stated that although a chain was stretched across his body while seated in the car to hold him in, in case of an accident, at no time during the ride was he brought into contact with the chain, but that at all times he felt himself held firmly in the seat by centrifugal force alone.[14]

The ride's only flaw was that, because of the high G-forces created by the motion of the car, some passengers sustained whiplash.

There was also the Old Mill, which was a boat ride through a dark tunnel containing tableaux ranging from the historical to the ghoulish. This ride sacrificed speed and illusion of peril for darkness and mass privacy. Through a narrow, serpentine sluiceway, boats were kept in gentle motion by a large paddle wheel, which was located conspicuously near the entrance to create excitement. Displays of scenery in the tunnels and caves afforded only occasional chaperonage for spooners. Three times through the ride was considered the equivalent of an engagement ring, and, sometimes, once did the trick. This ride was also responsible for the classic comedy act involving Sarah and Sam:

"You shouldn't have done it, Sam," Sarah said after the Old Mill ride.
"But I didn't do anything, Sarah!"
"Nothing, Sam?"
"Not a thing, Sarah."
"Well, *somebody* did!"[15]

The park's signature attraction was the Shoot the Chutes. This ride featured a toboggan that went down a water slide into a lagoon. The incline had an upturn at the bottom so that the boat would fly into the air before bouncing in and out of the water. When the boat came to a stop, it would be hoisted up the slide by a cable and returned to its original position.

The park did moderately well throughout the rest of the decade, even though Boyton only added a few new features, such as a ballroom

This early version of the Chute-the-Chutes ride, at Sea Lion Park, was designed for those pleasure seekers who preferred sightseeing to the thrills associated with the standard roller coaster.

4. The Parks

and a cage of live wolves. His main problem was attracting repeat customers since he wasn't adding new rides on a regular basis. In 1902, the combination of a declining customer base and a rainy summer caused a financial strain from which Boyton could not recover, forcing him to close the park. His major contributions to the amusement parks of the future were the charging of a single admission price and the popular water rides.

At the same time that Sea Lion Park was in operation, Coney Island's greatest showman was beginning to construct his park named Steeplechase. George Cornelius Tilyou, son of Peter Tilyou and nemesis of John McKane, began making money as early as 1876 through his ingenuity and by following a simple dictum—the public believed that an article had value only if it had a price on it. His first venture was to fill medicine bottles with salt water, and cigar boxes with sand, and sell them for a quarter each as souvenirs of Coney Island. After that venture, he invested his profits in the purchase of a horse and the construction of a stagecoach, and began transporting steamboat day trippers from the landing at Norton's Point to Culver Plaza in the middle of the island. Once there, the passengers were encouraged to stop off at his father's Surf House.

> By the end of the season he owned six horses and two stages; this was an enterprise successful enough to attract the attention of John Y. McKane, then riding high as political boss of the Island. McKane promptly got ideas about selling a franchise for the route; even more promptly, young Tilyou, as yet loath to buck McKane, sold all his assets and looked around for further opportunities.[16]

In 1882, at the age of twenty, Tilyou made his first venture into the entertainment business when he and his father built the island's first theatre, Tilyou's Surf Theatre, featuring only top-notch vaudeville acts. In 1886, he gave up the entertainment business when a new law permitted the sale of common lands by the town of Gravesend. In order to concentrate on the real estate business, he rented out his theatre and even produced his own newspaper, *Tilyou's Real Estate Telephone*; this journal, which was only printed once, gave the reader an in-depth view of the real estate situation on the island. As an example:

CONEY ISLAND NOTES
> The Hotel Brighton is being repaired where the heavy tides of the past winter damaged the brick foundation.

> Feltman is getting his large Hotel and Dancing Pavilion in readiness for business, as he anticipates an early opening for the season. Boats will land at the Old Iron Pier [in] the coming season.
> Stratton and Henderson will open their "Sea Side Hotel" with a company of first class artists about May 1.
> De Verna, it is rumored, intends building a large theatre at the Island, somewhat after the plans of the Metropolitan Opera House, New York.
> It is said that the Brighton will introduce American fireworks [in] the coming summer on their grounds.
> Racing will be inaugurated at Brighton Beach Fair Grounds about May 23rd.

Advertising in the paper boasted a thousand new flannel bathing suits, stocked by Tilyou's father at his new Sea Beach Bathing Pavilion, and the plant expansion of the great local "manufactory," makers of Dr. George T. Raymond's Pectoral Plasters, which were guaranteed to "cure whooping cough and all bronchial and lung diseases." George Tilyou, who knew a thing or two himself about selling marine products,[17] stressed the "hygienic advantages" of renting a cottage at Coney Island. "Convalescents from Typhoid Fever," he wrote, "those suffering from Malaria and Bronchial troubles, or those who desire and need rest from the cares and anxieties of their daily avocations can here derive a great benefit."[18]

In 1893, two events transpired that set Tilyou on his future course: the first was losing his nemesis, John McKane, who was on his way to Sing Sing; the second was visiting the Chicago World's Columbian Exposition on his honeymoon, where he saw his first Ferris wheel. On his return to Coney Island, he borrowed some money and ordered one. The ride was 125 feet in diameter, with 12 cars, each carrying 18 passengers. While awaiting its delivery, Tilyou rented some land and erected a huge sign stating, "On This Site Will Be Erected the World's Largest Ferris Wheel."[19] While this was merely hyperbole, it caused enough concessions to open on his land for him to make the down payment upon its delivery. Since the Ferris wheel was one of the island's first big attractions—especially after dark, when festooned with lights—he was able to pay it off completely within 50 days.

In addition to the Ferris wheel, Tilyou had other rides across Coney. There was the Aerial Slide, a precursor to today's Zip Line; the Intermural Bicycle Railway; and the Double Dip Chutes. Then came the realization that he should group all the rides together, enclosed by a fence, with admission charged at the gate. These ideas had been the brainchild of Boyton at Sea Lion Park, whose actions Tilyou studied closely. The entrance fee of a dime guaranteed "ten hours [of] fun for ten cents," which was a manageable amount for a working-class excursion.[20] The park competed with outside vendors on the beach and boardwalk, but it was still a very successful enterprise, mainly because once inside the enclosed park, all of the business belonged to Tilyou. And because many of the attractions were concessions, both their owners and Steeplechase benefitted from having them. The park had another benefit: the entrance fee kept out the undesirable inhabitants of Coney Island; even though Tilyou did not cater to the genteel middle class as did Thompson at Luna Park, he was able to maintain a level of respectability.

In examining the practices of Sea Lion Park, Tilyou realized that he needed a major ride, one that would be the symbol of his park. For that, he turned to horse racing, the most popular sport in the area, one that had been responsible for attracting the masses to spend the afternoon at the Gravesend, Sheepshead Bay, or Brighton Beach races. Tilyou not only found his ride, but named his park after it—Steeplechase. The ride consisted of large wooden horses that would be ridden by his patrons along a metal undulating track propelled by momentum which allowed the horses to race down inclines with enough speed to surmount the next hill. The course crossed a stream bed, and then over a series of hurdles. The ride also had realistic touches, such as attendants dressed as jockeys, buglers to announce the start of the race, half- and quarter-mile posts, and a finish line at the end. The *Brooklyn Daily Eagle* included the following description:

> The principle amusement attraction that will be new on the island this year is the grand national steeplechase race course, which is being built at the western extremity of Ocean avenue. The structure is a big one and forty-two wooden horses are to be operated on a track 1,166 feet long and twenty-five feet wide. The building is 600 feet long and 100 feet wide. There will be a grand stand, a judge's stand and a platform 50 × 500 feet in size for the accommodation of the patrons.[21]

Each horse carried two persons, usually a man and a woman, sitting close together. Normally, the women sat in front so that the man could help her hold on. The ride was mild in formation and speed, but it simulated a race, since by proper manipulation of weight, such as leaning forward just before moving downhill, a couple could slightly increase their speed and win the race. Jockeys from the racetracks in the Coney Island area during the early years of the 20th century used to wind up a day of riding on real horses by competing in the evening on the metal steeds at Steeplechase. Being tiny fellows, they ran the risk of defeat at the hands of a plump girl who knew nothing of track strategy. Probably the plumpest winners of all time at Steeplechase were Michael and Frances Rienzi, who, in a 1931 suit that reached the Court of Appeals, won substantial damages for falling off a horse. Had true justice prevailed, Mr. and Mrs. Rienzi would have been disqualified and fined for entering a sporting competition with an unfair advantage, since between them they weighed no less than 430 pounds.[22]

In 1901, Tilyou added another signature ride, this time on a concession basis. Visiting the Pan-American Exposition in Buffalo that year, he was attracted to an amusement called A Trip to the Moon, built by Frederic Thompson and his partner, Elmer Skip Dundy. The price of the ride was fifty cents, which was twice the price of any other ride at the exposition; despite this, it was experienced by more than 400,000 people in less than a year.

The ride consisted of a simulated trip for thirty passengers from the fairgrounds to the moon aboard the airship-ornithopter *Luna*, passing Niagara Falls, the North American Continent, and the earth's disc. After landing on the moon, the passengers then left the craft to walk around on a cavernous papier-mâché lunar surface peopled by costumed characters known as Selenites. Afterwards, the space tourists would visiting the palace of the Man in the Moon, complete with dancing "moon maidens," before leaving for the trip back to earth through a mooncalf's mouth. Relocated to Steeplechase (Tilyou gave the owners a minimum guarantee against 60 percent of the net), the attraction was as popular as it had been in Buffalo, before being again moved when Thompson and Dundy opened Luna Park.

Tilyou added other attractions. He had naphtha-powered boats cruising on Venetian canals, a miniature steam railroad, and he convinced LaMarcus Thompson (the creator or the Switch Back Railway) to build a scenic railroad with a guarantee of $40,000. He also built the largest ballroom in New York State, which featured four bands, each taking turns providing dance music for his patrons. Like Boyton, Tilyou charged one admission price, twenty-five cents, which allowed his customers to use any ride as often as they wished. Also, like Boyton, he

4. The Parks

The first of the three original iconic amusement parks built on Coney Island (the other two being Luna and Dreamland), Steeplechase (shown here in 1903) outlasted them all, remaining in operation from 1897 to 1964.

enclosed his park, which effectively eliminated the criminal and sordid elements that roamed Coney Island and preyed on innocent visitors.[23]

By 1905, Tilyou faced competition with the opening of Luna Park and Dreamland, two amusement parks, also in Coney Island, whose attractions were far more spectacular than his. Rather than fighting against these other parks, Tilyou welcomed them. His reasoning was that the more attractions there were, the bigger the crowds, the greater the gaiety, the more profit. Also, Tilyou did not rely on the spectacular for his success; his modus operandi was to concentrate on setting up opportunities for his patrons to amuse themselves. His mission, then, was to create attractions to facilitate this. By 1905, he was credited with the following rides:

> *The Wedding Ring*, later called the Razzle Dazzle and still later the Hoop-la. This was a great circle of laminated wood suspended

by wires from a central pole; as many as seventy persons at a time could perch insecurely upon it while four muscular acrobatic attendants rocked it back and forth. (This was 1905, and when a girl lost her balance her ankles would show, and she would have reason to clutch at her escort. Hoop-la!)

The Barrel of Love was a modest adaptation of the Switchback Railway. Passengers were strapped into seats in a revolving drum that rolled gently down one incline and up another. A nearby sign read: "Talk about love in a cottage. This has it beat a mile."

The Dew Drop: patrons climbed by leisurely stages to the top of a tower perhaps fifty feet high, climbed in, sat down, and were whirled feet first down and around, and around again and out, upon a billowy platform. (Did you see those *ankles*?)

The Whichaway: a swing that whirled its passengers eccentrically in any of four directions, but invariably catapulted a girl into her escort's lap.

The Earthquake Stairway: a flight of steps split down the middle so that one half could be jerked suddenly up while the other half was jerked a few inches down. A practical joke on the same level as the pail of water that tumbles down when a door is opened, this aberration was described as "the most unique and side-splitting fun maker in existence."[24]

By the 1890s, an important development in Coney Island was the increasing presence of women, especially young women. Concert halls and theaters that attempted to appeal to women and children began to pepper the strip in Coney Island, joining the gambling houses, saloons, and brothels that were formerly male enclaves. Dancing pavilions were especially popular with female patrons, who could find eight such halls at Coney, with cultural styles ranging from relatively refined establishments, such as Stauch's Restaurant and Dance Hall, to the seediest saloons, like the Silver Dollar and Perry's Cabaret.

A number of reporters commented on the extraordinary popularity of these pavilions and the dance craze among young women in this era, usually remarking on the differences between "appropriate" and "inappropriate" venues where young women could dance. One account noted: "In the most fashionable [dance hall] there is a good deal of promiscuous intercourse, flirting, and picking up of acquaintances but the dancing itself is usually proper and conventional." In either case, the large crowds found patronizing the dance halls and other amusements on the Bowery and along Surf Avenue reflected a widespread trend in changing male/female social and sexual dynamics. Tilyou understood these dynamics well and would incorporate them into his unique design for the innovation that would define Coney Island and make it world famous as the 20th century began.[25]

The author Charles Belmont Davis, commenting on Tilyou's methods, stated:

> [The] gigantic Ferris wheel, ponderous in its movement, and most admirably suited for those sentimentally inclined, especially as the guards always seem to arrange that each car shall hold but two passengers although they are rarely built for twenty. This, incidentally, has nothing whatever to do with that other

Before the advent of air conditioning and private swimming pools, untold thousands of overheated tourists ventured to Steeplechase Park to use its massive swimming pool.

most excellent revolving machine "the Barrel of Love." The barker here will tell you that "the ladies like this show the best of all." Here is the reason for this statement given by the student of nature who wrote the official guide: "The young men (and every man is young when there is a woman in the case) like it, because it gives them a chance to hug the girls; the girls (and every woman is a girl when there is a man in the case) like it, because it gives them a chance to be hugged."[26]

Steeplechase abandoned any pretense that recreation should uplift and encourage virtue. Amusements involved mechanical or gravity-driven motion, loss of balance, and reckless gaiety. "Instead of games of competitive skill, which demanded self-control, Steeplechase emphasized games of theatricality and of vertigo, which encouraged participants to shed self-consciousness and surrender to a spirit of reckless, exuberant play."[27]

When Fred Thompson departed Steeplechase to open Luna Park, he took the "A Trip to the Moon" ride with him. This wasn't a problem for Tilyou; he simply replaced it with another attraction from the Pan-American Exposition, Cummin's "Indian Congress and Life on the Plains." A Wild West show sanctioned by the United States government, the "Indian Congress" depicted the domestic life of the "red nomads" as well as their combat skills. Forty-three tribes and five hundred aboriginal Americans took part, including Geronimo.

To ensure that Steeplechase was always new, Tilyou continuously changed his attractions. In 1905, he eliminated the Canals of Venice and in its place constructed a 25-foot-wide and 25-five-foot-high pedestrian arcade from Surf Avenue to the 700-foot-long Steeplechase pier, erected in 1904 and containing a three-story bathing pavilion with two thousand changing rooms. Cruise ship passengers docking at the pier could use the pedestrian arcade to enter the park. In a circular pavilion on the beach, Tilyou retained the French Voyage, a walk-in boat, and the House Upside Down, a 2½-story structure with a German village restaurant on the first floor. On the second floor, all the furniture was nailed upside down.

Tilyou made more changes in 1906, first with his ballroom. He improved the orchestra stand in the center and then installed multi-colored lights above it that flooded the dance area. Previously, there were drab white statues along the walls, which he replaced with colorful paintings of Spanish dancers. Behind the ballroom, he constructed a miniature version of Manhattan's Flatiron building. The unwary visitor encountered a tempest of man-made wind (courtesy of an electric fan) that blew off their hats as they turned the corner. Also in this year, a Fads and Fancy building was erected to contain several smaller amusement devices.

The newest invention, the motor car, was also featured in 1907 in Steeplechase. Tilyou created an illusion entitled the "Automobile Sensation." Here, a full-sized car began a journey at top speed, and then appeared to stop. Then, with the wheels spinning, the car seemed to start again, with the scenery behind it moving backwards, giving the illusion that the car was moving forward. Suddenly, a pedestrian appeared in front of the car and was apparently struck head on, much to the horror of the viewing patrons.

The year 1907 also featured a new edifice called the Monte Carlo Building, which contained an amusement called the Human Roulette Wheel; this was a large spinning wheel on which riders were encouraged to play "king of the mountain," until they were forced off the center of the ride, piling up along the edge. The building also housed a hall of mirrors that gave its viewers a distorted vision of their reflection.

In this 1908 photograph, good-natured men and women wait to take a spin on the Human Roulette Wheel. The object of the ride—in addition to some opportunities for flirtation—was to stay on the spinning platform as long as possible; the last to remain earned the fleeting label of "King of the Mountain."

Next, they were subjected to the Jumping Floor, where a sudden movement of the floor sent them plunging head first into a wind machine known as the St. Augustine Tower. Finally, there was the Human Zoo in which the patrons descended down a narrow staircase into a cage where they were ridiculed by those who had already been there. Possibly this amusement was a model for the future Insanitarium.

One of the most spectacularl swindles conceived happened at Steeplechase in 1906. Architect Samuel Friede had designed an enormous structure to be known as the Globe Tower, which was to be built inside Steeplechase on land leased from Tilyou. The Tower was essentially a gigantic sphere, which would be a 700-foot-tall amusement park. The sphere was to contain four circuses, amusement rides, restaurants, a hotel, palm gardens, a vaudeville theater, a roller skating rink, a bowling alley, and slot machines. The globe would have eleven floors, each fifty feet high, with massive elevators moving between the floors. The top of the sphere would house floodlights and telescopes. The structure would be supported by eight enormous socles (pedestals) whose foundations would be thirty-five feet deep. Below the ground, there would be a combination parking garage, subway, and railway station, with a branch heading towards the Steeplechase pier. The cost of the amusement globe, according to Friede, would be $1,500,000, and he urged investors to join in the project.

There was a cornerstone laying ceremony on May 26, 1906, complete with speeches, band concerts, and fireworks that attracted a rush of investors. Another ceremony was held on February 17, 1907, when the first pieces of the foundation were laid. On May 19, 1907, the *Brooklyn Daily Eagle* was touting the concept as "perhaps the most ambitious undertaking on the island."[28] But by 1908 it became obvious that the entire project was a fraud, leaving Tilyou with the problem of removing thirty foundation piles on his property.

Disaster struck the park midway through the season of 1907. A fire that began in the Cave of Winds leveled most of the park and consumed thirty-five acres of the amusement district along the Bowery.[29] The day after the fire, George Tilyou, a showman in the face of adversity, set up a sign over the spot where the entrance to Steeplechase had been; it read:

> I have trouble today that I did not have yesterday.
> I had troubles yesterday that I have not today.

> On this site will be erected shortly a better, bigger, greater, Steeplechase Park.
> Admission to the Burning Ruins—10 cents.

Steeplechase's celebrated Funny Face had been lifted above the smoking ashes, crossed and recrossed with plaster patches, and carrying the legend, "A little worse for wear, but still in the ring." Each time, what had been built new was conspicuously better: the 1903 Coney Island fire had destroyed the Bowery, and now, as a result of the 1907 fire, the rebuilt Steeplechase was an improved park, bigger, offering more fun, and much of it housed within a great weatherproof glass pavilion.[30] This enclosure, the Pavilion of Fun, covered five acres and housed many of the rides that Tilyou had invented, such as the Whirlpool, the Barrel of Love, and the Human Pool Table. Even as he was rebuilding, Tilyou was making money, "We are scorched, but we still have twenty-five rides for twenty-five cents." Within a year, he was completely back in business.

Two of the rides in the Pavilion of Fun—the Whirlpool and the Human Pool Table—joined by the Human Roulette Wheel, were examples of Tilyou's idea of having patrons amuse themselves by bringing people together—"in the case of these rides by throwing bodies in all directions and often into the flesh of a member of the opposite sex." A British visitor in 1912 reported that when he slid down Steeplechase's "long bumpy slide, you did get awfully messed up with other people as you went down—strange girl's arms around your neck and everybody calling everybody a silly ass." And the Human Pool Table "certainly makes you acquainted with a lot of people without being introduced to 'em." Upon entering the Steeplechase ride, a couple had to go through a dark passage called the "dog house" on their hands and knees and then onto a brightly lit stage, at one point called the Insanitarium. There, the women found their dress blown up by compressed air from holes in the floor while a clown struck her male friend's backside with an electric prod and a dwarf wacked it with a slapstick. As they made their escape, the couple had to pass along a sliding floor and a pile of barrels that seemed to be just about to fall over their heads as they scrambled for safety—all in front of a crowd who had just experienced the same thing.[31]

The writer Kevin Baker captures this experience in his novel *Dreamland*, in which most of the story takes place in Coney Island.

His protagonists are Kid Twist, a petty gangster who is hiding out on Coney Island, and Esther, a factory girl in the needle trades, who longs to escape the dual horrors of the sweatshops and her oppressive family. The two meet on the beach amid the excitement and romance of Coney Island and go off together to Steeplechase, where they take the signature ride. Esther, a first-timer, has dismounted the horse and runs off ahead of Kid before he can stop her. Baker writes:

> She stopped to find herself on a stage—row after row of bleachers in front of her, every seat filled with laughing men and women pointing at *her*.
> A terrible little man in a clown suit rushed up to her waving some kind of club in his hands, [his] mongoloid face grinning hideously. He swung it at her, and she backed away, holding out her hands. He only kept advancing on her, swinging the cattle prod like a baseball bat.
> "Piece of wretch!" she shrieked, barely dodging away in time. "Wild animal!"
> He laughed, yelling her words back at her in his ridiculous, high dwarf's voice while he jabbed at her legs.
> "Piece of wretch! Wild animal!"
> She felt a terrible shock run through her body, as if a hand had wrapped itself around her heart. She fell back—and cold air rushed mortifyingly up her backside, blowing up the skirt of her mermaid bathing suit and making her jump in the air before the laughing crowd....
> Kid came running onto the stage shooing away the dwarf. The mongoloid clown smirked, and scooted around him—but there was something in his face that made him go on to torture other riders. Kid wrapped his arms protectively around her, guided her out past the Laughing Gallery and its barker:
> "Come on in! Only a penny! *You* be the one laughing this time!" ...
> *It was fun*, Esther told herself, feeling her heart pounding wildly. It was terrifying, she had beat it, she had got past the awful little man, had gone through it all and survived.
> *It was fun, and I like it.*[32]

Watching other's humiliations, having undergone them oneself, was part of Steeplechase's appeal. This type of experience pushed shy couples close together, encouraging them to let down their inhibitions. By alternating the roles of spectator and spectacle, Tilyou lessened the cruelty and sting of the moment. Patrons experienced hilarity rather than humiliation, though there was often something of a cruel edge to the humor.

A major attraction of Steeplechase was simply the sanctioned opportunity to witness the wholesale violation of dominant social boundaries. Momentary disorientation, intimate exposure, physical contact with strangers, pratfalls, public humiliation—conditions that in other circumstances might have been excruciating—became richly entertaining. The laughter of participants and spectators testified to their sense of release.[33] According to newspaper reporter Oliver Pilat,

> The amazing thing is that there are almost never any complaints about the Insantitarium. For one thing, victims cannot resist the temptation to look back at the stage from which they had escaped, and the momentary tortures of those who follow seem to ease their own humiliation. Also, if they have any sense, they realize that such monkeyshines are precisely the things for which they visited the park.[34]

At the Chute the Chutes the "apparent risk gives one a sense of personal daring very gratifying to us all, and as each boat load plunges down the chutes into the lagoon this finds expression in a cry for protection from feminine, and an answering shout of triumph from masculine, throats." Even more, a "sudden clutch of his arm when the boat goes through the mill-race has often brought a young man to realize how pleasant it would be to have the right to protect and cheer the maiden by his side."[35]

Steeplechase was a product of Tilyou's insight into human nature and his genius for inducing . "Laughter," he once said, "made me a million dollars."[36] Tilyou turned everything on its head. He called his park "Refinement's Pleasure Ground," yet its trademark Funny Face was a leering carnival mask. His talent lay in juxtaposing the two. At Steeplechase, the carnival spirit without vulgarity was distilled for middle-class Americans. Steeplechase's appeal can be attributed to the spirited, liberated, physical play at its core. Everything in the park revolved around the human body, with no holds barred. Tilyou put it this way: "We Americans want either to be thrilled or amused, and we are ready to pay well for either sensation."[37] Like Fred Thompson of Luna Park, Tilyou understood that adults "are just boys and girls grown tall."[38] But while Thompson added an imaginative, architectural dimension to Luna, Tilyou simply built an enormous glass lid over his. Beneath it, much as in Alice's looking glass, things that were small grew large, and those that once were large suddenly lost all proportion.[39]

Injuries and even deaths were not uncommon occurrences at Coney Island. The large numbers of people who frequented Coney prompted medical problems of all kind. To deal with such emergencies, Steeplechase had its own infirmary: it served those who suffered due to the summer heat, or from food poisoning, or simply from overeating, as well treating employees who might become sick or hurt. Primarily, though, it tended to those patrons who suffered a range of injuries, from cuts to friction burns to broken bones, from such rides as the Whirlpool, the Down and Out Tube, the Bowery Slide, and the Human Pool Table. Sometimes the accidents were grave. A man was killed on May 19, 1912, when he fell off the Wooden Donkey. The object was to ride on its revolving back for five minutes in order to win a five-dollar prize. On May 26 of the same year five patrons were injured when the cable on the Airship snapped and dropped one end of the car. The passengers tumbled out and fell to the ground; fortunately, the ride was slowing down and was close to the ground at the time. In August 1931, William Nevins lost his balance on the Venetian Gondola as he attempted to get a seat and fell to his death out of an open side. Four years later, John Barke, a ten-year-old boy, fell to his death from a Steeplechase horse. An especially dramatic accident occurred at the outdoor pool on August 1, 1933. The pool area was crowded with an estimated thousand bathers, and some, in an attempt to get out of the hot sun, congregated beneath the shaded west balcony. At three o'clock in the afternoon, a fight broke out between two men on the pool deck, and a lifeguard attempted to break it up; not only was he unsuccessful, but four other patrons joined in. Those above, on the balcony, moved to the railing in order to see the fight; their combined weight was too much for the structure, causing the entire balcony to collapse. An estimated eighty men, women, and children fell off the balcony. Some were lucky, falling only seven feet to the bathhouse roofs, but the remainder fell seventeen feet to the pool deck below. Although fifty-four people were injured, only a few of the injuries were serious.

Beyond the reported cases are numerous notations in James Onorato's diaries of legal actions filed against the park and of his appearances in court.[40] Additionally, the presence of Steeplechase's lawyers, or their investigators, and its insurance company in the infirmary, is a further indication that accidents were part and parcel of running an amusement park. One example was the case of *Reinzi v. Tilyou*, in which the plaintiffs asserted that they fell from a mechanical horse on the Steeplechase ride because the attendant had insisted on putting them on the same horse despite their considerable size and contrary to their wishes, and because a footrest on the horse had broken off. Steeplechase's lawyers followed the strategy of denigrating the ride itself. Quite gratuitously, the lawyers described the mechanical horse ride as "a somewhat undignified amusement."[41] In this instance, however, the Steeplechase attorney's ploy of casting aspersions on the ride was not sufficient to persuade the court to set aside a plaintiffs' complaint. During the trial, Thomas Hart, an investigator for Steeplechase's lawyers, testified that he just happened to be at the infirmary to investigate another case when the Reinzis were being treated. He further testified that he visited the infirmary between twenty and twenty-five times each summer season.[42]

Steeplechase's managers dealt with the risk and the reality of accidents in a number of ways. Onorato's diaries indicate that management emphasized safety and careful upkeep of the rides, including continuous safety inspections. Managers did, however, act to limit liability when the inevitable accidents did occur. Steeplechase's owners and managers attempted to assert their sovereignty (and, with it, their sovereign immunity) over the park, to stay beyond the reach of New York State laws. One method they used was to post signs at every ride indicating that their patrons rode at their own risk. It is impossible to assess how much control this gave Steeplechase over accident victims. As an example, the park tried unsuccessfully to rely on the sign posted at a ride called the Flopper in the case of Murphy v. Steeplechase Amusement Co., where the plaintiff fell off the ride and injured his knee. Murphy simply denied that he noticed the sign and its message.[43] Moreover, there is some indication that New York courts were disinclined to give much weight to such signs. Nevertheless, many injured patrons, whether or not they were made aware of the sign, may have agreed on the spot to accept minimal compensation for their pain in part because they assumed that the signs' presence would negate any right to recovery they might otherwise have.

There is also reason to believe that Steeplechase was fairly aggressive about attempting to head off liability before the injured patron left the park. According to Michael Onorato, park manager James Onorato's son, his father's practice for minor injuries, such as "a friction burn ... or a scraped knee and torn pants or anything short of sutures and bone-setting," was to treat the person in the infirmary, and to "try to bring closure immediately, usually with a statement of release for the price of the trousers or dress together with $50 to $150, in today's dollars, as compensation for the inconvenience."[44] This was probably done so that the patron would not have time to contemplate the amount for which he could sue. Onorato further notes that, after 1946, the park stationed an insurance adjuster in the infirmary in order to fend off litigation by getting an injured patron to sign a release.[45] Apparently, the park's increased aggressiveness in obtaining releases while the person was still in the park led to a significant decline in lawsuits.

This did not mean that the park was against rider safety. In fact, Onorato was meticulous in inspecting and repairing or even replacing the slightest worn part. He and his staff of thirty year-round employees would disassemble a ride completely during the winter months and then completely rebuild it. During the summer season they would inspect each ride before the park opened and walk the entire track of the Zip roller coaster and the Steeplechase horses, looking for even the slightest flaw.[46]

It is also apparent that when it could not avert a lawsuit or settle a claim, Steeplechase defended itself forcefully in court. From the onset, Steeplechase prepared for litigation. It is clear from the trial records in both the Murphy and Reinzi cases that the park's doctors and nurses were supposed to question the patron about the circumstances of the accident and make a record of the conversation in anticipation of possible litigation. Moreover, James Onorato seems to have enjoyed litigation as a competitive sport. His son recounts:

> He usually went loaded for the kill, and he was quite willing to let the jury know that he had won many cases of this kind. In later years, he would regale the family with how the plaintiff's lawyer would scream, "Objection! Objection!" and the park's lawyer would laugh and the judge would admonish the jury to disregard the statement about how Mr. Onorato won cases such as these.[47]

There is some justification for believing that the park's win in the Murphy case had an impact on subsequent trials. In his November 19, 1935, entry, Onorato recorded: "Went to court—Mildred Lucas v. T. R. Co. & S. A. Co.—$50,000. Whirlpool mixup—Murray Jenkins trying case for us. (Case dismissed on [Justice] Cardoza's [sic] decision by Judge Brennan."[48] Onorato considered the Murphy case important enough to keep the park's original copy of the decision in his diaries. While that particular case did not eliminate the prospect of liability, Onorato's diaries suggest that Steeplechase won in court far more often than it lost. Whether or not the park would have won most of its cases without this precedent is impossible to tell.

4. The Parks

The least known Coney Island amusement park, opened in 1905, was Brighton Beach Park. It was developed by New York showman William A. Brady. It was also the largest of the area's enclosed parks, covering seventy-five acres between the Brighton Beach Hotel and Manhattan Beach, including a mile-long boardwalk. The park was a recreation of the Pike, the amusement midway at the recent (1904) Louisiana Purchase Exhibition in St. Louis. Like the other amusement parks in Coney Island, Brighton Park had a signature attraction. In this case it was "The Great Boer War Spectacle," which it secured for its opening season. To house this attraction, an arena with a grandstand seating twenty thousand people was erected. Brady hired a thousand British and Boer veterans, including General Piet Conje, Zulu warriers, Kaffirs, mounted lancers and artillery to reenact various battles of the 1899–1902 war over a battlefield spanning fourteen acres.

Most of the park's other attractions lined an unenclosed midway called the Brighton Pike. More attractions were added at the beginning of Brighton's second season, including Ferrari's Wild Animal Arena, a scenic railway, a carousel, an Irish fairground called Donnybrook, and a pavilion called Happyland. When "The Great Boer War Spectacle" became dated, it was replaced in 1907 by Pawnee Bill's Wild West Show and Great Far East Show in the park's arena. Major Gordon Little, dubbed Pawnee Bill, was at various times a competitor and partner of Buffalo Bill and was an heir to his Wild West Show. His act combined Wild West and Far East set pieces, replete with elephants, camels, Russian Cossacks, South Sea Islanders, Chinese, and Turks. The following year (1908), the "Miller Brothers' 101 Ranch," whose cowboy performers included Will Rogers, occupied the arena. After this exhibition, Pain's fireworks took up residence there, presenting elaborate productions such as "The Destruction of Jerusalem," "Sheridan's Ride," and "Battle in the Clouds," a pyrotechnic spectacle that featured balloon flights and airships. The managers of Brighton Park promoted it as a family playground and sought to strike a middle ground between Coney Island proper and the "sporty" attractions of Manhattan Beach. Although it was twice as big as Luna Park, with attractions that included the mile-long Chase through the Clouds coaster, it was never as popular as its rival, nor did it draw comparable crowds.[49]

5
Luna Park and Dreamland

Frederic Thompson and Elmer Skip Dundy bought Paul Boyton's failed Sea Lion Park In 1903 and created Luna Park, a thirty-six-acre attraction more spectacular than Steeplechase. Dundy provided financial expertise, borrowing from speculators, such as the gambler "Bet-a Million" Gates and the rest from Wall Street bankers. The partners poured every cent they had into the venture. Dundy even spent the evening prior to the opening scraping together twenty-two dollars in change for the park's ticket sellers. When asked about the park, he took to referring to the project as "Fred Thompson's Coney Island sideshow." Thompson used his architectural background and experience in the "world's fairs" at Nashville and Buffalo to build an "electric Baghdad," by starting from scratch. He utilized only the idea, not the formal classical look of the White City[1] of Chicago's fair, including a dense forest of spires and colonnades, which he claimed "promoted release, dynamic motion, overwhelming transformation, and above all, exotic illusion." While Tilyou favored raucous gags and vaudeville tomfoolery, Thompson and Dundy found their inspiration in awe-inspiring sensation, extravagance, and excess, creating huge thrill rides that attempted to simulate people's most extreme fantasies about the modern era that lay ahead.[2]

As with the temporary structures of the world's fairs, Thompson's builders used a composite material called "staff," a blend of gypsum, alumina, glycerin and dextrin, reinforced with fibers such as burlap, to create a plaster-like imitation stone. Staff made possible quick exterior treatments, built up over steel or wood framing, and could be easily formed to resemble architectural styles and details from around the world. Luna founded a new and lasting paradigm for outdoor amusements—an architecturally unified and exotic garden of enchantment

5. Luna Park and Dreamland

The handwritten inscription on this stereopticon slide reads: 5572 Surf Ave. Entrance to Luna Park, a novel feature of Coney Island New York. Copyrighted 1903 by William H. Rau.

which specialized in the experience of imaginative escape from everyday life. When it opened for the first time at precisely eight o'clock on May 16, the main electrical switches in the park were thrown and the outlines of its building burst out of the early evening darkness.

As the *Brooklyn Daily Eagle* reported the next day: "It seemed that a huge mantle of light had been let down from the sky to disclose the domain of an unknown world." The newspaper added that never "here or elsewhere has there been such an opening to a pleasure park."[3] The *New York Times* said of the opening: "They took the lid off Coney last night, and a quarter of a million men and women got a glimpse of a swaying, rocking, glittering magic city by the sea. It was Coney Island's opening day, but Coney Island never experienced such a bewildering opening. First of all, there were more people there than had ever been at Coney Island at one time before. Then there were more dazzling, wriggling, spectacular amusements offered than had ever before been collected together at any one place at any time."[4]

Again, as with Steeplechase, the key was balanced contradiction. On the one hand the park would feature an elongated reflecting pool with a Shoot-the-Chutes water slide at one end and a two-hundred-foot tower at the other.[5] The tower recalled the 1901 Pan-American Exposition's breathtaking Electric Tower, which was studded with twenty thousand incandescent lamps. Luna Park's tower was only half as tall; however, with its lights that changed color every second, it was a visual confection, hence its name—the Kaleidoscope Tower. Twin circus rings flanked the tower and an electric fountain at its base sent up a spray of alternating colors. Acrobats, jugglers, and equestrian acts gave continuous performances on the twin stages and an aerial circus high overhead featured a slack wire artist performing in evening dress and a bicyclist on a trapeze. To top it all, Thompson enlisted Cameroni the Great to duplicate a feat he had performed at the Buffalo fair by descending from the top of the tower on a two-thousand-foot cable, with his hands tied behind his back, hanging by a leather strap held between his teeth.[6]

The press notices heralding Luna Park's opening proclaimed it a "Realm of Fairy Romance," but Thompson and Dundy's "colossal electric carnival" outstripped even the most inflated expectations of those who came to visit it. Architecturally, it was a wonderland, blending the visual elements of many lands, both real and imagined, into a single "delirium of something doing," outlined in orange, white, and gold. Luna's entrance gate was a gigantic arch covering half a city block. The court beneath the arch was a solid mass of electric lights and rising above it were "four monster monoliths, traced in electric lights and

A stereopticon slide takes the viewer inside Luna Park, labeled the "Heart of Coney Island." This twenty-two-acre amusement park opened in 1903 on what had once been the site of the Elephantine Hotel. Perhaps appropriately, an actual elephant can be seen crossing the bridge.

5. Luna Park and Dreamland

surmounted by great balls of fire, which shed light over the island."[7] At the entrance gate stood five Roman chariots, and ticket kiosks occupied by young women dressed in evening attire and Merry Widow straw hats emblazoned with red feathers. Beyond the gate, manned by helmeted, scarlet-coated Cerberi, were fifty-three buildings arrayed along the Court of Honor. At one side was a reproduction of the Piazza San Marco, with a campanile, an ornate loggia, and a grand canal plied by gondoliers coursing under an illuminated bridge. It faced the sculpted façades of three immense buildings where Thompson's illusion spectacles were staged.

Lining the Court of Honor were other buildings, housing such attractions as Hagenbeck's Wild Animals, Wormwood's Dog and Monkey Circus, a Chinese Theater, and various native villages. There was also a Helter Skelter bamboo slide, an Old Mill sluiceway, and a Grand Casino.

Luna Park clearly owed part of its inspiration to the urban planning movements of the early 20th century. The park's promotional pamphlet described its grounds in terms recalling the designs of the Chicago and Buffalo world fairs: "Broad promenades, wide gardens, splendid lagoons and gushing fountains surrounded on all sides by towers, battlements and handsome buildings, the whole illuminated by countless

This beautiful stereopticon slide (circa 1904) gives just a hint of the awe-inspiring appearance of Luna Park at night, lit up like a scene out of a fairy tale.

colored lights, make the scene one of unusual beauty and splendor."[8] The *Brooklyn Citizen* proclaimed that Luna Park's lagoons, promenades, hedges, and sculpture combined the virtues of a modern Venice and a beautiful seaside park.[9]

Like Walt Disney much later, Thompson recognized the need for a focal point in the pool and tower, an area that also facilitated the circulation of the crowd in and out of attractions on all four sides of the rectangle. And anticipating Disneyland, Luna offered scenic railroads and rides that were high enough to offer views of the park. While most successful amusement parks changed attractions to keep their offerings fresh, many of Thompson's rides were contracted on short-term leases, which led to a constant change. The park's attractions included its signature ride, the Trip to the Moon (which had already been at Steeplechase), the War of the Worlds (a strange miniature fantasy of the navies of the European powers attacking New York City, but losing the battle to Admiral Dewey's fleet), and Twenty Thousand Leagues Under the Sea, a submarine ride based on Jules Verne's famous book. It simulated an undersea journey from Luna Park to the North Pole. Along the way the voyagers encountered mermaids and strange sea creatures, glided beneath icebergs, visited an Eskimo village, and emerged at the North Pole, where they were greeted by a luminous, varicolored aurora borealis.

All of these amusements had appeared elsewhere, but at Luna, the constant change of attractions was successful. In 1904, the park had four million visitors. At Sea Lion Park and Steeplechase, one admission entitled the visitors to use all the rides; here, there was a general admission price of ten cents, with the attractions priced separately. The park's success forced the owners to raise a second deck around the pool to accommodate the overflowing crowds. Thompson changed the look of Luna Park each year, adding more and more architectural markers. "Wherever there was a chance to put up a tower or minaret to break the line of any roof or expanse, "Thompson noted in 1906, "I have stuck one on to please the eye."

"I have eliminated all classic, conventional forms in its structure and taken a sort of free Renaissance and Oriental type for my model using spires and minarets wherever I could," Thompson added. "It is marvelous what you can do in the way of arousing human emotions by the use that you make, architecturally, of simple lines. Luna Park is built on that theory—and the result has proved the theory's truth."[10]

5. Luna Park and Dreamland

Thompson and Dundy at first advertised Luna as "another world's fair," but before long they realized it was something better—an "'electric Eden,' unlike anything that had been built before." In constructing Luna, Thompson claimed that he had thrown all his architecture "books and plans onto the ash heap and decide to do something completely original. "I stuck to no style," he insisted. "[Luna Park] ... is utterly unlike anything else of its kind.... An exposition is a form of festivity, and serious architecture should not enter into it if it will interfere with the carnival spirit."[11] Thompson did, however, start from a very concrete notion of what the ideal pleasure park ought to be like and sought by every visual trick and device he could summon to transport visitors to a land of carnival pleasures and to hold them fast once they had surrendered themselves to it. To achieve its aim, Luna Park needed to be architecturally unified in its construction. Many of the park's elements, such as the graceful curves, colonnades, and minarets, came from the 1901 Pan-American Exposition that Thompson reconfigured for Luna Park. At Luna they became the carefully orchestrated backdrop of a stupendous carnival, where, for a modest sum, one could voyage to the moon or under the sea, encounter elephants and other exotic creatures, or be amused by the Sinhalese "stich dancers" or Hassan Ben Ali's Troupe of Hindus. Thompson spared no expense. If the Pan-American fair had two hundred thousand incandescent lamps for its 366 acres of exposition grounds, Luna must have an equal or greater number to decorate its twenty-two acres.

In executing the design of Luna Park, Thompson put to the test a theory of amusement architecture he had first explored at the Tennessee Centennial Exposition of 1897, where his Moorish palace won an architectural prize. All of Thompson's energy and resources were poured into a single purpose, to instill the carnivalesque spirit into every feature of his park. Everything that contributed to the air of gaiety, spontaneity, and otherworldliness was permitted on his architectural palette; anything that might diminish the effect was omitted. "Straight lines have no right in the place of honor of a great outdoor show," he wrote. The architecture "must be in keeping with the spirit of carnival. It must be active, mobile, free, graceful, and attractive." The fact that Thompson succeeded so completely in his purpose set Luna Park apart from anything yet created by the nascent American amusement industry. It was, as its promotors had promised, a "fairy realm."

It enchanted all who entered its precincts and sent them reeling into a zone of carnival transformation, albeit of short duration, and of simple pleasures. Luna Park was the handiwork of a midway magician who had wielded a "scintillate wand of fire." His park was a spectacular success as an "Everyman's World's Fair and a luminous Bagdad by the Sea."[12]

Like the rest of Coney Island, but more so, Luna was a "totally synthetic resort," where all was artifice, extravagance, and excess. It was, as Thompson himself put it, "bizarre and fantastic—crazier than the craziest part of Paris—gayer and more different from the everyday world." Thompson and Dundy filled their fantasyland with characters and animals as exotic as the architecture. There were camels to ride, diving horses, and elephants that slid down their own Shoot the Chutes ride.[13] When journalist Albert Bigelow Paine entered Luna for the first time, he reported being filled with "profound amazement [at this] enchanted, story-book land of trellises, columns, minarets, lagoons, and lofty aerial flights.... It was a world removed—shut away from the sordid clatter and turmoil of the streets."[14] At night this effect of being encircled in a fairyland, a "world removed," was even more intense as 250,000 electric light bulbs—the highest number ever assembled at any one site—lit up the towers, arches, and minarets of the park in an exuberantly ornate, yet stately, skylight visible for miles.

Realizing that most human beings occasionally craved speed, change, and illusion, Thompson also designed Luna to satisfy those needs. In order to accommodate daily crowds of greater than ninety thousand people, Thompson kept his consumers moving at a brisk pace. Twenty years earlier, Coney Island's entrepreneurs introduced fast food frankfurters and roller coasters; now, Thompson accelerated the tempo even more, shortening rides to one minute and theatrical shows to less than twenty. Thompson ordered his employees to promote "speed in the mind, heart, and steps of the most laggard visitors [because] to keep up the carnival spirit everybody and everything must be on the 'go.' The moment a crowd of folk ... catch the spirit, they walk faster, they laugh, they spend money, they have a good time."[15] To better understand his meaning, he encouraged people to "picture many white steeples, and numerous minarets, and innumerable highly decorated buildings of every conceivable architecture, from the prototype of a Turkish mosque to the styles obtaining among the more imaginative of the Japanese, with a strain of the architectural fashions which are credibly supposed to obtain in fairyland." Then "imagine swirling things, and tortuous things, and very quickly moving things," and "countless crowds of women in white and quite as many men in many colors, strolling, waiting, peering, laughing, being borne off in curious contrivances that rush and dash, being carried again by other curious contrivances that jump and dance."[16] Imagine life, in other words, as a perpetual and hyperactive carnival of pleasure.

Thompson's Human Toboggan Slide and Mountain Torrent created a demand for increasingly faster and more dangerous rides. The Human Toboggan Slide sent patrons sliding on their backs down a curving, undulating ramp cut out of a man-made mountainside; the Mountain Torrent was Thompson's attempt to combine the best elements of a water slide and a scenic railroad. It had an eighty-foot-high mountain with cliffs and cascades that carried boats down a sluiceway and under a great cataract that swept "helpless" victims along a sinuous water path.[17]

In addition to adding speed and danger, Thompson also exploited darker desires. He believed that, like children, adults enjoyed viewing (or vicariously experiencing) "the anxieties of others." The scene of a shipwreck or the aftermath of a train accident, he said, yielded "active pleasure," although his consumers were no longer satisfied solely by the "appeal to the eye." Now, he said, the customer demanded to "hear the boat crash or the train fall apart" or to feel "the sensation of going down some dizzy incline."[18] Some of his spectacles, such as an urban tenement fire (Fire and Flames) or the fall of the Turkish city of Adrianople in the "first Balkan War of 1912–1913 (Fire and Sword), were performed in an outsized, although conventional, theatrical setting. In 1907, the illusion "Night and Morning" allowed its visitors to vicariously experience a horror that belonged to an earlier time. In the 19th century a common fear was that someone in the state of catalepsy would be mistaken for dead and accidentally buried alive.[19] Edgar Allan Poe was one of the great popularizers of this "all-absorbing but ... too entirely horrible" theme. It appears in several of his stories, including "The Premature Burial," in which the narrator argues from personal experience that "a vast number of such interments have actually taken place."[20] Luna's victims began their untimely inhumation by entering a large, dark, oblong room shaped like a coffin. Through the glass ceiling they could see the drooping boughs of weeping willows and a "profusion" of consoling flowers. As the journey began, the coffin trembled and tilted and the world above receded as the room seemed to sink "into the underworld to the accompaniment of strange and weird noises, voices utter[ing] farewells, shrieks, and wails. Then the lid is closed and you hear the thud of gravel and earth." The illusion continued with a tour of hell and a concluding resurrection."[21]

In Thompson's opinion, his rides also engaged adults in a reenactment of their lost youth. Most of the mechanical devices designed for speed and movement at Luna derived from Thompson's idea of action-oriented boy's play. As an example, his Helter Skelter required customers to take an "automatic stairway to the top of a high tower," from which they slalomed down troughs of slick rattan, which plunged in a bouncing, snaking descent before depositing them onto a soft mattress, usually amid a crowd of spectators.[22] Two of Luna's most popular mechanical rides—The Tickler and The Virginia Reel—dispatched carloads of passengers careening down a serpentine route, spinning on casters and ricocheting abruptly off objects or each other. With the Tickler, the writer Elmer Blaney Harris remembered in particular, that "unless the neck is kept rigid one's head may be snapped from one's shoulders." He and his wife, Dora, each lost their grip on the ride, and ended up on "the bottom of the car, submerged under a plump young lady who held her mouth to keep her teeth in." The idea for Witching Waves, which opened at Luna in 1908, came from watching men at work in a steel rolling mill. The undulating sheets of metal grabbed the attention of Theophilus Van Kannel, the ingenious inventor of the revolving door, who turned this industrial inspiration into play. The ride was set up on successive segments of a flexible steel floor which simultaneously moved up and down, mimicking the ocean's waves and gently propelling riders in wheeled boats over the roiling surface.[23]

Many visitors to Coney Island demanded recreational activities far removed from the tedium of labor. "Visitors are not in a serious mood," Thompson explained, "they have enough seriousness in their everyday lives and the keynote of the thing they do demand is change." He adapted these expectations into a succinct motto: "Everything must be different from ordinary experience." Thompson combined illusion with play because "people are just boys and girls grown tall. Elaborated child's play is what they want on a holiday."[24]

Luna Park was an instant and overwhelming success. The speed with which Thompson and Dundy not only repaid their investors, but accumulated profits in the hundreds of thousands of dollars, was sufficient for others to enter the amusement park industry. Luna also established a standard by which all subsequent amusement parks would be measured. Luna's amazing popularity revised Coney Island's identification with vice by establishing a new reputation for hearty, joyful, innocent childhood so widely recognized that, in 1913, a department store in Oakland, California, named its indoor children's playground after the Brooklyn resort. In an effort to bring in all the business possible, in its inaugural season, Luna offered a nursery service "For Tired Mothers," and guaranteed, "Babies No Longer a Bar to Pleasure.... You Get a Check.... We Do the Rest." The promise underscored the origins of Thompson's amusements as temporary shelters from the encumbrances of respectable middle-class adulthood.[25] Photographs from the period show children in the Luna crowds, but the little ones were not the hardship cases he targeted. Thompson's amusements, as a newspaper writer observed near the end of the showman's life, were "for grown-ups and Peter Pans who never will grow up."[26]

Luna Park was also successful because Thompson was able to attract his target audience. Although he took their money, he was not interested in catering to recent immigrants or to the men and women who worked in the city's factories and sweatshops. They already went to Coney Island when they could afford it. Nor did it take aim at the carriage trade, whose pockets were deep, but numbers small; throngs were what he needed. The audience he targeted, in other words, looked like the New York counterpart to world's fair crowds. Some were small business owners and entrepreneurs, but the big money was in two rapidly emerging sectors of the city's population. The more important was the new and growing employee class of white-collar clerks, salesmen, and salaried managers who staffed or supervised the offices of New York's government, legal, financial, retail, and service economy, or hustled the goods and services of the urban marketplace locally or on the road. This class formed the critical foundation of the city's new commercial amusement economy, and it was Thompson's bread and butter.[27] The other target was the growing class of domestic tourists who visited New York for business or pleasure, who were drawn to Coney Island because of its reputation. This was a change from the mass of visitors to Coney Island in the Gilded Age. The *Brooklyn Daily Eagle* described them as "the folks who work in the factories, shops and offices for six days and some nights a week and they go to Coney Island because they ... can take the boisterous pleasures that ease the strain of work and confinement."[28] Additionally, Thompson and Dundy made a concerted effort to keep Luna Park safe for all visitors: they employed a park police force and claimed the right to eject troublemakers from the premises. Thompson proudly declared that Luna Park was "a place not for a thug, but for his mother and sister."[29] The park police also made sure that female visitors were protected from inappropriate male advances. Customer behavior within the park's borders was stringently monitored by the owners and attendants, which helped Luna to remain a family-friendly place of amusement. This formula for a successful, well-attended attraction became the model for many modern-day parks; indeed, Luna is widely considered the amusement park prototype.[30]

By 1911, Luna Park had erected 1,210 red-and-white-painted towers, minarets, and domes.[31] In Luna's second year (1904), Thompson purchased an additional sixteen acres; in this new area, he placed the Streets of Delhi, a remarkable spectacle that depicted the celebration in India when a new British monarch was crowned. The *New York Times* said of it: "There were gilded chariots and prancing horses, and trained elephants, and dancing girls, regiments of soldiers and an astonishing number of real Eastern people and animals in gay and stately trappings. The magnificence of the scene was such as to make those who witnessed it imagine that they were in a genuine Oriental city."[32] In 1904 alone four million visitors watched this show, five thousand at a time. Although, interestingly, this was one of the shows on which Thompson and Dundy lost money: its cost to stage the first summer was $240,000, which represented a $100,000 loss. He brought LaMarcus Adna Thompson's Scenic Railroad to the park and even changed the costumes of the female cashiers to Mexican hats and Bolero red jackets to create a new look. In 1905, the already dated Twenty Thousand Leagues exhibit was replaced with Dragon's Gorge, an indoor scenic railway which featured an entrance flanked by "two enormous dragons with outspread seventy-five-foot wings, five-ton heads, two-foot-wide eyes made up of enormous green electric lights and three-foot-long teeth protruding from open jaws. The railway was actually an enclosed coaster with a four-thousand-foot-long track and steep curves and grades. Its enclosure had a proscenium arch thirty feet high exposing a waterfall under which cars sped." Since it was no longer a novelty, the admission price on the

5. Luna Park and Dreamland

Trip to the Moon ride was reduced to ten cents. Finally in 1905, Luna added, as its spectacular, the Fall of Port Arthur, depicting the most dramatic event in the recent Russo-Japanese War, complete with working models of the torpedo boats used to sink the Russian fleet. In 1908, the Trip to the Moon was finally replaced with the Battle of the Merrimac and the Monitor, followed two years later by a Trip to Mars by Aeroplane. Thompson had created a very successful formula for Luna Park that attracted 31 million admissions in its first five years.[33]

Thompson spent so much money in successfully recreating Luna that, in April 1912, his creditors drove him out of business when they discovered that the park had debts totaling $665,000. Luna Park had probably begun its decline in 1907 when Elmer Skip Dundy died, which left Thompson rudderless. Ever since their initial partnering they had served as a check on each other; when Thompson would spend too much money on new exhibits, Dundy would invent a sudden financial stringency to serve as a check rein. Similarly, when Dundy spent too much time at the gambling table, only Thompson could lure him away to sleep on the pretext of a talk about a future attraction.[34] The new management, even while attempting to be more prudent fiscally, recognized the need for continuous innovation to draw more crowds each year and, as a result, added still more lights, towers, and spectacles in 1914 and 1915. Among them was Vernon Castle's Summer House Dance Hall.[35]

The third large amusement park created in Coney Island at the turn of the 20th century was Dreamland. Inspired by the success of Luna Park, Dreamland combined beauty, cleanliness, and higher prices than the other parks in order to attract a higher class of patron. It was built in 1904 by William Reynolds, a former Republican state senator and suburban housing developer. He constructed Dreamland using the same principles he had employed at Borough Park, which was a section of Brooklyn containing reasonably priced, detached private homes designed for middle-class families. Reynolds built Dreamland for the same upwardly mobile, respectable people who purchased his homes.[36] Reynolds had first planned to name the park Wonderland, touted as the "Gibraltar of the Amusement World."

Appealing to New Yorkers made uneasy by the influx of immigrants, Dreamland stressed the sharp physical contrast between its own spacious grounds and congested Manhattan. Disdaining Steeplechase's greater crowds, Dreamland instead promoted its quiet ambience. Using language reminiscent of the City Beautiful reformers, a 1904 guide expressed this idea: "One thing that strikes a visitor in making a journey round the park is that there is not one step in the place, all the walks are level or inclined, and none are less than fifty feet in length."[37] The basic objective was to replicate Luna's formula of exotic attractions and rides, but make everything bigger and better.

Dreamland distanced itself even further from the Bowery than did Luna Park. Spanning fifteen acres in Coney Island, it was built at a cost of $3.5 million. Like Luna Park, the entrance fee was ten cents, with a separate charge for the attractions. While only about half the size of Luna, its land was better situated as it was connected to the old Iron Pier on one end and Surf Avenue on the other. In its overall plan, Dreamland resembled a horseshoe facing out toward the ocean. The park advertised "Avenues Wide and Imposing—No Crowding."[38] In contrast to Luna, Dreamland had a classical appearance—all white buildings set around a stately lagoon. A 375-foot Beacon Tower, modeled after that of the Giralda in Seville, stood at one end, with a sunken garden surrounded by a balustrade and crossed by footbridges. A track on which chariot races were staged encircled the lagoon, and wide boardwalks surrounded the entire center court, around which various buildings of every style of architecture were arrayed. Dreamland's Beacon Tower dwarfed Luna Park's Kaleidoscope Tower, rising to a height of 370 feet, capped with a ball and eagle. It was white and gold in the French Renaissance style, with wide arches supporting a fifty-foot square base, decorated with bas-reliefs. In size and appearance it resembled John Galen Howard's[39] tower at the Pan-American Exhibition. It was studded with 100,000 incandescent lamps to produce the effect of "an ocean of electric fire."

In attempting to outdo Thompson and Dundy, Reynolds built two Shoot the Chutes side by side opposite the tower which extended three hundred feet out into the ocean on its own steel pier and was equipped with a "moving stairway" that ferried seven thousand passengers an hour to the top. Its boats carried twenty people at a time, careening downward into the lagoon. Visitors arriving at the pier by night by steamboat from Manhattan enjoyed a magical and majestic vista of Dreamland with its one million electric lights illuminating the skyline. A blanket of heavy fog that cloaked the park on the night of its opening

5. Luna Park and Dreamland

contributed to the overall effect. "Dreamland, when it had once passed at dusk into the realm of the electric king was made mysteriously weird and very, very beautiful," the *Brooklyn Daily Eagle* reported. "The tower that rose by day, a white shaft to a glorious conquest of Good Taste, by night became a beacon against the blackness of the heavens. It rose above the show, radiant beyond belief, a living, glowing thing that excited the admiration and praise of the most prosaic sort of folk."[40]

At the entrance the first venue that the park's patrons saw was a dance hall accommodating 25,000. Also on view was "The Creation," a replica of a classical nude female sculpture, measuring 150 feet wide and 75 feet high, and decorated in gold paint. After passing beneath the statue, visitors took a scenic boat ride along a thousand-foot canal, encircling the interior of a domed building that showed depictions of the Biblical "First Seven Days." Adding to the aura of "gentility," the young women at the cash booths wore "white college gowns and mortar boards."[41]

Dreamland matched Luna Park's Venetian City with its own recreation of the Doge's Palace and a half-mile-long gondola ride. Its "Fighting the Flames" was more spectacular than a similar attraction at Luna. There was also Dr. Martin Couney's Infant Incubators. Billed as a scientific exhibition of the care of premature infants, the incubator building was, in fact, a small hospital in the style of a German farmhouse, the lower half in brick, the upper part in half timber, topped by a tiled roof. A stork guarding a basket of terra-cotta babies decorated its front gable.

Dreamland's architecture generated professional interest as a tool to regulate the leisure behavior of urban residents. In 1904, the *Architects and Builders' Magazine* cited Dreamland as the prototype of the new popular resorts because of its "aid to civic betterment." As an oasis of splendor and respectability, the amusement park jolted a generation which knew Coney Island only as a sordid resort. Both Luna Park and Dreamland demonstrated that "intelligent architecture" could create profitable entertainment. At Dreamland, the beautiful tower, modeled after the Tower of Seville, and painted murals covering the canals of Venice, the Fall of Pompeii, and Switzerland buildings marked an important attempt to reorient the presentation of popular amusements.[42]

Dreamland was a combination of simulated tourism, thrill rides, and sideshow acts often veneered with grandeur and religious imagery

A bird's-eye view of Dreamland, circa 1904, includes the Shoot the Chutes ride, circus rings, Fire City, the "Pike," dancing pavilion and landing. Deep in the foggy background is a ship, returning weary travelers back to the grind of city life.

deemed suitable for a "respectable" middle-class crowd. On the East Promenade was located "The Canals of Venice," a 250-by-80-foot model with gondolas carrying passengers along 54,000 square feet of painted canvas of Venetian scenes. Nearby was a scenic rail ride called "Coasting Through Switzerland," with the latest refrigerated pipes to "keep this artificial 'Switzerland' as cold and as full of sweet pure air as can be found among the picturesque Swiss mountains." During the ride, patrons rode in red sleighs through a miniature Swiss valley and ascended, by means of a lengthy funicular tunnel, to an artificially chilled summit of snow-covered peaks. Dreamland also featured a British import, "Bostock's Circus" (which included a French cyclist riding on a tilted circular track above twenty fierce lions in "The Circle of Death"), which was part of "Bostock's Wild West Show," a fixture at world's fair midways that appealed to urban residents in much the same way as Buffalo Bill's Wild West Show. There was also "Ben Morris' Magic Show," and "The Seven Temptations of St. Anthony" (a spectacle for men, featuring paintings of voluptuous women "tempting" the saint).[43] On the West Promenade were attractions that were meant to educate. "The Destruction of Pompeii" was a cyclorama enhanced by mechanical and electrical effects depicting the eruption of Mount Vesuvius and the destruction of its surrounding area. "Under and Over the Sea" (a simulated submarine ride under the Atlantic), "The Baby Incubator Show" (moved from Luna), and a dog and a monkey show were also attractions, albeit more along "carney" lines; as such, these exhibits were located on the lower portion of the Iron Pier, where Dreamland leased out stalls for shooting galleries and other small concessions.[44]

Dreamland introduced several novel attractions. Midget City was a re-creation of 15th-century Nuremberg built to half scale and inhabited by three hundred little people. Residing there were shopkeepers, policemen, wagon drivers, and musicians, all of them dwarfs. There was a Lilliputian theater for tiny folk, a circus under a miniature tent, a livery stable, a midget Chinese laundryman, and even a midget fire department with a small steam fire engine hauled by two fat ponies that responded each hour to a false alarm in the town square. The *New York Times* noted that "grown folks who visit it can see into third-story windows of the houses without standing on tiptoe."[45]

Although Dreamland sought to disassociate itself from the boisterous clientele of Coney Island, it did not abolish the vertigo-inducing rides and wild animal shows common to amusement parks. Perhaps the scariest ride in the entire resort was Dreamland's Leap Frog Railway. Located on the Iron Pier that stretched nearly a thousand feet into the Atlantic Ocean, this ride consisted of two electric railroad cars, each one carrying up to forty passengers and traveling at a speed of about eight miles per hour, which hurtled towards each other on a single track, but at the point where a collision seemed inevitable, one car rode onto curved rails attached to the top of the other car, allowing it to travel up and over the other car and continue safely on its journey. The park's numerous other attractions included a Haunted Swing, a giant human bagatelle board called Chilkoot Pass, and Alberto Santos-Dumont's experimental airship, housed in a Japanese pagoda, which conducted daily ascents over the ocean.[46] In the highly popular "Fighting the Flames," fireman rescued women and children from a block-long line of burning buildings. This life-saving display thrilled spectators while reassuring them of the city's competency in providing essential social services. Far removed from the forests and jungles where wild animals roamed, city dwellers nevertheless took pride in vicariously conquering nature. Similarly, the furious chariot races held in Dreamland's hippodrome track surrounding the lagoon excited people seeking a link with the powerful civilizations of ancient Rome.[47]

Like Luna Park, Dreamland underwent dramatic changes nearly every year. "The Creation" was so popular that the park made Biblical themes a specialty by offering thrilling encounters with the hereafter. "Hell's Gate," a boat trip in a water flume to Hell, done in plaster of Paris, so captured the crowd's imagination that in 1906, a new exhibit, "The End of the World," replaced a boring scenic ride entitled "Touring Europe." This apocalyptic fantasy, basically a retelling of Dante's *Divine Comedy*, featured reproductions of Dore's pictures of the dead rising from their graves and the holy taking wing. The Orient encompassed several exotic attractions, including "The Hanging Gardens," "Herod's Temple," and "Salome's Dance of the Seven Veils," and concluded with a spectacular reenactment of "The Feast of Belshazzar" and "The Destruction of Babylon."

"The Orient," featuring La Belle Sultana performing the "Dance of the Wicked," was advertised thusly by a skilled barker: "This way to the Feast of Belshazzar! One hundred and fifty Oriental beauties! The warmest spectacle on earth! Anywhere else but at Dreamland it would be consumed by fire!" The following year (1907), "The Hereafter" stage show portrayed the destruction of the world by fire, backed up by two hundred singers performing portions of the libretto from Berlioz's *The Damnation of Faust*. In 1906, the exotic Village of Moqui and its Indians appeared in the space formerly occupied by Midget City, and the timely display of the San Francisco Earthquake replaced Fighting the

5. Luna Park and Dreamland

Flames. The following year, when earthquakes were passé, the exhibit was replaced by a scenic railway, "The Great Divide," which simulated travel across the Rockies with a mechanical volcano that pleased thrill seekers by erupting as they passed by.

Despite the high-minded rhetoric and elegant pseudo-architecture, Reynolds knew from the beginning that visitor's tastes were hardly refined. In fact, Dreamland hired circus and sideshow impresario Samuel Gumpertz to develop spectacles, promoting him to general manager in 1909. Gumpertz featured freak shows and exotic villages along with replicas of the Siege of Richmond.

Dreamland engaged well-known stage performers, such as comic singers Andrew Mack and Peter Dailey, to act as concessionaires. Actress Marie Dressler, who popularized the song "Heaven Will Protect the Working Girl," had charge of a corps of young boys who staffed the park's popcorn stands.

By 1911, the white paint was already peeling off the staff buildings, forcing Dreamland to undergo a major facelift, this time abandoning the purity of white for cream and firehouse red. Dreamland's goal of simultaneously sustaining exclusivity and large crowds proved elusive, despite its seemingly bigger and better attractions. Dreamland's managers touted the educational and scientific nature of their shows, and yet, as a citadel of refined amusement, it was a bit out of place at Coney Island. Perhaps the sheer size of the buildings overwhelmed the crowds, for it could never match Luna Park's popularity. Its ultimate success was left unresolved, and when a catastrophic fire destroyed the entire park in May 1911, the site was leased out for parking and for various rides and attractions, becoming the location of New York's aquarium in 1957.

In all their diversity, the Coney Island amusement parks anticipated later 20th century theme parks, especially with their emphasis on an integrated architectural fantasy. But they also hearkened back to earlier traditions of dime museums, circuses, and fairgrounds, which they brought together in an enclosed park, often in seeming contradiction to each other.[48]

Both Luna Park and Dreamland heralded a "new Coney Island" arisen, so it seemed, from the ashes of the old Bowery, reduced by fire. "Coney is regenerated," crowed the *New York Times*, "and almost every trace of Old Coney has been wiped out. Frankfurters, peanuts, and

Dreamland's large central tower at night; at its peak, the park was said to be illuminated with a million electric lights.

popcorn were among the few things left to represent the place as it was in the old days."[49] The two parks were now locked in a specular competition. One thousand people, including sixty firemen with engines and extension ladders, took part in Luna Park's production of "Fire and Flame," in which an entire city block was set ablaze. A factory building

5. Luna Park and Dreamland

Another stereopticon slide, this one featuring the Chute-the-Chutes (a.k.a. Shoot the Chutes) ride. This wildly popular attraction had been moved from Coney Island's Sea Lion Park in 1895.

collapsed nightly, bit by bit, in a glare of fire and pyrotechnic smoke. While all about it was the clamor of horsecars, wagons, and pushcarts with which the firemen had to contend. In Dreamland's near identical production, twice that number took part with engines and wagons. Both parks added spectacular new attractions. Dreamland installed "Hiram Maxim's Airships" in its forecourt, equipped with gondolas that revolved around a 150-foot-high tower. The park's rides included "Over the Great Divide," a scenic rail trip through the Rocky Mountains, which wound in and out of tunnels, through canyons, and over a seventy-foot-wide trestle.

Dreamland went even further on the "morally instructive" theme when they again engaged Henry Roltair, who had brought "The Creation" from the St. Louis Exposition in 1904 to the park, to present other spectaculars. He began with "Arabian Nights Up to Date" which recast the Arabian Nights tales, and "Pharaoh's Daughter," in which a scene came to life. Thompson took full advantage of Luna Park's size in placing attractions. Night and Morning was followed by other "dramatic spectacles," including "The Great Train Robbery," "Days of '49," The Burning of "*Prairie Belle*," and "Crack of Doom." These shows were presented on a 700 foot wide stage, and employed hundreds of actors and required elaborate effects. A full sized locomotive crossed the stage

A stereopticon slide of Dreamland's miniature railroad, advertised in 1910 as "the world's smallest locomotive and train ever built."

during "The Great Train Robbery," in which an outlaw gang held up a train, fled to a mining town, and was pursued to a mountain hideout. "The Burning of The Prairie Belle," a reenactment of life along the Mississippi, concluded with the burning of a river steamer. Thompson created "Crack of Doom" that depicted a mining town engulfed by floodwaters produced by a tank that held 65,000 gallons of water because he believed that "Your average person does not want a conception to be suggested to him. He wants a conception to dazzle, to stun him on the head like the crack of doom."[50] "The thing is hideously convincing," wrote one delighted observer."[51] He was continuously at work transforming the park's appearance. "A stationary Luna Park would be an anomaly,"[52] he explained. By 1907, the park had 1,326 towers, domes, and minarets, and 1,300,000 electric lights, employed 1,700 people; and housed hundreds of exotic animals, including twenty-five elephants. "The very name 'Luna' and the weird and fantastic charms of the moon have been preempted by Fred Thompson in the layout and character of this park," wrote the *Brooklyn Daily Eagle*, "About the court of Luna are corralled all those feats of worriers bold, highway robbers, knights and other adventurers, together with the gruesome and ecstatic imagination of nether worlds and the tom-tom pageant, romp and tinsel display of the present world."[53,54]

The Luna Park that Thompson built to satisfy the appetites of "those millions of insatiable one" was a flickering theatrical world endlessly metamorphosing like the grown up children inhabiting it. Recent scholars and chroniclers of popular amusements have tended to discuss Luna Park as though it was the same in 1912 as in 1903, obscuring the essential dynamism of the enterprise. "You see," the showman said in a 1906 interview conducted inside a plaster volcanic crater at Luna Park; "this being the moon, it is always changing."[55] After opening in 1903, the park underwent major changes in 1906, 1908, and 1912. Much of the 1904 addition was devoted to the Indian Dunbar, with three hundred natives and dozens of camels and elephants; it flopped and was torn down after one season. With each season, new decorative features and amusements replaced some of the previous year's shows or were expanded for the sake of surplus and variety. In Thompson's world, too much of a good thing—was an essential virtue.

The heavily capitalized amusement parks, constructed to produce monetary returns, expanded the entertainment level at Coney Island. But after the initial novelty of Luna Park and Dreamland wore off, they shared the usual constraints of modern life: clock bound, dependent on technology with emphasis on monetary calculation. The amusement park's freedom was illusionary. Its owners admitted as much; it was not innocent play, but a business.

In theory, drinking, dancing, and amusements could easily take place in one's own neighborhood. A trip to Coney did not necessarily involve a spending a great deal of money, for after purchasing transportation, the sun, sea, and sand were basically free. The *New York Times* said as much in 1868, "Those who mind their own business and do not seek to form acquaintances with strangers who may be wolves in sheep's clothing may enjoy themselves plentifully, and come away with ... as much money as they landed with, after deducting the price of a bathing-dress and a dish of baked clams."[56]

A major change that the parks made in Coney was life inside and outside its environs. Outside was licentiousness, gambling, drinking; inside, the parks' dictum was that fun must be innocent and respectable, never crossing "forbidden limits"—although this was sometimes a matter of definition. George Tilyou declared, "[T]he day of the confidence men and sharpers in amusement places is practically over." For Tilyou, deliberate swindling differed from his brand of "harmless hoodwinking" through the use of outrageous come-ons. However, Tilyou also posted signs strictly prohibiting entertainers from using even mildly objectionable language: "Performers playing in this house are requested not to use any *Vulgarity* or *Slang* in their act and to kindly omit the words *Damn* or *Liar* or any saying not fit for ladies and children to hear.... Our audiences are mostly ladies and children, and what we want is only *Polite Vaudeville*." Those who violated this edict were subject to "immediate discharge on the first offence."[57] Frederic Thompson admitted that Luna Park might be "frisky," but it knew where to "draw the line."[58] But also, in the case of these amusement parks, large outside investments necessitated organization and discipline.

The respectability of the parks and their visitors did not go unnoticed by those observing the Coney scene. The writer Albert Bigelow Paine reported reassuringly that the trip home at the end of a long day at Coney Island showed that the patrons were not the "old Coney crowd." Adults and children, both, were orderly, and men behaved like gentlemen and gave up their seats to women:

> By some process, the petty grafter seems to have been eliminated, and to have taken his victims and confederates with him.... Now we found that the lemonade was real lemonade in reasonably clean, large glasses, the restaurants were wholesomely kept, while the concert-halls supplied decent, even if not the highest order of, dramatic entertainment, and were patronized by thoroughly respectable men and women.
>
> Remembering that the Bowery used to be the worst section of old Coney, we went over there. But even the Bowery was changed,—laundered, as it were.... Of course it was still a whirl of noise and exhibition and refreshment, but the noise was within the limits of the law and order, and the exhibition and refreshment were more wholesome. Indeed, kinetescope shows of a gay but harmless variety seemed to prevail where once painted and bedizened creatures attracted half besotted audiences with vulgarity and display."[59]

With the opening of Luna Park and Dreamland, Coney Island furthered its quest for respectability. The park's enclosures made them morally safe. Admission fees meant that people could not wander in and out, and patrons were ejected by private police if they got too rowdy. Even though the admission fee at the parks was only ten cents, it was still high enough to exclude vagrants and the very poor. In addition, because of Jim Crow practices, the parks were only open to whites, which increased their exclusivity.

Class was also a factor in determining respectability. When people visited the Coney Island parks, they often dressed and acted in a manner higher than their stations: factory girls posed as department store girls, and stenographers pretended to be middle class.[60] Because higher classes were considered to have higher morals, these bumps in social status contributed to an overall appearance of greater respectability. It was an axiom of bourgeois culture that the upper classes, because of their whiteness, wealth, and lengthy American pedigrees, possessed an innate respectability that the working class could not strive to emulate.[61]

Brooklyn Life magazine praised the effect of the enclosed parks on the formerly disreputable Bowery area of Coney Island. Less than a month after Luna Park's opening, an editorial opined:

> Coney Island is doing for itself what no amount of police supervision has been able to do for it. It is reforming itself. Steeplechase Park, by providing no end of innocent entertainment for the people at minimum expense, began the good work. It remained, however, for Luna Park to bring about the most extraordinary change. This new resort—which is above reproach morally—has simply done wonders in the way of revolutionizing the amusement habits of thousands upon thousands who formerly fooled away their time and money in low concert halls and other more or less questionable resorts.[62]

From the viewpoint of the upper and middle classes, the parks revolutionized Coney Island, making it a place where people could engage in hours of fun without debasing themselves. While Steeplechase and Luna Park were approved of by these people, they wholeheartedly supported and patronized Dreamland. It was advertised heavily throughput its inaugural season in the magazine *Brooklyn Life*,[63] and was highlighted frequently in the magazine's "Summer Amusements" section.[64] Clearly, the magazine thought that Dreamland was special, when it wrote, "Both by day and night it offers no end of entertainment, the shows being all so good and of such variety that few are satisfied except by taking in the whole list."[65] Neither Luna nor Steeplechase ever received such an endorsement from *Brooklyn Life*.

Apart from its religiosity and didactic shows, Dreamland also featured a popular open-air café in the middle of the park. According to *Brooklyn Life*, "The spaciousness of the main portion of the place [is] one of Dreamland's greatest charms."[66] It was an open space, not one of the attention-grabbing amusements that drew patrons back to the park again and again. At a time when New York City was becoming increasingly crowded and the amount of space that one occupied was a marker of economic standing, the open space indicated to members of the upper class that Dreamland was a respectable place for them to be. The enclosed space protected customers from interactions with undesirables, but was also large enough inside so that a trip to this park could be a relaxing luxurious day in the open air. This combination of exclusivity and excess appealed to the middle and upper classes, which in turn raised Dreamland to a higher level of respectability.[67]

An additional lens with which to view Coney Island, specifically Luna Park and Dreamland, was that of the City Beautiful Movement, a reform philosophy of North American architecture and urban planning that flourished during the 1890s and 1900s. Its advocates believed that such beautification could produce a harmonious social order that would increase the quality of life. The success of this philosophy is credited with the beautification of such cities as Washington, D.C., Baltimore, Cleveland, and Denver, among others. Its connection with Coney Island came with the construction of a model city known as the "White City," which had modern transportation systems and no poverty; this had initially been an exhibit at the World's Columbian Exposition of 1893 in Chicago, which visited by George Tilyou. While the only attraction that Tilyou took from that exposition was the Ferris wheel, and not the idea of the "White City," he witnessed the popularity of the Chicago Midway, which gave him a new kind of amusement venue that was more entrepreneurial than civic minded. Tilyou wanted to create a place with wide commercial appeal, where pleasure seekers could enjoy mental stimulation and physical thrills. The city beautifiers had targeted Coney Island for edification through civic art. The problem was that entrepreneurs, rather than professionals, masterminded the Coney amusement parks. The ideals that Coney Island overtly expressed were the opposite of the heroic visions of order and stability embodied in the City Beautiful programs. Coney's lavish architecture and sculptural arrangements were designed to contribute to a riotous carnival atmosphere. Along the way, they helped to nurture indifference and even resistance to the elite values that official civic sculpture sought to transmit.

Coney Island was a legacy of the midways of the turn-of-the-century world's fairs that did in fact exist at the Columbia Exposition, not because the organizers wanted it, but included it nevertheless to prevent the appearance of an unauthorized tenderloin district of the kind that had cropped up at the 1876 Centennial Exhibition. Unfortunately, the midway proved to be so popular that the noted American

5. Luna Park and Dreamland

landscape architect Frederick Law Olmsted urged that the midway become part of the "White City" because, according to him, visitors there all looked so miserable.[68] Coney Island became sort of a permanent midway, with all of its amusements and few of its pretensions.

Architecture and sculpture were an important part of Coney's amusement parks because the decorations functioned as advertisements for the attractions. They played a crucial role in the amusement park experience and were the subject of careful planning. While the designs of Coney Island shared a few features with those in the exhibitions, they were essentially a parody on the City Beautiful ideals. Consequently, the sculpture at Coney Island, particularly in Luna Park and Dreamland, served a different purpose from those in the "White City."

Frederic Thompson, the creator of Luna Park, had a background in draftsmanship and art which shaped his attitude toward architecture as both a form of entertainment and a means of crowd control. Luna was developed on the basis of a carefully thought out system. But unlike the expositions, Luna Park would make no attempt to teach. Instead, Thompson viewed laughter, emotional release, and commercial success as the desired effects of his architecture, a fact he never attempted to hide.[69]

> Theatrically speaking, architecture is nothing more than scenery.... Everyone, I take it, knows that a "bally-hoo" is a device calculated to attract the attention of people and to guide them into a show[70]—a brass band, an automation, a lightning calculator, a dancing dervish, anything which can collect a crowd and hold it until the "barker" can get in his fine work. All showmen use them, but I think I am one of the very few who have ventured to make architecture shout my wares. I have tried hard to make it as much a part of the carnival spirit as the band, flags, rides, and lights. I have tried to keep it active, mobile, free, graceful, and attractive, and I have always preferred the remarks, "What is that?" or "Why is that?" to "Isn't that a beautiful building?"[71]

Anyone who considered Luna Park too vulgar could visit its competitor, Dreamland. In contrast to Luna Park, however, was deliberately more conventional and seemingly closer to the City Beautiful vision, at least on the surface. The park itself housed the usual compendium of wild rides and bizarre amusements, including a huge "hatchery," where premature human babies were actually displayed in mass incubators. As with Luna Park, the object of Dreamland's artwork and sculpture was to bring in customers. As an example, the gigantic, nude, winged

A panoramic view of Dreamland, taken shortly after the destructive fire of 1911. Fortunately, the all-wooden roller coaster appears to have escaped the flames.

women at the entrance to the "Creation" show might be an angel or Eve, and thereby contribute to the uplifting message of the Genesis-inspired exhibit. But, then again, she might also be merely a big naked lady whose presence provoked perfectly reasonable winks and snickers.[72]

6
The Nickel Empire

By 1912, Coney Island was undergoing changes from its amusement park heyday of only a few years earlier. Of the five enclosed parks that were constructed beginning in 1895, only two, Steeplechase and Luna Park, were still in existence. Sea Lion Park had been sold to Luna Park, and both Dreamland and Brighton Park were lost to fires and not rebuilt. The Manhattan Beach Hotel was razed in 1911 and the Oriental Hotel was demolished five years later, followed by the Brighton Beach Hotel. Through it all, however, Coney continued to prosper. The 1917 season proved to be the most successful on record, and the outbreak of World War I did not interrupt this prosperity. Even the imposition of Prohibition in 1919 did not have an injurious effect on the island, basically because of the lure of the beach.

Over time, Coney Island's beach had become a narrow strip, eroded by the tides and carved up by commercial bathing concessions. Public access to the beach was further impeded by jetties, fences, and other obstacles. Bathing areas controlled by so-called "bathhouse barons" were extremely congested, and many who wished to use them could not afford the fees imposed. In 1911, the city sought to alleviate this condition by erecting the Municipal Bathhouse. The next year, the West End Improvement League proposed the construction of a much-needed boardwalk at Coney Island that would ensure entry to the beach, resulting in a lengthy legal battle. This was finally settled in 1915 by the State Supreme Court, affirming public ownership of the beach. The result was that the bathing house proprietors were ordered to remove any structures that prevented access to the beach, which included Steeplechase Park. When some of the bathhouse owners resisted, public employees, some of them armed with axes, destroyed the structures.

Steeplechase's problem with the city in this respect centered on the park's policy of offering its paying customers free use of its fenced "private beach" in front of the property. Also, having a title to the property was advantageous since, over the decades, sand had built up and extended their property. However, when their right to deny beach access to the public was challenged, they lost the court case in 1913. Although they showed title to "a conveyance in fee to land extending out into the Atlantic Ocean," the judge ruled that the public had a right to use the beach in the area between low and high tides.[1]

With the beach now opened, three other factors contributed to a "new" Coney Island. The first occurred in 1920, when the subway reached the island. Now express trains from Times Square could reach the Stillwell Avenue station in forty-five minutes—thirty-five minutes from downtown. The subway allowed as many as a million people to reach Coney on a daily basis. The second factor was the construction

A train—no doubt carrying a large group of beachgoers—arrives at the Stillwell Avenue station in Coney Island.

6. The Nickel Empire

of a boardwalk to accommodate those crowds. This was first proposed in 1915, after public access to the beach was secured. The *Brooklyn Daily Eagle* wrote on this point: "There is no reason why the city should not do something to give the people of the city full enjoyment of the rights they have been awarded by the court."[2] Nothing was done at this time, however, because of World War I. With the subway bringing enormous crowds to the beach, boardwalk construction was begun in 1921, and "Coney Island's Fifth Avenue" was completed on May 15, 1923, at a cost of $3 million. The third change was the opening of Nathan's. Nathan Handwerker, an employee of Feltman's, saved three hundred dollars throughout 1915, and opened his own hot dog stand in 1916. He had tremendous success for two reasons: first, he was a block closer to the subway than Feltman's; and secondly, he only charged five cents for his product, half the price of Feltman's hot dogs. Coney Island now became what was known as the "Nickel Empire"—five cents for the subway ride, five cents for a hot dog, and five cents for most rides.

The Nickel Empire saw another evolution in the demographics of Coney Island: the introduction of immigrants into the population mix. During the 19th century, the Coney visitors went from the wealthy in Manhattan Beach to the middle class in Brighton Beach, to the lower-middle-class seeker of recreation. Now they were joined by the immigrants from eastern and southern Europe, who poured into Ellis Island between 1880 and the closing of the immigrant door by the Immigration Act of 1924. Not only did this influx have an effect on the number of people coming to Coney Island, but also the number living there. The resort's permanent population had always been low—under two thousand in the 19th century. Now, it swelled to seventy-five thousand in the 1920s, with the infusion of Italians, Greeks, Jews from eastern Europe, and emigrants from other European countries. In addition to classes of people at Coney, there were new nationalities and cultures. In 1924, French Prime Minister Edouard Herriot visited Coney Island and marveled at the scene: "To understand the crowd, one must go to Coney Island, the inexhaustible human river flows along the streets, past the Italian or Greek rotisseries, which turn out an uninterrupted sausage called hot dogs, past the naively pretentious astrologers' booths, the tattoo artists and the hideous four-legged woman. One is carried along into the torrent with all the languages and all the races of the globe." Commenting on the new boardwalk, he added, "Around this

Nathan's Famous Frankfurters (shown here in 1947) began its celebrated existence in 1916. Bearing the name of co-founder Nathan Handwerker, a German emigrant who, along with his wife, Ida, started selling hot dogs for a nickel apiece on Coney Island, Nathan's Famous remains in operation a century later.

city of cheap pleasure for cheap people, New York has built a magnificent promenade, three kilometers long and swept by the air of the sea. Families which cannot go to the rich watering places come in hordes on Sunday to enjoy the municipal beach. It is like the Promenade des Anglais turned over to the proletariat."[3]

Michael Immerso points out in *Coney Island: The Peoples Playground* that there were other observers whose opinions of Coney were more critical. The poet Federico Garcia Lorca, after a visit to Coney Island in 1929, spoke of being among "vomiting multitudes."[4] Sir Percival Philips, an English visitor stated in the London *Daily Mail*: "Coney Island is a slum, New York transported to the sea front by underground trains that function like a machine gun, for five cents the East Side worker is whirled by tunnel under a river and a city to a free beach." Arriving at his destination, Sir Philip found the beach overrun by "sweltering humanity in bathing costumes, packed sardine fashion on a foreshore of burning sand." Visitors to Coney Island, he wrote, were assailed on all sides by "incessant noise," oppressed by a "confusion of tongues," and suffered from "thirst, insatiable and insistent."[5]

Intellectuals, especially in the United States, despaired at understanding why wage earners would be attracted to seaside crowds. A revealing example was American art, theater, and literary critic James Huneker's question, "Why, after the hot, narrow, noisy, dirty streets of the city, do these same people crowd into the hotter, narrower, noisier, dirtier, wooden alleys of Coney?"[6] Huneker assumed that urban working people would seek a leisure site that reflected an escape from the city and its crowds, but this was the vision of the elites. Reformers hoped to enlist the working classes (and especially their children) into an uplifting love of nature, the purpose being to separate them from the city's masses. The *New York Times* found that "a tumble in the surf" was a "healthful and resting exercise," especially for those "forced to ply their busy tools in almost air-tight shops where the blast of furnaces consume what little air they may have."[7] Organizations like the Fresh Air Fund sponsored summer vacations for tenement children in the homes of suburban and rural families, beginning in 1877. The scout and summer camp movements hoped to bring children from all social ranks into a personal engagement with nature.[8] More important, perhaps, in reaching out to youths from wage-earning families were the urban playgrounds. With its roots in philanthropy, the Playground Association (founded in 1907) attempted to organize games on city playgrounds to lure youths away from the unsupervised streets.[9]

There was also a touch of nostalgia in the words of the reformers. Hostility toward the novelty and flash of Coney Island often showed a desire to return to the old "picturesque features of ocean commerce." Typical were the sentiments of O. Henry, who lamented the passing of beach sand and clam chowder remembered from his youth at Coney and the coming of the "phony red-flannel eruption of Mt. Vesuvius" at Dreamland.[10]

After the turn of the 20th century, another change came about at Coney Island: the purposeful addition of children as participants in the revelry. Children had come to Coney in the 19th century along with their parents, but they were a distinct minority. Coney's Bowery was very unfriendly to minors and the amusement parks appealed to adult sensibilities, with the playful sexuality of Steeplechase, the orientalism of Luna Park, and the religious fantasy of Dreamland. Kathy Peiss uses Steeplechase as an example of entertainment directed at adults:

> Steeplechase incorporated into its notion of mass entertainment cultural patterns derived from working-class amusements, street life and popular entertainment. Like them, the park encouraged familiarity between strangers, permitted a free-and-easy sexuality, and structured heterosexual interaction. This culture was not adopted wholesale, but was transformed and controlled, reducing the threatening nature of sexual contact by removing it from the street, workplace and saloon. Within the amusement park, familiarity between women and men could be acceptable if tightly structured and made harmless through laughter. At Steeplechase, sexuality was constructed in terms of titillation, voyeurism, exhibitionism, and a stress on a couple and romance.[11]

Grown-ups may have acted like children, but they seldom brought the kids along when they went to the parks. Additionally, the thrills and adventures that excited them—the dance halls, the freak shows, and even the dioramas—had little appeal for children.

Gradually, this began to change. In 1920, Steeplechase introduced Babyland at one corner of the Pavilion of Fun, featuring two child-sized slides, hobbyhorses, and a kiddie carousel. In the summer of 1925, the National Association of Amusement Parks promoted new children's rides at member parks.

Beginning in 1906, an annual baby show was held at Coney Island, complete with a carriage parade of twelve hundred participants and a contest judging the most beautiful, fattest, smallest, and most strenuous baby. Done for fun, the contest became an integral part of Coney's Mardi Gras celebrations.[12] By the 1920s, the baby parade became a way of civilizing the boisterous participants. It worked so well that the parade began to attract a "family crowd" rather than the throngs that formerly became involved in drunken brawls. As the "family" idea became more and more the essence of the parade, mothers began dressing up their babies to look like famous adults. As an example, the first prize in 1913 went to an infant dressed as Fatima. Other children were dressed as the boxer Jack Dempsey, and mayor Jimmy Walker.

Although children slowly became part of Coney Island, even more important to this transformation were new ways to express wonder. A new middle-class ideal of fun abandoned some traditional delights and found new ones. While human curiosities prevailed on the Coney Island Bowery and even Dreamland, the most "respectable" of its major amusement parks, middle-class sensibilities had already begun to turn against this traditional expression of wonder by 1900. A *Scientific American* article of 1908 fully revealed this new attitude: "Most of these humble and unfortunate individuals, whose sole means of livelihood is the exhibition of their physical infirmities to a gaping and unsympathetic crowd, are pathological rarities.... A more refined and a more humane popular taste now frown upon such exhibitions."[13] In the 1920s and 1930s, popular magazines explained how standard freak types (giants, bearded ladies, obese people, dwarfs, etc.) were really victims of glandular malfunctions. Sideshow barkers' claims that they displayed a member of a "lost tribe" of pygmies or "natives" with tails lost credibility when global exploration demystified distant places and people.[14]

Even at Coney Island, the freak show was becoming discredited. While in the early 1900s newspapers had reported the latest additions to the sideshows in the same way that they would announce a new Broadway musical, by the late 1920s the *New York Times* was reporting that sideshows were growing "more conservative," not only because of a scarcity of "dog-faced men, mermaids, and many-legged livestock," but because of "the marked slump in the credulousness of metropolitan throngs." The "broad and dignified boardwalk" at Coney Island, along with the "tall shoulder-to-shoulder apartment houses and retail enterprises ... reminiscent not of the erstwhile leading honky-tonk center of the nation, but rather of [upscale Brooklyn neighborhoods like] Washington Heights and Williamsburg,"[15] were finally closing in on the old freak shows and catchpenny amusements.

New York City also had a hand in the changes at Coney: first, with the erection of the Municipal Bathhouse in 1911, which competed successfully with the private operators and, later, with the construction of the boardwalk. The free beach and its boardwalk seemed to promise an opportunity for universal uplift or, at least, democratization of access.[16]

But those for whom the boardwalk and the Municipal Bathhouse were built did not always share the values of the city's governors. The masses simply broke the rules when there was an alternative that would benefit them. Many arrived via subway, with swimming suits under their clothes, or changed in the bungalows of locals for a small fee, avoiding the pricier bathhouses. They hid peddlers from the police during periodic crackdowns (preferring the peddlers' convenient services to the distant and expensive cafés and licensed vendors on the streets). During summer weekends the beach was so crowded that the capacity of the bathhouses was entirely insufficient. This massive amount of humanity, sometimes reaching 750,000 persons on a given day, defeated the dreams of the reformers. Added to this, the 1920s saw the addition of new massive roller coasters lining the back of the boardwalk, which appealed primarily to a youthful crowd looking for thrills.

The roller coaster was perhaps the only constant in the history of Coney Island. First built in 1884, forty-seven coasters were erected between that year and 1949. Some of the most famous constructed in the 20th century were:

The Cannon Coaster (1902, 40 ft. high). So called because the designers had the cars enter the mouth of a cannon at the top of the tracks. From there, the cars passed through its bore,

Thrill-seeking turn-of-the-century tourists hang on to their seats as they make a fast turn on one of Coney Island's roller coasters.

6. The Nickel Empire

accelerating downhill, and then leapt over a gap in the tracks. After this failed to work, the gap was filled in. The coaster still drew crowds, however, because of the stories that were circulated involving casualities that supposedly occurred during test runs when the gap existed.

Rough Riders (1907, 60 ft. high). This was a new type of coaster that derived its power from a third rail which was operated by a motorman with a throttle so that he could accelerate the cars' speed traveling uphill and retard it on steep downgrades, if needed. Attendants wore Spanish-American War uniforms, and the trains carried passengers past murals depicting that war. On June 22, 1910, the train's power mechanism jammed, causing two cars to overturn. As a result, seventeen riders were pitched from their cars at the top of the track, resulting in three deaths. Another accident occurred on August 17, 1915, when the train derailed and jumped the track, resulting in the death of the driver and two passengers.

Drop-the-Dip (a.k.a. Trip to the Moon) (1907, 60 ft. high). This coaster opened on June 6 and was constructed with oversized dips, giving it some of the steepest drops of any coaster to date. Despite the ride's small size (only 450' × 65') and the fact that a ride only lasted ninety seconds, at twenty-five cents per ride, it would have grossed $20,000 a season if it had not burned to the ground during the Steeplechase fire on July 28.

When reconstructing the coaster, Christopher Feucht added more hills and angles, making for a more thrilling ride. This resulted in long lines of paying customers, many requesting re-rides. It was considered the first modern high-speed roller coaster. Because of the acute hills and turns, Feucht invented the lap bar to hold the passengers in the cars; formerly, riders either held on to the cars or were restrained only by a leather strap.

Another interesting note concerning this coaster was that, in 1915, Feucht, in order to avoid an increase in his rent, moved the entire coaster across the street and reconstructed it within a twenty-four-hour period. It was moved once again, in 1924, to Luna Park, and its name changed to "Trip to the Moon."

Giant Racer (1911, 50 ft. high). This 900-foot-long two-track coaster was built of steel rather than wood, which allowed it to survive the fire that destroyed Dreamland. It was built at a cost of $180,000. In 1916, to increase its revenue, the entire structure was moved as it occupied a section of the beach which, the courts ruled, impeded the public's right to free access. Also, the entrance to the ride was moved seventy feet closer to Surf Avenue, which increased its gross revenue by $3,700 in 1917. The coaster suffered a terrible accident in 1911 when one of its cars left the tracks fifty feet above the street, killing two female occupants. There was another bad accident, this one on February 28, 1925, just prior to the season opening, when three workmen were testing the ride. As the cars were moving up an incline, a coupling pin broke as the train neared the top, causing the last two cars to slide backwards and crash into a barrier.

Mile Sky Chaser (1923, 80 ft. high). At a length of 3,850 feet, this enormous coaster ran along Luna Park's perimeter, mainly on the west and back sides. It was originally built as an attraction inside the Brighton Beach Amusement Park in 1910, and was known then as the Chase Through the Clouds. When the park was destroyed by fire in 1919, the coaster was abandoned until 1923, when it was moved to Luna Park; it remained in use until 1944, when Luna burned down.

Thunderbolt (1925, 86 ft. high). This was the only coaster erected on top of a building, the two-story Kensington Hotel, after the top story was removed. The hotel then became a residence, which was featured in the 1977 Woody Allen film *Annie Hall* as the boyhood home of Alvy Singer (Allen's character). The Thunderbolt had two serious accidents during the first two years after construction. A woman was killed on August 25, 1925, when she was thrown forward and hit her head on the metal bar in front of her. Another accident occurred on July 26, 1926, when a three-car train stalled partway up a hill. After stopping, the cars suddenly began sliding backward down the track, crashing into the following train. As a result, twelve passengers were injured, one seriously. It remained in operation until 1982, and was demolished in 2000, when it was replaced by an all-steel coaster.

Tornado/The Bobs Coaster (1926, 71 ft. high). This coaster was built on a very narrow lot, only seventy feet at its widest point, tapering down to fifty feet along Coney Island's Bowery. It was constructed at a cost of $250,000 when it opened on Memorial Day and earned $300 per hour until the advent of the Great Depression. It was extremely popular because of its exciting drops, tight turns, and crossovers. In 1937, a high school boy was pitched out of a twenty-person car, falling to the tracks below, where he was run over by a following train. It was announced that the Brooklyn District Attorney would investigate this accidental death, but the furor died down and the coaster's operations returned to normal. In 1977, much of the ride was damaged by arson, and then torn down in 1978.

The Cyclone (1927, 85 ft. high). The success of the Thunderbolt and the Tornado prompted the construction of this coaster. The ride's top speed was sixty miles per hour, and the time from start to finish is one minute and fifty seconds. The construction was a combination of lumber and steel, and its final cost to build was reported at between $146,000 and $175,000. On May 28, 1985, a twenty-nine-year-old man was killed while riding the Cyclone when he stood up during the ride and struck his head on a crossbeam.

During the 1920s, despite the disapproving glances of the respectable, the lower-class bathers changed in public or "dripped" on the subway ride back home, still dressed in bathing suits and saving money by not renting a place to change. It was simply part of enjoying themselves at Coney, practically for free. And for their part, the city leaders were also satisfied by repeatedly extending and improving the boardwalk, allocating police protection, providing competent lifeguard protection, and eventually building a sewage treatment plant in Coney Island to reduce shoreline pollution.

The combination of the boardwalk and the beach provided a way for all classes of people to use Coney Island. While the lower classes used the free beach and boardwalk, the middle classes could simultaneously partake of the amusement parks. Also, through new investment in the area, including new theaters, a boxing ring, and a new large hotel, the Half Moon, the middle class began investing in bungalow vacation rentals.

The trend towards more investment in Coney Island did not, however, continue with the widespread use of the automobile, especially after World War I, because it gave those who could afford it alternatives. No longer would the well-off have to endure the crowded conditions at Coney and the "drippers" on the subway. Now, New York families could visit the "Jersey Shore" (i.e., Long Branch, Bradley Beach, Atlantic City, and Asbury Park), the Rockaways, and Coney's biggest competitor, Jones Beach.

The return to the "old" Coney Island was also retarded by the persistence of the "nickel empire." With the decline of the middle class and the emphasis on thrills from the Wonder Wheel, built in 1920, and the roller coasters and away from the amusement parks. With the demise of Dreamland in 1911, leaving only Luna Park and Steeplechase, all of Coney began spiraling down.

When Frederic Thompson left Luna Park in April of 1912, he took with him all of the models, designs, and plans that he had drawn up for that season. Barron Collier, a streetcar advertising expert, founder of the Boy Scouts in the United States, and the largest landowner in Florida, took over Luna Park. He immediately began to enlarge the park's infrastructure. Collier and his associates added new buildings and rides, including one called the Coal Mine, in which donkeys pulled the customers, seated in carts, through dark tunnels. By 1913, Luna had raised their employee count to 1,500, possessed 1,450,000 lights, and 2,054 towers and minarets. Another spectacle, "The Fall of Adrianople," which took place on a stage measuring 475 by 175 feet, was added for this year. Collier built a Turkish city on the stage, complete with a castle and a fort armed with foot-long guns which were fired on an invading army made up of Bulgarians, Serbs, Montenegrins, and Greeks, all of whom were attempting to capture the city. The battle raged in front of a grandstand holding 1,800 patrons.

In 1914, a show entitled "Great Sea Divers" was added. To accommodate it, an 80,000-gallon tank was constructed, in which a ship was placed. A sudden explosion rocked the ship and sank it. Submarine men in diving suits then entered the tank and swam to the bottom to salvage the ship's valuables.

6. The Nickel Empire

For the 1915 season, Luna added more visual attractions than had previously existed at other parks. The first was the Oriental Village, depicting life in Turkey, Arabia, and Egypt. It consisted of whirling dervishes, dancing girls, acrobats, and magicians, as well as native workers plying their trades. The park also installed a Village of Midgets, based on an earlier version that had existed in Dreamland, featuring an entire town in miniature, including houses, shops, a tiny theater, and a farm with miniature animals. A new and interesting attraction that Luna added was "The Trip to Niagara," which took place entirely indoors. As the patrons entered, they boarded a train that took them above the falls and then back to the park. They could also sit and watch as the lights played on the waterfall.

Unfortunately for Luna, the park's owners and managers, including the general manager, Oscar C. Jurney, did not have the genius exhibited by George C. Tilyou and Frederic Thompson. They brought in rides and attractions that mirrored contemporary events, but rarely ones that excited the public. As a result, while the park drew millions of visitors each season, it earned less money than expected. An example of this was an unusual attraction that Jurney brought to Luna in 1917, entitled "The Scenic Spiral Wheel," also called "The Top." It was a forty-five-ton, seventy-foot-diameter steel wheel that was tipped backwards so that one edge was touching the ground. A roller coaster track spiraled around the outer rim from the top to the bottom. As the four-car train moved toward the edge of the wheel, its weight caused the wheel to slowly turn so that it moved in a circle. The amusement proved to be more interesting to watch than to ride, and, consequently, it only lasted four years.

The park's management changed the rides continuously, not because they were attempting to keep their patrons coming back to see something new, but because they were guessing which ones would be successful. As a result, Luna fell back on its usual productions, in this case reproductions of World War I battles prior to the involvement of the United States in 1917. First was "Aerial Night Attacks," which featured a German Zeppelin attack on a miniature French village. Also depicted were miniature submarine attacks on Allied shipping. And finally, "Over There," which was comprised of 150,600 square feet of miniature soldiers in battle.

In 1924, Barron Collier scored somewhat of a coup when he

replaced Oscar Jurney with Arthur Jarvis as the park's general manager. Jarvis was an expert at developing spectacular roller coasters, including Dreamland's Giant Racer; Brighton Beach's Trip to the Clouds; and Drop the Dip, located on Coney Island's Bowery (later relocated to Luna); and Luna's Mile Sky Chaser, which he built covering three sides of the park. This was the island's highest and longest coaster; it contained six drops, several of which were more than seventy feet in length. This ride became immensely popular, and had thrill seekers standing in long lines, waiting to step aboard. In its first year it carried a million passengers.

In 1925, Jarvis began replacing older rides with newer ones. There was the Tumblebug, in which a train of five connected saucers that moved around a circular and undulating track, each saucer seating six people who were holding on to a central grip wheel to avoid knocking into their fellow passengers. Although billed as "family oriented," the ride was reminiscent of the mildly flirtatious nature of Steeplehouse's attractions.

As the Depression worsened in the early 1930s, Luna's fortunes waned. Less and less money was put back into the park, and reducing the admission prices did little good. Only a fraction of the lights were illuminated and the untended rides looked tired and shabby. In 1933, there were two major changes: first, Collier hired a new general manager, Rex Billing, who made a number of changes to the rides and attractions in the spring before the season opened; the second was that, in May, Luna went into bankruptcy.

Since the park had spent money to refurbish the rides and bring in new ones, the bankruptcy judge ruled that opening the park was the best way to bring in income and repay the park's creditors. Consequently, Luna was allowed to reopen during the second week in June. Unfortunately, with the country still in the grip of the Depression, there just wasn't enough business to solve the park's financial problems. By 1934, Luna was out of bankruptcy, and, while he could have leased the park to other operators, Collier decided to operate it himself. Luna was reopened in July, but did so poorly that it was sold after the season.

The new owners immediately began to bring in new rides, but the situation was the same—the ownership simply did not know what the public wanted, and the Depression continued to linger. In 1939, with the park carrying a $400,000 mortgage, the park's bank leased it to

6. The Nickel Empire

Harry Meinch, a Coney Island amusement operator and an owner of Meinch & Feldman, a supplier of shooting galleries. At the end of his first season, Meinch gave up, and an attorney, Milton Sheen, along with a group of associates, leased Luna for twenty-one years, beginning in 1940. They invested $100,000 in new rides and equipment and eliminated the entrance fee. Their tenure only lasted one year, however, and in 1941, Edward and Harry Lee Danzinger leased the park. The Danzinger brothers were British film producers who would later be responsible for a number of American television shows. As had some of their predecessors, they brought in new ideas, rides, and money. Their main deterrent to success was the Second World War. The government's rationing allowed the park to remain open, but its iconic symbol—the profuse number of lights—had to be dimmed so that Luna could not be seen by overhead enemy planes or offshore submarines.

In 1944, Luna finally succumbed to Coney Island's usual disaster—fire. Just before the park opened for the season, a fire destroyed the L.A. Thompson Scenic Railway. It was reopened in August seven days before another fire, this time a major one, ravaged most of the park. The problem now was finding the money to rebuild. Luna could have claimed $400,000 in insurance money, but the owners were fearful that the mortgagee, Farmer's Bank and Trust Company, would fight for the money since they held a $600,000 mortgage on the property. A secondary difficulty was finding building materials during the war.

Luna did not reopen in 1945, during which time the owners and the bank were battling in court over the insurance money. Finally, in September 1946, Farmer's Bank sold the park to Fred Trump (Donald Trump's father) for $275,000. Trump announced that he would raze the fire-damaged park and use the site for constructing low-income housing. During construction in 1949, another fire destroyed the remainder of Luna as it was being torn down. The area was then turned into a parking lot.

From 1947 on, several investors made offers to buy the Luna property. There were rumors that Walter O'Malley, owner of the Brooklyn Dodgers, wanted to build a baseball stadium and relocate there when the club was planning its move from Ebbets Field. The team wound up in Los Angeles instead, after negotiations with Robert Moses broke off. According to Charles Denson, author of *Wild Ride! A Coney Island Roller Coaster Family*:

Every time amusement or recreational development plans were initiated, they fell through. It soon became apparent that this was not a coincidence. What no one realized at the time was that a silent hand was being played behind the scenes by two of New York's most devious developers, Robert Moses and Fred Trump. Their plans would cost Coney Island dearly.[17]

Steeplechase attempted to attract working-class patrons by first issuing a combination ticket which permitted the bearer to use every ride in the park for one admission price. Additionally, the park advertised in working-class newspapers, and offered a variety of special rates. Also, Steeplechase managed to succeed by appealing to both the working and middle classes simultaneously. For the former it was sexuality; the latter, romance, and making them both respectable by staying within acceptable limits.

George Tilyou added a number of outdoor attractions through the early 1910s, including the Ocean Roller Coaster on the beach side of the park, the Airship Ride, the Venetian Gondolas, and an automobile ride on a quarter-mile track that accommodated full-sized autos. George Tilyou died in 1914 and was succeeded by his eldest son, eighteen-year-old Edward F. Tilyou.

Under Edward Tilyou's management, the park continued to be innovative, but with more emphasis on the outdoor rides. The older popular attractions, particularly in the Pavilion of Fun, were retained, but following George Tilyou's lead, most of the outdoor attractions were replaced with more thrilling rides. The biggest changes in Steeplechase's outdoor amusement attractions occurred in the early 1920s, with the addition of the Frolic, a circular spinning ride where the suspended cars tilted outward, a Dodgem bumper-car ride, the Witchway, a swing that whirled passengers around, and a Caterpillar flat ride. In 1915, he converted an unused space above the restaurant near the balcony and built a skating rink on it.

Capitalizing on the success of Steeplechase's namesake ride, the park bought the Racing Derby Carousel in 1920. This ride featured sixteen groups of horses racing four abreast on a 315-foot-circumference platform at speeds approaching twenty-five miles per hour. The horses were set in a six-foot-long track and would move back and forth as the carousel rotated. Unlike the Steeplechase horse race, in which a rider's weight could affect the outcome, here, it was impossible to influence a patron's chances of winning because the cables that moved the horses back and forth were set up in a crisscross pattern beneath the platform. It was an exciting race lasting one mile, with a free ride given to the winner, and was purposely located near Surf Avenue so that it could be seen by passersby outside the park.

With the opening of the Reigelmann Boardwalk in 1923 and the widening of Surf Avenue during the following year, Steeplechase had the opportunity to again add to their outdoor amusements. A new roller coaster, The Limit, was erected on the south side of the park, along with the Old Mill Tunnel of Love water ride beneath the Tilyou apartment, and Noah's Ark, which catered to the parents of young children. This amusement was an old-fashioned fun house that rocked like a boat. Inside was a mirror maze, moving floors that nearly knocked patrons off their feet, and hidden compressed air jets that blew women's skirts high in the air. There was also a menagerie of animals that Noah and his wife saved from the flood.

After the 1928 season, Steeplechase began to spend money on the Pavilion of Fun. The heated indoor pool was demolished. The park spent $4,000 in 1929 to erect the Hey Day ride in place of the pool. This featured steerable cars on an elliptical-shaped track that were attached via a slot in the platform to a cable running underneath it. The driver could spin the car around to face backwards as it was pulled around the track counter-clockwise. Another car ride, the Custer Cars, which were small gasoline-powered automobiles that ran on a serpentine track, was installed next to the boardwalk.

The Pavilion of Fun also contained some novel "fun devices." The revolving Funny Mirrors had a six-inch-wide row of nails encircling the mirrors. When a patron came along, the individual received a mild shock when he leaned on the rails to see the reflections in the mirror. If he tried to take a seat to look into the mirrors, the seat would suddenly collapse, sinking four or five inches below the floor. A stereoscopic viewer nearby had a blowhole at its pedestal so that when a women looked at the mirror, her dress blew upward. The California Red Bats exhibit, placed in a small cage at the top of a steep ship's ladder, were merely two miniature baseball bats painted red and accompanied by a sign inside urging, "Don't tell anyone!"

Just before the stock market crashed in 1929, Steeplechase began spending money on the boardwalk. The Boardwalk Carousel was constructed for the 1930 season. It because known as the 72H carousel and contained seventy-two horses and two chariots. The ride's music was provided by a band organ. Additionally, The Whale replaced Noah's Ark and an eight-car Whip was installed. Even with the economic fallout of the Great Depression, Steeplechase continued to bring in new rides and acts. For the 1933 season, the park brought in a one-ring circus, which was set up next to the Limit roller coaster. Instead of having the circus manned by employees, acts were brought in by outside impresarios. The shows were free and featured Rosie the elephant, Leon's Performing Dogs, a tumbling act, three men with a bucking mule, and a clown act, all big hits with children. Since facilities for children were becoming a priority, a children's wading pool had been built in 1932, along with an elongated semi-circular diving pool erected between the big pool and Surf Avenue. The big outdoor pool was where the park's beauty contests were held, with the judging done in mid–August. This contest had been running since 1922. Added to it in 1933, was the Grandma's Bathing Contest in mid–July. In the 1930s, acts were changed frequently; new acts included the Riding Waltons, a group of bareback equestrians that were once with Ringling Brothers–Barnum & Bailey; Pelot & Wilson, a juggling clown act; and Silver & Company, a man-and-woman trapeze act.

Basically, however, expensive new attractions were postponed at Steeplechase as well as at other amusement parks. An additional problem was that a lack of new orders forced many ride manufactures into bankruptcy. In 1933, Steeplechase did place an order for a new innovative ride called the Flying Turns. Essentially, this was a bobsled ride consisting of a train of two passenger cars on swiveling rubber wheels, which ran through a cylindrical wooden chute made of cypress wood. The cars ran from the top of the ride around a tight figure-eight course, making nearly perpendicular turns. The Flying Turn cost $50,000 to build and was a huge success when it was officially introduced in 1934.

Aside from the Depression, Steeplechase suffered two more setbacks during the 1930s. On December 19, 1935, the Steeplechase pier was damaged by a barge that was being used to work on some nearby rock jetties. It broke loose from its mooring and smashed into the pier, destroying a house that was situated on the pier's end. To save money, the pier was never rebuilt to its original length. Three years later, on September 16, 1939, disaster struck again when garbage beneath the boardwalk caught fire and spread into the park. The flames, fanned by

6. The Nickel Empire

an afternoon onshore wind, threatened the entire park, but two fire boats, with the aid of fifty-two pieces of fire-fighting equipment, managed to contain the blaze, bringing it under control two hours after it started. The Pavilion of Fun was saved because it was repeatedly doused with water and because the park's own fire crew worked to save it. Edward Tilyou estimated the cost of the fire to be $500,000. Lost were the Flying Turns bobsled ride, the Bicycle ride, the House of Glass, the Cake Walk, the Barrel of Fun, the band stand, the entire circus backstage area, and a 220-foot portion of the Steeplechase horse track. Tilyou, being as resourceful as his father in combatting tragedy, ordered his workers to spread sawdust over the water-soaked areas and reopened the park at 7 p.m.

The fire was simply a continuation of a bad year, not only for Steeplechase but for all of Coney Island. In addition to the Depression, the island had to contend with competition from the World's Fair at Flushing Meadows Park, in Queens. Since the world's fair was scheduled to have a two-year run, Tilyou decided to clean up the fire damage. Insurance only paid $92,501.10 for the damaged rides; as a result, the Flying Turns was not rebuilt, the cost of lumber and steel being too high, and while the 220 feet of the signature horse race ride was replaced, only the inner four horse tracks were left in operation. The only good outcome from the fire was the lease negotiations on the park's western five acres. The yearly cost had been $30,000 per year on a ten-year lease. The family that owned the property, the Hubers, cut the price by half, worried that Tilyou might sell the park because of the fire.

There was, thankfully, a good outcome for Tilyou when he paid a visit to his competitor, the World's Fair. Again, in comparison to his father, who discovered the Ferris wheel at Chicago's World's Columbian Exposition, the son discovered the Parachute Drop at the Flushing's World's Fair. The Parachute Drop was the main attraction at the Fair's Fun Zone, and Tilyou knew it would be a tremendous benefit to Steeplechase. The design had been created by Retired Naval Air Commander James H. Strong, and was patented in August 1936. The structure was comprised of a strong, high, steel tower, with electric motors to tow the chutes upward. A series of eight guide cables, arranged in a circular formation, were set up to prevent swaying and dangerous contact with the tower. Commander Strong originally invented the tower as a training device for American parachutists in the armed forces; he later had the idea to use it as an amusement park ride when motorists stopped by his estate in Hightstown, New Jersey, to ask for a ride when he was testing it.

Strong agreed to sell the attraction to Tilyou, after the fair ended, for the exorbitant price of $150,000 and an additional lease agreement that paid Strong a commission of 10 percent on the first $25,000 of ticket sales, plus 7.5 percent of the sales on the second $25,000. It was also agreed that all replacement parts would be paid for by Strong. Although he eventually expected to make a profit, the acquisition of the Parachute Drop was a huge gamble for Tilyou. The ride could not be placed inside Steeplechase because if it was, it would therefore be part of the combination ticket (the admission price entitled the bearer to one ride on every attraction); as a result, Tilyou placed it on the boardwalk, with an admission price of thirty cents (twenty-seven cents plus three cents tax). Another financial problem was that the ride was labor intensive, requiring three operators for each chute. It was also sensitive to wind conditions, and, in order to make a profit, there had to be steady crowds.

To increase the opportunities for the maximum number of rides on the Parachute Drop, Steeplechase changed its boardwalk entrance. Previously, the entrance was enclosed so as to offer protection from the rain; the new entrance was now completely open, with a direct view of the tower when it was erected. Other changes were made to the boardwalk, mainly to the concessions, which were now placed in a brick building, and a new ride, the Silver Streak, was set up at a cost of $9,750. This was a circular flat ride on a thirty-degree tilt, with passenger cars containing two persons traveling around the perimeter at thirty miles per hour. The area in front of the pavilion, where the Flying Turns once stood, was refashioned as a lawn where the new gas-powered Express Train ride operated. Inside the pavilion, the Flyers ride was moved to the center of the building, and a new Bicycle Carousel amusement was set up in its place. The Gondolas ride was eliminated altogether.

In 1941, with the park on a better financial footing, Steeplechase began to spend more money on new attractions. First, during April and May, the Parachute Drop was put in place on a large, reinforced concrete base just west of where the Flying Turns ride once stood. When finished, the tower stood 262 feet tall and had a capacity of twelve

6. The Nickel Empire

thirty-two-foot diameter chutes. Passengers were strapped into a canvas seat and were then hoisted to the top of the tower. At the top, a mechanism automatically tripped the descent, which allowed the passengers to free fall to the ground, slowed only by the partially opened but limp chutes which blossomed to their full capacity. On the ground, rubber dampers cushioned the landing. The ride was a success, giving the passengers the same feeling as a parachutist jumping out of an airplane. Additionally, the 80-foot-high Giant Swing was revamped with six-passenger aluminum Buck Rogers–style rocket cars, at a cost of $4,100. Additionally, a brand new twelve-car Whip was installed on the Surf Avenue side of the park.

World War II had the same effect on Steeplechase as it did on the nation as a whole. Specifically, much of the park's gaiety was curtailed by wartime regulations. The park was allowed to remain open for the sake of public morale, but with restrictions; at night, regulations required that any park lighting had to be set in accordance with dim-out conditions so that it couldn't be seen by overhead enemy aircraft or by offshore submarines. This regulation required the use of soft blue and dark purple bulbs. Even the light inside the Pavilion of Fun had to be dimmed, creating a dark and dreary Steeplechase. The war affected the park's ability to purchase new rides and to obtain materials for repairs. As an example, Commander Strong had to receive a rubber ration for the upkeep of the Parachute Rides' shock absorbers. Labor shortages also had an impact on Steeplechase, as many employees either volunteered for service or were drafted. This situation led to the hiring of the elderly and women for the 1943 season, and to the cutting back on the park's hours, including remaining closed on Mondays. Even so, it was difficult to staff the park. By 1945, only the rides outside the Pavilion of Fun were operating until the war officially ended that year.

The war had another effect on Steeplechase that could have put the opening of the park in 1944 in jeopardy, and it concerned both the managing of the park and the Tilyou family. James Onorato, the park's manager, was drafted at the age of thirty-six; Edward Tilyou was dying; his brother Frank was in the navy; and his younger brother George C. Tilyou, Jr., wasn't prepared for the task of managing the park. President Franklin D. Roosevelt came to the rescue, however, when he limited the draft age to thirty-five, thereby allowing Onorato to continue managing Steeplechase.

Edward Tilyou died after a long illness, on June 19, 1944, which immediately caused problems for the operation of the park. Frank Tilyou was now back from service in the navy, but neither he nor his younger brother George had any real experience in running the park. Even when Edward was in the throes of his illness, he continued to travel extensively and maintained tight control of Steeplechase. After Edward's death, the two brothers and their sister Marie simply followed his successful formula in running the park, aided by the fact that Luna Park had burned down during the summer of 1944. More problems came after the war when the family began to split apart. While George, as the elder brother, inherited both the title and salary as president of the Tilyou Realty Company, he and Frank disagreed about how the park should be run. George and Marie wished to follow the ideas that Edward had set in place, but Frank and another sister, Eileen, were in favor of change. Because each owned equal quarter shares in the company, the fractious Tilyou family was usually divided into two opposing camps.

In 1945, with the war over, Steeplechase began to return to normal, which included changes, first to the park's method of bringing in income. The park instituted what it called "Season Bathing," which was essentially a pool club for members. These membership fees brought in extra income. The next change concerned the combination ticket. Instead of giving its patrons one ride on every amusement in the park, the ticket now entitled the holder to fifteen rides for a dollar. Added to this, as a means of increasing the gate, social, political, and religious groups became eligible for discounted daily tickets, and tax-deductible free tickets were given to orphanages and some church organizations.

In 1947, some modernization began. The ballroom was cut by half to install a television studio and, in 1948, some new rides were purchased, including the Scrambler and the C-Cruise, as well as twenty new Dodgem bumper cars. For the children, Steeplechase added a Kidde Boat ride and a Kidde Roto Whip.

The problem that Steeplechase faced in 1949 had nothing to do with the park, but with disease. A polio epidemic swept New York City, causing the citizenry to avoid places where large numbers of people congregated—and, naturally, this included amusement parts. By August of that year, sixty new cases of polio cases were being reported each day, mainly in the borough of Brooklyn. To combat the problem, Steeplechase

6. The Nickel Empire

began adding more chlorine to the swimming pool, to no avail. No one used it, and the park's business fell off by 25 percent. The scare lasted throughout the season, culminating in the cancellation of the Mardi Gras festivities.

More changes came in 1951, first with a price increase on the combination ticket from twelve rides for a dollar to eight rides for seventy cents—except on Thursdays, when the same price would entitle the patron to use twelve rides. The television studio was now used to broadcast singer Kate Smith's show, and the park hired their first female lifeguard.

The year 1953 proved to be another troubled one for Steeplechase. On November 7, an odd natural disaster struck the park. At 4:30 a.m., night watchman George Butler called James Onorato to inform him that he could not complete his rounds because the water from the Atlantic was washing in the direction of the park. While the ocean had never reached Steeplechase before, the ocean water, combined with the rising water from Coney Island Creek on the east, met, and put the entire island under a foot of sea water. At 6:00 a.m., a postal worker, driving by the park, spotted a fire at the site of the Boardwalk Carousel. Before the fire department could arrive, the entire ride was aflame. Although the ride's sprinkler system contained the fire and fifty-two of the wooden horses survived, the damage exceeded $50,000. Since the water damage to the park was not expected, no preventive steps had been taken, especially to the motors that drove the amusements. As a result, Onorato brought in pumps to drain the water from the Pavilion of Fun's cellar, the sprinkler pits, and the swimming pool. To avoid replacing the motors, he had them cleaned and placed in a hothouse to dry out.

In 1954, Mary E. Tilyou, the widow of George Tilyou, Sr., the founder of Steeplechase, died at the age of 84. She had been a trustee of George's estate since his death and a moderating influence on her four children, who had been running the park since Edward's death. At this point, Steeplechase was only operating as a going concern because of the expertise, ability, and dedication of James Onorato. The four children had been diverting capital from the park and continuously battling with one another. Steeplechase's image was suffering as well, due, in part, to its lack of vibrancy. The park needed younger, more eager employees, but as the park paid its workers only minimum wage, it could only retain the loyal, elderly staff members. So, from 1955 to 1957, without new capital and renewed interest from the family, Steeplechase began to resemble a museum.

Not that the year 1955 was entirely uneventful. On April 22, the Steeplechase pier burned down, and on August 6, two patrons were stuck thirty feet in the air on the Parachute Drop ride for twenty-seven minutes, which necessitated the sending of two workmen to the top of the Drop to fix the jammed mechanism from above. On the plus side, the park received some much-needed positive publicity that year when Arthur Godfrey began broadcasting a one-hour television show from the Steeplechase studio; the program showed the still-operable rides, with members of the Coney Island families appearing as unpaid extras. In 1956, the publicity almost turned against the park when a sixteen-year-old boy was shot by a careless friend who was holding a loaded rifle at the Pavilion of Fun's Shooting Gallery. The park escaped the blame for the incident by giving out their address on Surf Avenue and not the park's name, causing newspaper readers to assume that the incident happened at a shooting gallery outside the park.

Even though new ideas were needed, there were only minor changes to the park's rides during the next several seasons, although the rebuilt Steeplechase was open at the end of the summer in 1958. A more important change took place in December of that year when George C. Tilyou, Jr., died. His daughter, Marie H. Tilyou, assumed the presidency of the Steeplechase Amusement Company, a title that had been held by James Onorato since 1932. Onorato was then given the title of treasurer along with a $500 raise, and was retained as the park's general manager. Onorato received offers from other amusement park operators, including Walt Disney, but preferred to continue running Steeplechase, a job he had had all his life.

Marie Tilyou, in her position as president, attempted to turn Steeplechase's fortunes around. Between Edward's death in 1944 and George Jr.'s death in 1958, the park had only added two new adult-oriented rides. Her main problem, however, was Coney Island itself. Many of the old-timers who had taken pride in their businesses—be they ride owners or concessionaires—either retired or sold out. New owners of these establishments usually ran them into the ground, or had them closed down by city safety inspectors. Additionally, during the 1950s, as the conditions in Coney Island were declining, the prices for rides and food and drink were rising, since the business owners began taking their customers for granted, believing them to captive consumers. The percentage of these customers with automobiles was increasing however, allowing them to discover new and better amusement destinations. By 1960, the comparison between the well-kept grounds of Steeplechase and the rest of Coney Island was painfully obvious.

Compounding the decline of the Coney Island neighborhoods, Steeplechase was struck with another natural disaster when heavy surf, driven by Hurricane Donna during high tide, flooded the park. The Pavilion of Fun, to cite just one example, was flooded with two feet of water. As a result, the park was forced to close two weeks early, losing not only the receipts for that period but also the income from the Pfizer Chemical Company, which had leased the entire park for one day for their annual outing. The total damages amounted to $35,000.

The year 1961 saw two unusual occurrences in the park. First, on July 19, Steeplechase had to stop selling tickets two hours after opening because, at that time, there were 8,800 paying customers in the park, which was far more than normal after the Second World War. And, on August 16, the total number of patrons in the park reached more than 18,000, the highest number in the history of Steeplechase, making 1961 one of the last of the good years. Second, on August 19, a fight broke out in the Insanitarium when six men took offense at being separated from two girls who had accompanied them due to the use of the electric cattle prod; they also failed to see the humor in the use of the blowhole on the women. Following the brawl, the blow-hole operator was hospitalized with a fractured collar bone and a lacerated forehead that required twelve stitches.

In 1962, Frank Tilyou's son Frank Jr. began working in the park to gain experience in running Steeplechase. He partnered with his father to create the Frank Development Company. Their idea was to revitalize Steeplechase by bringing in the rides from the Seattle World's Fair when it closed. To accomplish this, they offered to buy out the interests of every family member. Marie Tilyou, who was still the president of the company, refused the offer because she believed it was too great a gamble. In the same year, the Huber family, owners of part of the Steeplechase property, decided that they would not renew the lease; instead, they wanted to sell it. Fortunately, when the lease was originally signed, George C. Tilyou, Sr., had a clause inserted, giving the park the right of first refusal in the event of a sale. While the family could not afford to purchase the land, they would have lost too much of the park by refusing and so, in 1964, agreed to a purchase price of $800,000.

In 1963, the park nearly suffered damage from another fire, when the Ravenhall Baths, situated next to Steeplechase, were consumed by flames on April 28. As the fire spread towards the park, Steeplechase employees formed a bucket brigade and manned fire hoses to successfully save the park.

Finances continued to be a major problem for Steeplechase. Because the park charged less for its rides than other businesses in Coney Island, it revised its ticket policy during the 1962 and 1963 seasons, raising prices by assigning each ride a certain number of ticket punches; when attendance lagged in 1964, the old system was restored. Season Bathing also became a problem: while it was profitable, the city was insisting on a new and expensive filtration system. To avoid the additional outlay, the pool was closed in 1963.

When Frank Jr. died in 1964, Steeplechase came under the control of four women—Marie, who had no children, was still in charge of the park; Frank's widow, Nickie, who may have wanted control of the park if she could have gotten it for her two sons; George's widow, Adele, whose children had no interest in the park; and Eileen, whose children also had no interest in running Steeplechase. Faced with the dual problems of rising crime in Coney Island, which had become a major factor in Steeplechase's declining business, and the usual interfamily squabbling, Marie decided to sell Steeplechase.

On September 20, 1964, Steeplechase closed permanently in an emotional ceremony at the Pavilion of Fun, and in 1965, Marie sold the park to Fred C. Trump for $2.5 million. Trump then sold off the rides and demolished the rest of the park buildings, planning to erect high-rise low-income buildings on the site, although this never materialized. The land was eventually sold to the city for $4 million. Since it was too expensive to tear down, the only reminder of Steeplechase now in existence is the Parachute Tower, which has become a landmark.

7

Decline and Rebirth?

The beginning of the end of Coney Island started long before the demise of its great amusement parks. The first negative impact centered around two forms of transportation: the automobile and the subway.

The automobile made alternatives to the crowded island increasingly accessible in the years after World War I. Those who could afford it and were seeking diversity in their pleasure choices could now travel to places out of reach of the nickel empire crowd. The Jersey Shore became a favorite destination of the motoring population. New Jersey also began attracting motorists by establishing state parks, such as Island Beach State Park. New York State also became involved in the state park idea beginning in 1924, by reclaiming costal land and beaches to create fourteen new parks accessible by automobile on the new state highways. The largest of these parks was Jones Beach, situated an hour from the city by car. Additionally, the bridges on these highways were too low to allow buses to travel on them and there were no railroad connections near to these parks. This was attributed to one man, Robert Moses, a city planner who began his career in 1924 as president of the Long Island State Park Commission and chairman of the State Council of Parks. He was the person who, more than anyone, was responsible creating parks without access other than by automobile. It was also he who had vetoed the Long Island Railroad's proposed connection of a branch spur to Jones Beach. Basically, this was done to restrict the use of state parks by poor and lower-middle-class families. "To him they were lousy dirty people, throwing bottles all over Jones Beach."[1]

The other form of transportation that affected Coney Island to a great degree was the subway. The middle- and upper-middle-class beachgoers that formerly summered in Brighton Beach and Manhattan

Beach were replaced by those New Yorkers who has access to the subway system anywhere in the city and possessed five cents for the ride.

Internally, Coney also began to change. Dreamland, a park that catered to the more refined patrons, was not rebuilt after the fire that destroyed it in 1911 and, more and more, the amusement park shows or spectacles were replaced by thrill-type rides, especially the roller coasters. On top of all this came the Depression, making it very difficult for the park operators to make a living. The typical commuters to the island spent as little as possible—a nickel a the ride and perhaps another nickel for a hot dog at Nathans, or they brought their own food. They also avoided the bathhouses as another means of saving money. "A million [p]eople, treading gingerly among broken glass and filth that seem never to be cleaned up, jammed the beach so full on a Sunday that they could hardly see the sand."[2]

From the early 1920s until after World War II, it was Robert Moses who had the greatest effect on the fortunes of Coney Island. In point of fact, Coney Island was the only beach in the New York Metropolitan area accessible by public transportation, prompting this comment from Robert Moses's biographer, Robert Caro, "[Coney Island was] the lone bathing beach reachable by public transportation, and therefore the one to which, because of Moses's class-separating policies, the city's poor were herded." Cars were allowed in Coney Island, but parking spaces were difficult to obtain. Moses insisted that fifty cents be the cost to park one's car in a city lot on a weekend, a charge that the Board of Aldermen cut by half in 1934. A member of the board commented that most of the car owners who traveled to Coney were "poor people," those individuals who could not afford to pay fifty cents."[3]

Moses's involvement with both Jones Beach and Coney Island revolves around the construction of the Belt Parkway in the late 1930s. This road would now allow automobile owners to travel east towards Long Island from lower Brooklyn. As far as Coney Island was concerned, it allowed access to all of it from Norton's Point to Manhattan Beach and actually increased the number of visitors to the island. Also, while parking was initially priced at fifty cents, it was cheaper and easier to travel to Coney Island for entertainment than it was to drive into Manhattan or to the other side of Brooklyn to see a game at Ebbets Field. Whether or not Moses took into consideration the fact that the Belt Parkway helped Coney Island is open to conjecture.

7. Decline and Rebirth?

Parking was not the only situation that Moses became involved in where Coney Island was concerned. His dislike of the Coney beachgoer was patently obvious.[4] The Coney Island beachgoers were just not the Jones Beach group that he favored. His power over the Coney Island crowd covered not only the beach, but also the boardwalk. He blamed the profusion of litter on the itinerant candy and refreshment salesmen who sold to Coney's undisciplined inhabitants. In a single June day in 1934, he had no fewer than 350 peddlers arrested. By 1938, his powers increased to the point that he could campaign against the hundreds of fast-food, souvenir, and cheap-amusement businesses that proliferated on the island. Further, he banned advertising, human pyramids, gymnastics, speechmaking, phonographs, and loudspeakers at or near the beach. He also attempted to curb the "ballyhoo" of the sideshow barkers and posted signs outlining his rules and regulations governing deportment on the island. The *New York Times* commented on the regulations:

> Beach attendants now wear sailor suits instead of drab khaki. Chair pushers are garbed in special uniforms, too. A few of the millions visiting the beach have been fined $5 for sitting on newspapers on the sand. Others have paid small fines for undressing beneath the boardwalk, playing poker on the beach, and walking on the Boardwalk in bathing suits.[5]

Moses's overall goal was not simply enforcing a series of rules and regulations, however; he wanted a family beach area free of "catchpenny" devices and mechanical amusements. These he wanted replaced with parks, play areas, and more extensive beaches. This transition also included a shift from areas now devoted to amusements to one containing residences. "There is no use bemoaning the end of the old Coney Island fabled in song and story," he noted. "The important thing is not to proceed in the mistaken belief that it can be revived. There must be a new and very different resort established in its place.... There must be more land in public ownership, less overcrowding, stricter enforcement of ordinances and rules, better transportation and traffic arrangement, less mechanical noise-making and amusement devices and sideshows, and a more orderly growth of year-round residents." As far as Moses was concerned, the old Coney Island had to be eliminated for the public good, a belief that he shared with then-mayor Fiorello LaGuardia. In 1939, the mayor stated, "I feel that the present Coney Island layout is an anachronism. The best proof of this is that it is difficult for present holders of property and operators to make their investments pay under the old type method of resort amusement." Moses's interventions were beginning to increase the speed of decline in the Coney Island amusement business, which had already been hurt by the lack of investment during the Depression.[6]

Consistent with his idea that Coney Island should be a place for families, unencumbered by trashy rides in the amusement zone and with enough space for those who wished to use the beach, Moses put together a report in 1939, outlining his plans for Coney. First, he complained that each beachgoer had only sixteen square feet of sand available to them on many Sundays, or as he put it: the "same as required for a coffin." To remedy this, he did two things: first, he moved the boardwalk back from the water because the width of the beach had shrunk to virtually nothing—high tide in fact lapped under the boardwalk in places. Moses proposed rebuilding the jetties that sustained the beachfront, tearing down the boardwalk along this stretch, and rebuilding it three hundred feet inland; secondly, he added huge quantities of white sand to the extended beachfront. He insisted that a "civilized community" might do a little more by way of recreation for its citizens between the tight places of the cradle and the grave." Moses described the existing beach space with the "out-of-doors over-crowding of our tenements." Moses completed his plans by 1941. He oversaw the moving of the boardwalk inland and hired crews to add fresh sand; at the same time he continued authorizing his destruction of the carnival aspects of the island. To Moses's way of thinking, both had to be done for the good of the populace.[7] As reported in the *New York Times*, Moses "wants to broaden beaches, improve traffic arteries and—perhaps most important—to supplant Boardwalk hot dog and apple-on-the-stick snacks with long stretches of playgrounds, landscaping and modern bathhouses.[8]

The proposal that Moses made as park commissioner in 1937 was both comprehensive and expensive. The plan which would have cost $16.1 million had it been implemented fully as it called for improvements to the beachfront, not only in Coney Island, but also in Rockaway and at South Beach in Staten Island.

Reaction to Moses's proposal for Coney Island was overwhelmingly negative, and many observers jumped to the conclusion that this was merely the first step in turning Coney Island into a resort in the mode of Jones Beach than the Coney Island of old. The *New York Times* put it this way: "Let us confess to a certain pang at the thought of a tidy Coney Island,"[9] It was this belief that Moses wanted to replace all of the amusement areas of Coney Island with parks, playgrounds, parkways, and picnic grounds that led to the scaling back of his 1937 proposal, two years later.

Interestingly, the idea of turning Coney Island into natural parkland, and simultaneously plowing under the honky-tonk aspects of the area, was not new. In 1890, a bill had been filed in Albany that would have appropriated up to $500,000 to create a park between Norton's Point and West Brighton. The proposal faced immediate opposition from the King County political leaders, especially John Y. McKane, then the "boss" of Gravesend, so the plan was scrapped. It was resurrected, however, in 1899, by Bird S. Coler, the Brooklyn politician who gained some measure of fame by opposing the Brooklyn Rapid Transit's double fare policies on its lines to and from Coney Island. Coler's proposal, however, met the same fate as the earlier plan.[10]

In 1937, in a letter to Mayor Fiorello LaGuardia, Moses gave his ideas on why Coney Island was in the condition that it was, and what should be done about it. "Public authorities were actuated more by a desire to please the large property owners than to provide proper accommodations for the public," Moses wrote. As far as what should be done next: "[A]ny future plan for Coney Island must be based on the supposition that most of the summer patrons will come by rapid transit, that they will have comparatively little money to spend on mechanical amusements, and that more and more they will come for exercise and healthy outdoor activity."[11]

Moses's plan was not exactly radical. In the years following the First World War, the vast majority of visitors to Coney Island did not partake of the amusements; their aim was to enjoy a relaxing day at the beach, with perhaps a custard or a glass of beer on the way home. Of course, with the advent of the Depression, the most money spent at the beach was the five cents to get there and another five cents to go home. While there was always money spent on amusements and rides, both in the parks and outside, Coney Island's revenue came from a small percentage of the island's visitors.[12]

There has been some debate as to whether Moses's 1937 plan would have led to the complete destruction of the amusement areas of Coney Island. According to the plan, there would be "less mechanical noise-making and amusement devices and side shows, and a more orderly growth of year-round residents," which would have meant that there would have been no overt move to destroy all of the "old Coney Island." But was this true? Looking at the plan, virtually all of the amusement area would have been occupied by Luna Park and Steeplechase Park, and almost all of the rest of the area would be devoted to parklands.

Brian J. Cudahy, in *How We Got to Coney Island: The Development of Mass Transportation in Brooklyn and Kings County*, argues that the charge that Moses wanted to turn Coney Island into another Jones Beach is "without basis and does a disservice to what he actually proposed." As proof, he cites the fact that while Moses's 1937 plan was not enacted principally due to the fact that there was no funding available, while his new plan for Coney Island in 1939 was approved. The new plan was the movement of the boardwalk inland to open up more sand area for the island's visitors, and while it did destroy some of the amusement area, it did not include new parkland. There was, however, no question of Moses's motives about the destruction of Coney Island in the 1940s, especially after the closure of Luna Park in 1944 and his dealings with property developers, most notably Fred Trump.

Robert Caro, in *The Power Broker: Robert Moses and the Fall of New York*, gives an example of Moses's quest for parkland, and also his use of his power:

> He [Mayor La Guardia] and Moses had been arguing over a twenty-five-acre tract of land in Coney Island owned by the Dock Department but unused. Moses wanted all the land for a park; the Mayor was in favor of a Board of Education plan to use a few of the acres for a school. When he [Mayor La Guardia] impudently mentioned to reporters that "the location of a school on the border of a park is ideal," the reporters went to Moses for comment. "I thought this administration wanted playgrounds. Either they do or they don't," he said. And he added what the [New York] *Herald Tribune* called "some even more uncomplimentary remarks about the Mayor." La Guardia hastily scrambled for cover. "I can't believe my Park Commissioner made any such statements," the Mayor said. "No controversy exists, and none can be made out of it." And the school idea was dropped. "He didn't want to fight with Moses no matter what," Lazarus writes.[13] As long as he didn't fight, LaGuardia had learned, Moses would provide him with a seemingly inexhaustible cornucopia of political benefits. If he *did* fight, Moses would humiliate and defeat him. The little Mayor had learned—the hard way—that it was better not to interfere.[14]

7. Decline and Rebirth?

Despite the enormous crowds that traveled to Coney Island during the summer months leading up to the Second World War, the idea persisted that Coney's best days were over. In 1936, *New York Times* columnist Meyer Berger commented that "the world had moved and Coney Island has not kept pace." He added that the resort "saw its best days between 1903 and 1921."[15]

Even though Berger's observations would prove to be true in the long run, one individual, Benito Mussolini, believed in Coney. When he was drawing up the plans for a world's fair to be held in Rome in 1942, he instructed his people to contact the Coney Island Chamber of Commerce for a plan and a description of the Coney Island amusement area so that he could duplicate Coney Island in the marshland between Rome and Ostia.[16] The *New York Times* had some editorial fun with this idea when it wondered if "the hot dog will retain its identity in the journey from Coney Island to Rome." There were also satirical jibes regarding how certain Coney Island amusements might be changed to suit the needs of the totalitarian regime: "Instead of throwing baseballs at dolls, zealous party members could heave dummy hand grenades at effigies of all good enemies of fascism.[17] All such speculation proved pointless when the war erupted in Europe in 1939, bringing all plans for a Roman world's fair came to a halt.

Still, as late as 1940 there seemed a possibility that Coney Island would have a renaissance. Robert Moses's annual report for that year included one significant sentence: "Further reconstruction and reclamation must wait until time has demonstrated that the mechanical features and commercial developments of the old Coney Island cannot survive."[18] This optimism came from the two major parks, Luna and Steeplechase. Frank Tilyou hoped to obtain "a sizeable share of ... the bonanza from the New York World's Fair of 1939, by attracting out-of-towners with money in their pockets rather than the usual crowd who "come for the bathing dressed in their bathing suits and don't spend a red penny."[19] While a large amount of new business from the World's Fair never materialized, both Steeplechase and Luna Park were able to purchase new rides from the fair, especially the Parachute Jump by Steeplechase. Luna Park bought a glass-sided tank from the fair for Captain Coswell, whose specialty was to grapple with six man-eating sharks. Milton Sheen, the newest owner of Luna, explained, "People want blood for their dimes these days."

The owners of Steeplechase erected the popular Parachute Jump ride on the boardwalk, instead of inside the park's parameters, so that a separate admission could be charged. This photograph was apparently taken long after the ride's closure.

7. Decline and Rebirth?

Concessionaires, large and small, were anxious to cash in on an expected fever of war-bred gaiety waiting for the city of New York to get into a financial position to undertake large-scale improvements on the island. A few of them had a hunch that the old notion about the ultimate fate of Sodom by the sea might yet come true. Someday a fire would sweep the whole place clean, they predicted, and force reconstruction because of the huge crowds that continued to visit Coney.[20]

The same problem remained into the 1940s and 1950s: record crowds, but little patron involvement in the amusement business, which led to little investment in the parks and also little in what was left of the amusement areas; even the freak shows suffered. In 1943, a concessionaire at Coney summed up the situation:

> Not much dough there. You can't do clipping [swindling] anymore. You clip a guy today and they call it grand larceny. See these barkers. They're mostly guys with bum tickers. The old-style grifters, they gave up. What's the use? These people nowadays, they want their money's worth.[21]

Robert Moses would have certainly taken heart at this sentiment from the concessionaire as proof that his actions were bearing fruit. While his pulling back of the boardwalk certainly improved the beach, his destruction of much of the amusement areas was, in his eyes, equally beneficial. As the *New York Times* noted, "Veterans of the island concede that the carnival has ended." Many property owners saw the writing on the wall, and they were unwilling to invest and improve with the prospect of additional condemnations for redevelopment.[22]

In 1950, however, there was an opportunity for Coney Island to resurrect itself. A company called Ball Park Movies, Inc., bought the Luna Park site and announced plans to construct an entertainment complex featuring amusements, a swimming pool, a drive-in movie theater, a parking lot, and retail stores. With this eventuality, the business community began to support a resurrection of Coney Island, especially when new development money began to flow into the area, supporting the idea that Coney was on its way back. The euphoria, however, was short-lived because, just after the deal was closed, the city officials of New York began to raise objections to the new plan.

An article in the *New York Times*, on March 14, 1950, revealed the city's tactics. The New York City Planning Commission suddenly decided to bring drive-in movies under its jurisdiction "in order to protect the health and general welfare of the people of the city." This made no sense, especially since the article mentioned that the Coney Island drive-in plan was "vehemently opposed by the city's Traffic Commission." It became obvious that the city did not want the site developed for the purposes of amusement, despite its support by the Coney Island Chamber of Commerce and its business community.

Seven months after the article was written, the traffic-control ploy by the city was seen as an obvious charade when housing developer Fred C. Trump announced that he had purchased the Luna lot from Ball Park Movies on October 8, 1950. Trump was a controversial figure with a gift for backroom politics, and his surprise seizure of the property meant that something big was happening. It wasn't commonly known at the time that power broker Robert Moses was secretly running the city planning commission through his allies, and was making a play for the Luna site by pressuring Ball Park Movies to drop its plans to construct an entertainment center.

Beginning in 1949, Robert Moses began his quest to complete his highway and housing projects by systematically condemning and demolishing neighborhoods in every borough. This effort was especially devastating to Coney Island, an area that he despised because of its honky-tonk atmosphere. Ten years earlier, Moses began using his position as New York City's park commissioner to engineer a large-scale land grab of Coney Island's beachfront property, resulting in the permanent loss of boardwalk businesses. Interestingly, Moses did not take these properties for use by the city, but, rather, by private developers to erect housing. This is why the entertainment complex envisioned by Ball Park Movies could not go through and why Fred Trump, a housing developer, became involved.

The sale to Trump had an immediate negative effect on Coney's property owners. Not only wouldn't there be any return to the old Coney Island, but urban renewal would simply be used to create housing. Within two years, Feltman's sold out, and the old Half Moon Hotel became a nursing home.

With the backing of the city's powerful, Trump, after buying the Luna site, began trying to assemble a large amount of property adjoining the site to create one large parcel. He bought the old Velodrome site on West 12th Street and Neptune Avenue, but could not amass the amount of land he needed because the owners of businesses and property on the West 8th Street side of the Luna property refused to sell.

This included the Bonsignore family, who owned the L. A. Thompson roller coaster, which was still in operation at this time. Their refusal to sell would not, however, allow them to keep their properties because, in 1953, the family received notice that their land was being taken by the city for urban renewal. "Moses was a beachfront pirate," John Bonsignore said. "He ruined everybody. The city came around and inspected all the properties and then made an appraisal. It went in front of a judge and he favored the city condemnation order. After the property was taken, the city immediately turned it over to Trump. It was such common knowledge that Trump was behind the scenes, that there was no attempt to hide it. By the end of 1954, La Marcus Thompson's L. A. Thompson roller coaster, after standing for half a century, was demolished by the city.

Fred Trump's ability to become a major player in the changing fortunes of Coney Island depended on two factors. First, according to historian Charles Denson, was Trump's ability to take advantage of the loopholes in the New Deal programs, such as those designed by the Federal Housing Authority to promote residential development because of the housing shortage during the Depression. These loopholes allowed Trump to obtain federally guaranteed mortgages, which he used when constructing single-family homes in Brooklyn and Queens. Basically, the Federal Housing Authority was a welfare program for contractors and developers to enrich themselves.

Second, after World War II, Trump, who up until this point had concentrated on single-family homes and small developments, now began to form political alliances so that he could become involved in large-scale government-subsidized housing. These alliances included two men who would become mayors of the city—Abraham David "Abe" Beame and Robert F. Wagner, Jr. Also involved were Abraham "Bunny" Lindenbaum, a well-connected attorney, and Kenny Sutherland, the Coney Island political boss. With these contacts, Trump built Shore Haven in 1947, a thirty-two-building complex on fourteen acres of Coney Island Creek landfill, purchased from the city.

In 1954, Trump was called to testify by the federal government during the Capehart hearings, which was looking into "real estate profiteers" who had bilked the public through rent gouging. Trump was accused by the state of overbidding on his construction estimates and then pocketing the difference, which amounted to $4 million in public funds. As a result of the hearings, Trump's reputation was destroyed, and the Federal Housing Authority placed him on their blacklist. It was because of the blacklisting and the ensuing scandal that Trump was forced to sell the Luna Park property, in 1956, to the New York City Housing Authority. The sale of the Luna Park property for housing dealt a severe blow to Coney Island. While some visitors still traveled to Coney by car, without sufficient parking, more and more tourists sought out other destinations for recreation. In the 1950s, Moses built an overpass from the subway to the boardwalk, claiming it would facilitate foot traffic to the beach; however, it also destroyed the businesses in the area. At the same time, Moses leveled sixteen square blocks of Coney Island for additional housing, which would be erected by the still-disgraced (but politically well connected) Fred Trump, whose new scheme was to use New York State financing instead of monies from the federal government.[23]

Another project that involved Moses was the New York City Aquarium. Initially it was housed in Castle Clinton, which was located in Battery Park, in lower Manhattan. Moses guaranteed the Board of Estimate that he could build a brand new one for $2 million, and that the New York Zoological Society would foot the entire bill. In truth, the Zoological Society could never have raised that amount of money. In the end, the new aquarium would cost $10 million, plus another $1 million to acquire the land, all of which was paid for by the taxpayers. And because of the huge cost of the aquarium, a high admission fee had to be charged—it had been free at the Castle Clinton site. As a consequence, the people who frequented Coney Island—the poor—could not afford the admission price. Basically, the main beneficiaries of the new aquarium were the wealthy who had automobiles; to accommodate them, Moses built a large parking lot next to it. But they did not come, and the attendance at the new facility never matched the one in Manhattan.

By the late 1950s, Moses gained enough power with his control of the New York City Housing Authority not only to continue with his agenda of cleaning up the entertainment district in Coney Island, but doing it on a permanent basis by replacing it with residential development. His method was to re-zone the island from commercial to mixed business and residential use, with the key being the continued existence of Steeplechase, the last of the Coney Island parks, which would provide

7. Decline and Rebirth?

Coney's rides and games, and that the re-zoning would destroy the tawdry areas, which would be replaced with apartment buildings. Additionally, in 1957, he moved the New York Aquarium to the old Dreamland site, and, to provide parking, tore down even more of the amusement area. At this point, the Coney Island residents and the Coney Island Chamber of Commerce rose up to block some of Moses's ideas, including new beach and park development in the Manhattan Beach area. A local businessman summed up the situation as follows: "It would be criminal to tear down the Bowery and Surf Avenue.... Where would the poor people go—to the *Riviera*?" The Nickel Empire might be damaged, but it was still alive.[24]

The overall problem was that the reformers did destroy much of the seedier side of Coney Island without replacing it with something of value—not exactly what Robert Moses had in mind during his labors in the 1940s and '50s. Instead, the longtime residents of Coney—the immigrant Jewish and Italian families and their descendants who could not afford the rents in the new high-rise buildings—were forced out of the area during the late 1950s. Their place was taken by a new migration, this time Black and Hispanic welfare tenants. By 1967, the western end of Coney Island was declared a Poverty Zone and was thereby slated for urban renewal.[25]

This change in the racial makeup of Coney Island brought dramatic changes to the area. By the 1930s and '40s, residential Coney Island had evolved into a stable, working-class and lower-middle-class neighborhood. With its full occupancy, dual-ethnic character, and moderate-income families, the year-round island community near the beach was similar to other parts of Brooklyn, the Bronx, and Queens. The island's amusement section, Coney's main economic activity, also stabilized into New York City's premier summer resort. By 1957, when Luna Park was no longer in existence, Steeplechase still flourished, and even with the destruction wrought by Robert Moses on the area, Coney Island still had a larger concentration of outdoor rides and games than anywhere on earth. Attendance at Disneyland in California, opened just two years earlier, was no match against the tens of millions of seasonal visitors who flocked to Coney.

The 1960s brought dramatic changes to Coney Island, both to its residential and commercial areas. The changes were swift and sudden. The population change began after the war when white, middle-class families started moving to the suburbs, and other parts the city were not replaced by other white families. This situation had a twofold effect on Coney Island. First, the minority population which had been 2 percent in 1950 had grown to 13 percent by 1960. Second, as far as housing was concerned, Coney Island was split into two parts. In 1964, twelve 24-story apartment buildings, housing 6,200 families and sold as coops, were erected in Brighton Beach. Next, those Black and Hispanic families who were displaced, were moved to the area formerly known as "The Gut," which was situated between the amusement area and Sea Gate and which now had become a dilapidated bungalow colony. This sudden invasion forced out the Jews and Italians who had lived in the area for decades.

In 1964, the stability of the area suffered another blow when Steeplechase closed. In 1965, Marie Tilyou, who had retained the controlling interest in the park, described Steeplechase as a "gorgeous rosebud in a garbage can." She also complained about the "horrible types one sees in the summer," and worried about even more change in the area with "urban renewal."[26] Critics have suggested that these comments showed the reason for Marie Tilyou's refusal to keep Steeplechase going. Another example concerned the park's continuous moneymaker, the pool; ostensibly, the reason for its closure was the cost of a new filtration system. Another was the "whites-only" mentality of patrons of the pool that led to an informal exclusion of racial minorities, although this was denied by James Onorato, son of Steeplechase's manager.

After Fred Trump failed to gain permits to erect a housing development on the Luna site, he sold it to the city, which simply left it vacant. In April of 1968, with 600,000 people at Coney, a riot ensued, further diminishing the area's reputation.

The 1970 census underscored the continuing trend—35 percent of Coney's population was now made up of minorities, almost triple that of just ten years earlier. With shops and businesses along Mermaid Avenue (the area's main thoroughfare) boarded up, synagogue buildings taken over by Baptist or Pentecostal churches, scores of two- and three-family houses bulldozed, the amusement area became a shadow of its former self.

During the 1970s Coney Island continued its descent to slum status, aided by New York City. Steeplechase was a major reason for families to visit Coney; without it, the only attraction was the shrunken

7. Decline and Rebirth?

amusement zone, and that was quickly becoming a breeding ground for crime. The accidental fires that consumed Coney in the past now became arson, taking down more and more building and rides. On top of this, the Lindsay administration began moving Harlem residents into Coney Island, many of whom ended up in substandard housing lacking heat. In some instances, the old Coney still survived, represented by Nathan's Famous Hotdogs and the Cyclone roller coaster, but, in general, the muggers, drug addicts, and roving gangs made the area completely unsafe. In 1976, one resident of the area commented of his neighborhood: "It is a great dumping ground."[27]

Despite this, there continued to be efforts to revive Coney. Astroland opened in 1963, and, in 1979, an effort was made to bring in casino gambling when Coney Island entrepreneurs and local politicians took notice of the recent success of casinos in Atlantic City. This idea was opposed, however, by the Trump interests who had holdings in Atlantic City, and by those who believed that such a move would bring additional crime into the area. The 1980 census showed the continuous decline. Over 69 percent of Coney Island's year-round residents were minority members, and more than a third of the total population was living below the poverty line.

The mid–1980s brought hope for renewal. There was an ambitious plan to build an amusement park on the lot once occupied by Steeplechase, including some additional adjoining property. This would be a $350 million state-of-the-art amusement park, also called Steeplechase. The first order of business was to be the restoration of the Parachute ride, now a national landmark and a symbol of Coney Island. The park's planners, former Disney employees, mapped out forty-seven rides and attractions that would restore Coney to its former glory, including the Luna Shuttle, Dreamland Puppet Theater, Pavilion of Fun, and Old Coney Parachutes. Unfortunately, the dream never materialized. There were problems raising the required capital, because potential investors thought that the risk was too high and were unwilling to gamble on Coney's future.

In 1994, Mayor Rudy Giuliani opted for a new baseball stadium in Coney Island, and in 1998, he used $67 million of the city's and state's monies for construction. Not only was a new amusement park not constructed, but part of the initial plan was to construct two- and three-story houses along Mermaid Avenue. The idea was to have the Blacks and Hispanics living in the area take possession of these homes and develop the same feeling towards Coney Island as the Jews and Italians who preceded them.

By the dawn of the 21st century, history began to repeat itself in Coney Island, with new players, and, unfortunately, with the usual results. Thor Equities, a real estate development company which for years had been quietly buying up property in the old amusement area, went public with its plan for Coney. The project, which would encompass fourteen acres and cost an estimated $2 billion, was slated to contain: a large Bellagio-style beachfront hotel, which included a rooftop landing pad for blimps; a state-of-the-art spa; an enclosed water park; amusement park–type rides; an indoor mall; open-air cafés; arcades; bowling alleys; movie theaters; and a fifty-story luxury apartment building. If Thor Equities had its way, yesterday's summer resort for New Yorkers would become tomorrow's year-round playground for all of America.

The problem with Thor's proposal was its insistence on building the luxury apartments in the amusement area, which was contrary to the recommendations of the Coney Island Development Corporation composed of local business owners and city functionaries. This organization was against any zoning changes in the amusement area because of past problems with developers. The Development Corporation wished to leave the amusement area as it was, putting residences and stores in other parts of the island.

This is not the first time that Coney Island had been involved in a standoff between proponents of the amusement area against those who wished to build residences. A skirmish occurred in the early 1900s between such factions, resulting in a legal judgment that Coney's historical amusements took precedence over the wishes of the residents. This time, however, there were huge amounts of money at stake due to the scale of Thor's plans. Because the equities company could not prevail, they decided to follow a "scorched earth" policy. In 2006, they bulldozed the amusement displays that remained on their property and evicted business tenants from the part of the boardwalk they controlled, satisfied to wait for the next mayor who might look upon their ideas favorably. The next mayor, as it turned out, was Michael Bloomberg, and he, like his predecessors, did not want housing in the amusement areas.

7. Decline and Rebirth?

In 2009, the City of New York purchased 6.2 acres of land in Coney Island and put out a request for bids on a state-of-the-art amusement facility. This was won by Central Amusement International, which was already operating a small park, Victorian Gardens, at the Wollman Rink in Central Park. Central Amusement then constructed—in a period of one hundred days—a new amusement park, complete with nineteen rides, six games, and five food kiosks, and called it Luna Park. Again, it looked as if Coney Island was set to stage a comeback, especially when other companies added new rides (including two new roller coasters), and Luna Park expanded, adding new amusements as well. The problem was the continued existence of Thor Equities and their land in the heart of the amusements area, which was not only vacant, but filled with trash. As a symbol of their neglect, they had previously erected a lighted "Welcome to Coney Island" sign at the point where visitors disembarked from the subway. The sign was still in place, but most of the bulbs were now missing.

In 2014, business leaders in the area succeeded in convincing Thor to clean up their land, which was done, but not on a continuous basis, resulting in the return of the same condition. In 2008, the Bloomberg administration purchased slightly less than seven acres of Thor's property for $95.6 million, giving Thor a profit of $50 million and control of over seven remaining acres, prompting Coney Island real estate experts to believe that Thor is simply waiting to gain another huge profit at taxpayer expense.

What will the future bring for Coney Island? In 1905, Richard Le Gallienne wrote the following in *Cosmopolitan* magazine:

> Man needs Coney Island to-day, because he had always needed Coney Island.... Coney Island exists and will go on existing, because into all men, gentle and simple, poor and rich—including women—by some mysterious corybantic instinct in their blood, has been born a tragic need of coarse excitement, a craving to be taken in by some illusion, however palpable.
>
> So following the example of those old notions, whose place she has so vigorously taken, America has built for herself a Palace of Illusion, and filled it with every species of talented attractive monster, every misbegotten fancy of the frenzied nerves, every fantastic marvel of the moonstruck brain—and she called it Coney Island. Ironic name—a place lonely with rabbits, a spit of sandy beach so near to the simple life of the sea, and watched, and watched over by the summer night; strange Isle of Monsters, Preposterous Palace of Illusion, gigantic Parody of Pleasure—Coney Island.[28]

Chapter Notes

Preface

1. William Judkins Hewitt, "The Amusement Park," *Billboard*, July 25, 1907, 45.
2. Robert W. Rydell, and Rob Kroes, *Buffalo Bill in Bologna: The Americanization of the World, 1869–1922* (University of Chicago Press, 2005), 74.
3. Lauren Rabinovitz, *Electric Dreamland: Amusement Parks, Movies, and American Modernity* (New York: Columbia University Press, 2012), 32.
4. Kayhy Peiss, *Cheap Amusements: Working Women and Leisure in Turn of the Century New York* (Philadelphia: Temple University Press, 1986), 134–135.
5. James Huneker, *New Cosmopolis: A Book of Images. Intimate New York* (New York: Charles Scribner's Sons, 1915), 154.
6. R. W. Malcolmson, *Popular Recreations in English Society, 1700–1850* (Cambridge: Cambridge University Press, 1973), 47.
7. Gary Cross, "Crowds and Leisure: Thinking Comparatively Across the 20th Century," *Journal of Social History*, Vol. 39, No. 3 (Spring 2006), 632–633.

Introduction

1. "A Cool Resort in Hot Weather," *New York Times*, July 10, 1866, 5.
2. "New York in the Surf: Sunday Bathing at Coney Island and Elsewhere," *New York Times*, July 16, 1866.
3. "A Day at Coney Island," *New York Times*, August 20, 1877.

Chapter 1

1. Oliver Pilat and Jo Ranson, *Sodom by the Sea: An Affectionate History of Coney Island* (Garden City, NY: Doubleday, 1941), 117.
2. *Long Island Star*, July 1, 1824.
3. The road may have been constructed of oyster shells, hence the name.
4. *Long Island Star*, July 21, 1825.
5. Edo McCullough, *Good Old Coney Island* (New York: Charles Scribner's Sons, 1957), 23.
6. *New York Times*, February 3, 6, 1878.
7. Coney Island House Register, Brooklyn Public Library, Brooklyn Collection.
8. A circular wooden platform covered by a tent.

9. *New York Times*, May 30, 1855.
10. *Harper's New Monthly Magazine*, Vol. 57, Issue 341 (October 1878).
11. *Rockland County Messenger*, August 14, 1851, 2.
12. *Coney Island and the Jews* (New York: G.W. Carleton, 1879), 7.
13. Charles Dawson Shanly, *Atlantic Monthly*, Vol. 34, Issue 203 (September 1874), 306.
14. "To Coney Island," *Scribner's Monthly*, Vol. 20, Issue 3 (July 1880), 354–355.
15. *Brooklyn Daily Eagle*, April 15, 1844.
16. Charles Dawson Shanly, *Coney Island*, 308.
17. A tavern or eating house serving regular meals, usually a British usage.
18. *Brooklyn Daily Eagle*, August 26, 1846.
19. Townsend Percy, *Percy's Pocket Dictionary of Coney Island* (New York: Leypoldt, 1880), 77–94.
20. Stephen F. Weinstein, *The Nickel Empire: Coney Island and the Creation of Urban Seaside Resorts in the United States*, Phd dissertation, Columbia University, 1984.
21. *Brooklyn Daily Eagle*, July 13, 1888.
22. *Coney Island Sun*, September 14, 1878, reprinted the ads from the *New York Herald*.
23. *New York Herald*, July 16, 1865.
24. *New York Times*, July 3, 1863.
25. *Brooklyn Daily Eagle*, April 14, 1929.
26. *London Times*, September 9, 1881; Bayrd Still, *Mirror for Gotham: New York as Seen by Contemporaries From Dutch Days to the Present* (New York: New York University Press, 1956), 226.
27. *New York Herald*, July 21, 1884.
28. *Brooklyn Citizen*, July 9, 1887.
29. George Templeton Strong, ed., *Diary*, trans. Alan Nevins and Milton Thomas (New York: Macmillan, 1852), entry at August 15, 1851.
30. Charles Dawson Shanly, *Coney Island*, 306–313.
31. David Nasaw, *Going Out: The Rise and Fall of Public Amusements* (New York: Basic Books, 1993), 81.
32. Julian Ralph, "Coney Island," *Scribner's Magazine* XX (July 1896), 16–17.
33. "Coney Island Point," *New York Times*, March 31, 1879.
34. Jason Heard, *Reforming the Sodom by the Sea: Coney Island, Prize-Fighting, and Class Stratification*. www.columbia.edu/cu/cjas/print/coney island_prizefighting.pdf.
35. "Dixon Again Victor," *National Police Gazette*, October 7, 1893.
36. New York State had legislatively criminalized prizefighting in 1859 and made it a misdemeanor. The Horton Law expanded the definition of this misdemeanor to include "public or private sparring exhibitions." This language gave rise to many "athletic associations," such as the Coney Island Athletic Club, which promoted "sparring exhibitions for points."
37. *Brooklyn Daily Eagle*, January 16, 1900.
38. Raymond De L'Epee, "M'kane's Sodom-By-The-Sea," *New York Times*, October 15, 1893.
39. "Coney Island Park Plans," *New York Times*, June 11, 1899.
40. Oliver Pilat and, Jo Ranson, *Sodom by the Sea*, 71.
41. http://www.majorwager.com/forums/race-track/108730-coney-island-horse-racing-history.
42. *Brooklyn Daily Eagle*, July 3, 1854.

43. *Ibid.*, July 5, 1854.
44. Charles Dawson Shanly, *Coney Island*, 311.
45. *New York Times*, July 4, 1862.
46. *Ibid.*, July 7, 1862.
47. *Brooklyn Daily Eagle*, July 3, 1862.
48. *Ibid.*, April 14, 1929.
49. *Ibid.*, June 19, 1875.
50. The former name of Norton's Point.
51. *The Manufacturer and Builder*, Vol. 11, Issue 5 (May 1879).
52. *Brooklyn Daily Eagle*, July 2, 1878.
53. *Ibid.*, August 20, 1878.
54. *Ibid.*, November 11, 1896.
55. *New York Times*, May 27, 1896.
56. *Brooklyn Daily Eagle*, August 4, 1880.
57. *Scientific American*, September 7, 1889.
58. Brian J. Cudahy, *How We Got to Coney Island: The Development of Mass Transportation in Brooklyn and Kings County* (New York: Fordham University Press, 2002), 67–101.
59. *Scientific American*, November 17, 1906.
60. Jon Sterngass, *First Resorts: Pursuing Pleasure at Saratoga Springs, Newport & Coney Island* (Baltimore: Johns Hopkins Press, 2001), 81.
61. James Blaine Walker, *Fifty Years of Rapid Transit* (New York: Law Printing, 1918), 274.
62. *New York Times*, May 17, 1879.
63. *Ibid.*, July 20, 1879.
64. *Ibid.*, July 7, 1883.
65. Cudahy, *How We Got to Coney Island*, 60.
66. *New York Times*, March 20, 1879.

Chapter 2

1. Michael Immerso, *Coney Island, the People's Playground* (New Brunswick: Rutgers University Press, 2002), 17.
2. Wicked Half-Mile, *Harper's Magazine*, May 4, 1901.
3. *Brooklyn Daily Eagle*, September 5, 1890.
4. *New York Times*, April 1, 1887.
5. "M'kane Greatly Alarmed: Exposing the Rottenness at Gravesend," *New York Times*, March 31, 1887.
6. "Days When Mckane Ruled Gravesend," *Brooklyn Daily Eagle*, January 19, 1913.
7. Coney Island—John McKane, http://www.westland.net/coneyisland/articles/mckane.htm.
8. *Brooklyn Daily Eagle*, November 7, 1893.
9. Walter Creedmoor, "The Real Coney Island," *Munsey's Magazine*, August 1899, 747.
10. Edo Mc Cullough, *Good Old Coney Island* (Charles Scribner's Sons, 1957), 38–40.
11. *Brooklyn Daily Eagle*, September 16, 1878.
12. *New York Times*, October 8, 1882.
13. *Brooklyn Daily Eagle*, January 15, 1884.
14. *Ibid.*, July 2, 1878.
15. *Brighton Beach Daily Music Programme*, July 31, 1881.

16. Michael Immerso, *Coney Island: The People's Playground* (New Brunswick: Rutgers University Press, 2002), p. 18–19.
17. *Kings County Rural Gazette*, March 28, 1874.
18. *Brooklyn Union and Argus*, August 28, 1877.
19. "The Summer Exodus and What It Testifies," *Century Magazine* 38 (July 1889), 469.
20. *Coney Island and the Jews* (New York: G.W. Carlton, 1879), 17–18.
21. *Brooklyn Daily Eagle*, September 20, 1877.
22. *Brooklyn Union*, July 2, 1883.
23. *Brooklyn Daily Eagle*, May 24, July 8, 1880.
24. *Coney Island and the Jews*, 20–21.
25. *Ibid.*, 24. Also, this was no empty threat on the part of Sanger. The people he was referring to were the German Jews who had immigrated to the country in the 1840s and 1850s and began the great banking houses—Henry Leman, Samuel Sachs, Marcus Goldman, and Jules Bache.
26. *New York Tribune*, July 24, 1879.
27. *New York Commercial Advertiser*, July 23, 1879.
28. *New York Evening Post*, July 22, 1879.
29. *New York Evening Mail*, July 23, 1879.
30. *Philadelphia Ledger*, July 25, 1879.
31. Stephen F. Weinstein, *The Nickel Empire*, 538.
32. *New York Times*, June 26, 1878.
33. *Brooklyn Union and Argus*, July 13, 1878.
34. *Brooklyn Daily Eagle*, May 23, 1880.
35. *Ibid.*, November 20, 1880.
36. In fee or in fee simple—the highest form of real estate ownership.
37. *New York Times*, May 17, 1881.
38. Named after W. Fontaine Bruff, president of the line. Bruff was an Englishman by birth; an engineer by profession.
39. *Brooklyn Daily Eagle*, December 8, 1881.
40. Presumably Brooklyn and New York.
41. *Brooklyn Daily Eagle*, July 12, 1887.
42. J. Sweet, *A Day on Coney Island* (New York, 1880), 8.
43. Edo McCullough, *Good Old Coney Island*, 243.
44. *New York Times*, June 25, 1877.
45. *Ibid.*, August 7, 1877.
46. *Brooklyn Daily Eagle*, March 25, 1884.
47. The Rev. Austin Parsons Stockwell and William H. Stillwell, *History of the Town of Gravesend, New York* (Brooklyn, New York, 1884), 46.
48. The Brighton Beach Hotel specifically stated that it favored Jews, while Paul Bauer claimed Corbin's manifesto was merely "an advertising dodge." Jon Sterngass, *First Resorts* 108.
49. *New York Times*, June 7, 1885.
50. *Ibid.*, April 4, 1888.
51. McKane, "Coney Island."
52. *Brooklyn Daily Eagle*, February 25, 1884.
53. *Ibid.*, July 25, 1886.
54. *Ibid.*, July 26, 1886.
55. Brothels.
56. *Brooklyn Daily Eagle*, April 11, 1887.
57. *Ibid.*, June 9, 1887.
58. *Ibid.*, June 29, 1887.

Chapter 3

1. *Brooklyn Daily Eagle*, March 2, 1894.
2. "New York in Summer," *Harper's New Monthly Magazine*, Vol. 57, Issue 341 (October 1878).
3. *Brooklyn Eagle Almanac* (Brooklyn 1888), 123.
4. Stephen F. Weinstein, *The Nickel Empire*, PhD Thesis, Columbia University, 1984, 477–478.
5. *New York Times*, October 7, 1906.
6. Walter Creedmoor, "The Real Coney Island," *Munsey's Magazine*, August 23, 1899.
7. *Brooklyn Daily Eagle*, May 27, 1899.
8. *Ibid*.
9. Jon Sterngass, *First Resorts*, 254–255.
10. Robert Wilson Neal, "New York's City of Play," *The World Today*, June 1, 1906–December 1, 1906.
11. Richard Le Gallienne, "Human Need of Coney Island," *Cosmopolitan*, Vol. 30, May–October 1905.
12. Joe Nickell, *Secrets of the Sideshow* (Lexington: University Press of Kentucky, 2005), 68.
13. Jose Marti, ed., "Two Views of Coney Island," in *Inside the Monster: Writings on the U.S. and American Imperialism*, 165–175. *New York Monthly Review*, 1975, 166.
14. Djuna Barnes, "If Noise Were Forbidden at Coney Island a Lot of People Would Lose Their Jobs," 1914. A total of forty-two vintage articles were reprinted in *New York, Djuna Barnesed*, ed., Alyce Barry (Los Angeles: Sun & Moon Press, 1989), 142–149.
15. John F. Kasson, *Amusing the Million: Coney Island at the Turn of the Century* (New York: Hill & Wang, 1978), 53.
16. Joe Mckennon, *A Pictorial History of the American Carnival*, Vol. 2 (Sarasota, FL: Carnival Publishers of Sarasota, 1972), 100–101.
17. Fred Olen Ray, *Grind Show: Weirdness as Entertainment* (Hollywood, CA: American Independent Press, 1993), 8.
18. Nate Eagle, a sideshow impresario and a great talker, was once complimented by a carnival owner with the following words: "You have all the ingredients necessary to rise in your profession—a deceptively honest face, a genius for legitimate fraud, no conscience, a golden tongue, and a feeling that a quarter in someone else's pocket is a personal rebuke." Derek Nelson, *The American State Fair* (Osceola, WI: MBI, 1999), 95.
19. Robert Bogdan, *Freak Show: Presenting Human Oddities for Fun and Profit* (Chicago: University of Chicago Press, 1990), 97.
20. Oliver Pilat, and Jo Ranson, *Sodom by the Sea*, 180–191.
21. Michael Immerso, *The People's Playground*, 134–136.
22. Joe Nickell, *Secrets of the Sideshows*, 303.
23. George Conklin (as told to Harvey W. Root), *The Ways of the Circus: Being the Memories and Adventures of George Conklin, Tamer of Lions* (New York: Harper & Brothers, 1921), 165.
24. Tom Rinaldo, *Robbery on the Midway* (Privately printed, n.d.), 3, 8.
25. Edo McCullough, *Good Old Coney Island*, 308.
26. Oliver Pilat and Jo Ranson, *Sodom by the Sea*, 215.
27. Michael Immerso, *Coney Island, the People's Playground*, 99.
28. Guy Wetmore Carryl, "Marvelous Coney Island," *Munseys Magazine*, September 1901.
29. John F. Kasson, *Amusing the Million*, 62.

30. W. C. Boyce, "Modern Amusement Parks" (self-published brochure, n.d.).
31. *New York Times,* September 4, 1911.
32. An essential action.
33. Guy Wetmore Carryl, "Marvelous Coney Island," *Munsey's Magazine,* September 1901.
34. "Sues Coney Coaster for Wife's Death," *New York Times,* October 3, 1911.
35. C. B. Davis, "The Renaissance of Coney," *The Outing Magazine,* Vol. 48, August 1906, 515.
36. Arwen Mohun, "Designed for Thrills and Safety: Amusement Parks and the Commodification of Risk, 1880–1929," *Journal of Design History,* Vol. 14, No. 4. *Technology and the Body* (2001), 295.
37. Richard Snow, *Coney Island: A Postcard Journey to the City of Fire* (New York: Brightwater Press, 1984), 45.
38. Program, Coney Island Souvenir, Brooklyn Historical Society, Brooklyn, New York.
39. Richard Snow, *Coney Island,* 226.
40. *Ibid.,* 61.
41. John Kasson, *Amusing the Million,* 8.
42. *Ibid.,* 9.
43. Ida M. Tarbell, *New Ideals in Business: An Account of Their Practice and Their Effects Upon Men and Profits* (New York: Macmillan Co., 1916), 29–49.
44. David Nassaw, *Going Out,* 3.
45. Aldous Huxley, "Work and Leisure," *Literary Review,* August 30, 1924, 1; Maxim Gorky, "Boredom, 63," *The Independent,* 1907, 309.
46. Pilat and Ranson, *Sodom by the Sea,* 98–106.
47. *Ibid.,* 108–111.
48. *Brooklyn Daily Eagle,* July 14, 1879; June 13, 1897; June 20, 1897; July 1, 1898.
49. *New York Times,* May 6, 27, 1906.
50. *New York World,* June 5, 1885.
51. *Frank Leslie's Illustrated Newspaper,* August 24, 1878.
52. Saint Monday is the tradition of taking Mondays off. In his autobiography, Benjamin Franklin refers to the practice, saying of his youthful employment in a London printing house, "My constant attendance (I never making a St. Monday) recommended me to the master."
53. *Brooklyn Union and Argus,* August 20, 1877.
54. *Brooklyn Daily Eagle,* May 12, 1879.
55. *New York Times,* May 6, 1877.
56. *Illustrated Christian Weekly,* August 24, 1878.
57. Reprinted in *The Irish-American,* September 5, 1885.
58. *Brooklyn Union and Argus,* August 29, 1877.
59. *Brooklyn Union,* June 9, 1885.
60. *Brooklyn Daily Eagle,* July 1, 1883.
61. *Ibid.,* August 3, 1888; July 31, 1889; July 7, 1892.
62. *The Irish-American,* September 14, 1878.
63. Stephen F. Weinstein, *The Nickel Empire,* 193.
64. The three men who ruled the Republican Party in Brooklyn when Ulysses S. Grant was president.
65. John F. Kasson, *Amusing the Million,* 102.
66. Walter Creedmoor, "The Real Coney Island," *Munsey's Magazine,* August 1899, 745.
67. Gravesend Board of Health, Minutes, Vol. 14, 225–226 (May 3, 1886), Brooklyn Public Library.

68. *Kings County Rural and Brighton Gazette*, April 19, 1885.
69. *Brooklyn Daily Eagle*, May 7, 1887.
70. *New York World*, August 2, 1896.
71. *New York Times*, August 20, 1877.
72. *Ibid.*, July 21, 1868.
73. *Harper's Weekly*, August 10, 1878.
74. David Nasaw, *Going Out*, 81.
75. *Brooklyn Daily Eagle*, September 7, 1890.
76. Robert O. Harland, *The Vice Bondage of a Great City, or the Wickedest City in the World* (Chicago: The Young People's Civic League, 1912), 71.

Chapter 4

1. Raymond M. Weinstein, "Disneyland and Coney Island: Reflections on the Evolution of the Modern Amusement Park," *Journal of Popular Culture* 1 (Summer 1992), 131.
2. Richard E. Snow and David E. Wright, "Coney Island: A Case Study in Popular Culture and Technical Change," *Journal of Popular Culture* 9 (1976), 966.
3. Neil Harris, *The Artist in American Society* (New York: George Braziller, 1966), 28.
4. John F. Kasson, *Amusing the Million*, 37.
5. *New York Times*, May 17, 1903.
6. *Scientific American*, July 11, 1885.
7. *New York Times*, April 1, 1887.
8. Gates v. New York Recorder Co., 156 N.Y. 228, 230 (1898).
9. *Ibid.*
10. *Ibid.*
11. *Scientific American* (July 19, 1879).
12. Gary Kyriazi, *The Great American Amusement Parks: A Pictorial History* (Secaucus, NJ: Citadel Press, 1976), 17–18.
13. Stephen F. Weinstein, *The Nickel Empire*, 3.
14. *Scientific American* (September 22, 1900).
15. Oliver Pilat, and Jo Ranson, *Sodom by the Sea*, 114, 117.
16. Edo McCullough, *Good Old Coney Island*, 288–289.
17. Sand and seawater, to the tourists.
18. Oliver Pilat, and Jo Ranson, *Sodom by the Sea*, 133.
19. *Ibid.*, 295.
20. LeRoy Ashby, *With Amusement for All: A History of American Popular Culture Since 1830* (Lexington: The University Press of Kentucky, 2006), 136.
21. *Brooklyn Daily Eagle*, March 29, 1897.
22. Oliver Pilat, and Jo Ranson, *Sodom by the Sea*, 229.
23. http://www.westland.net/coneyisland/articles/steeplechase1.htm, 5.
24. Peter Lyon, "The Master Showman of Coney Island," *American Heritage*, Vol. 9, Issue 4 (June, 1958).
25. John S. Berman, *Coney Island* (New York: Barnes & Noble, 2003), 19.
26. Charles Belmont Davis, "The Renaissance of Coney," *The Outing Magazine*, Vol. XLVIII, No. 5 (August 1906), 519.
27. John Kasson, *Amusing the Million*, 59.
28. *Brooklyn Daily Eagle*, May 19, 1907.
29. Michael Immerso, *Coney Island: The People's Playground*, 77.
30. Edo McCullough, *Good Old Coney Island*, 202–203.

31. Gary Kyriazi, *The Great American Amusement Parks*, 89.
32. Kevin Baker, *Dreamland* (New York: Harper Perennial, 2006), 82–83.
33. John F. Kasson, *Amusing the Million*, 16.
34. Oliver Pilat, and Jo Ranson, *Sodom by the Sea*, 139.
35. Edwin Slosson, "Amusement Business," *Independent* 57 (July 21, 1904), 136.
36. *New York World*, September 15, 1907.
37. Reginald Wright Kauffmann, "Why Is Coney?" *Hampton's Magazine*, August 1909.
38. Frederic Thompson, "Amusing the Million," *Everybody's Magazine* 19, September 1908.
39. Michael Immerso, *Coney Island: The People's Playground*, 77–78.
40. James Onorato was Steeplechase's second, and final, general manager. He held the office from 1928, when he was nineteen, until the park closed in 1964.
41. Brief for the Appellant, Reinzi v. Tilyou, 252 N.Y. 97 (1929), 19.
42. *Ibid.*, 217.
43. Murphy v. Steeplechase Amusement Co., 21–22.
44. Michael Onorato, ed., *The Diary of James J. Ororato, 1997*, 337.
45. *Ibid.*
46. http://www.westland.net/coneyisland/articles/steeplechase2.htm.
47. *Ibid.*, 326.
48. *Ibid.*, 182.
49. *Ibid.* 74–76.

Chapter 5

1. This is a reference to the 1893 Chicago World's Fair, which contained Beaux-Arts buildings and others that featured classical Greek and Roman designs.
2. John S. Berman, *Coney Island* (New York: Barnes & Noble, 2003), 34.
3. *Brooklyn Daily Eagle*, May 17, 1904.
4. *New York Times*, May 17, 1904.
5. Judith Adams, *The American Amusement Park Industry: A History of Technology and Thrills* (New York: Twayne, 1991), 40.
6. Michael Immerso, *Coney Island: The People's Playground*, 64.
7. *New York Times*, May 17, 1904.
8. *Luna Park Souvenir and Programme Book*.
9. *Brooklyn Citizen*, May 17, 1903.
10. *New York Times*, February 6, 1907.
11. Frederic Thompson, "Amusing the Million," *Everybody's Magazine*, Vol. XIX (September 1908), 385.
12. Michael Immerso, *Coney Island: The People's Playground*, 66–68.
13. Rem Koolhaus, *Delirious New York: A Retroactive Manifesto for Manhattan* (New York: Monacelli Press, 1994), 29–30.
14. Albert Bigelow Paine, "The New Coney Island," *Scribner's Magazine* 68 (August 1904), 535.
15. Frederic Thompson, "Amusing the Million," *Everybody's Magazine* 19 (September 1908), 378.
16. Frederic Thompson, "Amusing People," *Metropolitan* 32 (August 1910), 609.
17. "Mechanical Joys of Coney Island," *Scientific American* 99 (August 15, 1908), 108–110.
18. Frederic Thompson, "Amusing People," 605.

Notes. Chapter 5

19. Paul Barber, *Vampires, Burial, and Death: Folklore and Reality* (New Haven: Yale University Press, 1988), 98–99.
20. Edgar Allan Poe, "The Premature Burial," in *Collected Works of Edgar Allan Poe* (Cambridge, MA: Harvard University Press, 1988), 954–955.
21. The description of "Night and Morning" appears in an untitled clipping, dated May 18, 1907, in the Thompson clipping file, New York Public Library.
22. Elmer Blaney Harris, "The Day of Rest at Coney Island," *Everybody's Magazine*, July 8, 1908, 33–34.
23. Ibid.
24. *Brooklyn Daily Eagle*, July 28, 1907.
25. Promotional brochure, *Luna Park: The Heart of Coney Island* (1903), in the collection of the Brooklyn Historical Society.
26. "Toy Makers for Grown-Ups," *New York Journal*, May 5, 1916.
27. David Nasaw, *Going Out*, 4–5, 43–46.
28. *Brooklyn Daily Eagle*, August 5, 1897.
29. David Nasaw, *Going Out*, 88.
30. LeRoy Ashby, *With Amusement for All*, 138.
31. Judith Adams, *The American Amusement Park Industry*, p.121.
32. *New York Times*, May 16, 1904.
33. Michael Immerso, *Coney Island*, 71.
34. Oliver Pilat and Jo Ranson, *Sodom by the Sea*, 151.
35. Woody Register, *The Kid of Coney Island: Fred Thompson and the Rise of American Amusements* (New York: Oxford University Press, 2001), 141.
36. *Brooklyn Daily Eagle*, July 13, 1907.
37. *Ibid.*, May 8, 1904.
38. Ad in the *Brooklyn Daily Eagle*, May 8, 1904.
39. A famous architect of the time.
40. *Brooklyn Daily Eagle*, May 15, 1904.
41. Stephen F. Weinstein, *The Nickel Empire*, 220–223.
42. Bart Ferree, "The New Popular Resort Architecture, Dreamland, Coney Island," *Architects' and Builders' Magazine* 36 (August 1904), 499.
43. Rem Koolhass, *Delirious New York*, 55.
44. *Scientific American*, July 5, 1905, 29–30.
45. *New York Times*, May 8, 1904.
46. Dumont was a Brazilian who flew the first heavier-than-air ship in Europe.
47. *Scientific American*, July 5, 1905, 29–30.
48. Gary S. Cross, and John K. Walton, *The Playful Crowd: Pleasure Places in the Twentieth Century* (New York: Columbia University Press, 2005), 40–45.
49. *New York Times*, May 15, 1904.
50. Frederic Thompson, "Amusing People," 607
51. Reginald Wright Kauffman, "Why Is Coney?," *Hampton's Magazine*, 220–221.
52. *New York Times*, May 6, 1906.
53. *Brooklyn Daily Eagle*, May 9, 1907.
54. Michael Immerso, *Coney Island*, 73–74.
55. "The Annual Awakening of the Only Coney Island," *New York Times*, May 6, 1906.
56. *New York Times*, July 21, 1868.
57. Kathy Peiss, *Cheap Amusements*, 129.
58. Frederic Thompson, "Summer Show," *The Independent* 62 (June 1907).
59. Albert Bigelow Paine, "The New Coney Island," *Century Magazine* 68 (1904).
60. Kathy Peiss, *Cheap Amusements*, 65.

61. Christine Frieman, *Redefining Respectability: Women and Coney Island at the Turn of the Century*, M.A. Thesis, Sarah Lawrence College, May 2010.
62. "The Looker-On," *Brooklyn Life*, June 6, 1903, 4.
63. *Brooklyn Life Magazine* chronicled the activities of Brooklyn's upper crust, from 1890 to 1931.
64. "Summer Amusements," and the "Looker-On," *Brooklyn Life*, May 28, 1904; June 18, 25, 1904; July 9, 16, 30, 1904; August 13, 1904.
65. "Summer Amusements," *Brooklyn Life*, July 30, 1904.
66. "The Looker On," *Brooklyn Life*, July 30, 1904.
67. Christine Frieman, *Redefining Respectability: Women and Coney Island at the Turn of the Century*, 2010 dissertation, 26–27.
68. John F. Kasson, *Amusing the Million*, 22–23.
69. Frederic Thompson, "Amusement Architecture," *Architectural Review*, July 16, 1909, 89.
70. The critic and writer Lindsay Denison provided an example of ballyhoo. As the barker is talking, "as if by accident the curtain [to his exhibit] is drawn aside, exposing to view a bit of the stage and a glimpse of the performers, "Look! Look!" he yells. "Quick! See! Get a Free Look! There! There, before the curtain closes! It won't cost you a cent if you hurry!" There is a rush of half indifferent idlers [who] suddenly become interested. The crowd outside the speaker's sphere of influence catches the movement and in a moment he has an audience." Lindsay Denison, "The Biggest Playground in the World," *Munsey's Magazine*, August 1905, 565.
71. Frederic Thompson, "Amusement Architecture," 89.
72. Michele H. Bogart, "Barking Architecture: The Sculpture of Coney Island," *Smithsonian Studies in America Art*, Vol. 2, No. 1 (Winter 1988), 3–17.

Chapter 6

1. http:www.westland.net/coneyisland/articles/steeplechase2.htm.
2. *Brooklyn Daily Eagle*, January 14, 1915.
3. Oliver Pilat, and Jo Ranson, *Sodom by the Sea*, 316.
4. Federico Garcia Lorca, "Landscape of the Vomiting Multitude (Coney Island Dusk)," in *Poet in New York* (New York: Grove Press, 1955), 39.
5. Sir Percival Philips, "Coney Island the Incredible," *London Daily Mail*, August 19, 1929.
6. James Huneker, *New Cosmopolis*, 154.
7. *New York Times*, July 16, 1866.
8. *Journal of Women's History* (Winter 2001), 47–88.
9. Henry Curtis, *The Play Movement and Its Significance* (New York: Cornell University, 1917), 60–65.
10. O. Henry. "The Greater Coney Island," in *Sixes and Sevens* (Garden City: Doubleday, 1919), 221–223.
11. Kathy Peiss, *Cheap Amusements*, 109.
12. The Coney Island Mardi Gras, based on the one in New Orleans, was an end-of-summer final fling, first organized in 1903, complete with a parade and floats. It was not a religious celebration, but, rather, a secular one created and promoted by the island's businessmen.
13. "Circus and Museum Freaks, Curiosities of Pathology," *Scientific America Supplement* 65, April 4, 1908, 222.
14. Hanna Lees, "Side Show Diagnosis," *Colliers* 99 (1937), 224.
15. Bertram Reinitz, "Coney Enters the Steel Age," *New York Times*, June 16, 1929.

16. Edouard Herriot, "America, the Land of Joy," *New York Times*, August 17, 1924.
17. Charles Denson, *Wild Ride! A Coney Island Roller Coaster Family* (Berkeley: Dreamland Press, 2007), 67.

Chapter 7

1. Robert Caro, *The Power Broker: Robert Moses and the Fall of New York* (New York: Vintage Books, 1975), 318–319.
2. *Ibid.*, 335.
3. *Ibid.*, 687.
4. *Ibid.*, 335.
5. *New York Times*, June 30, 1934.
6. Michael Immerso, *Coney Island*, 159–160.
7. New York City Parks Department, *The Improvement of Coney Island* (New York: City of New York, 1939), 1–3.
8. *New York Times*, December 8, 1937, 24.
9. *Ibid.*
10. *New York Times*, July 13, 1899, 14.
11. Letter from Robert Moses to Mayor Fiorello LaGuardia, published in *The Improvement of Coney Island, Rockaway, and South Beaches* (New York: Department of Parks, 1937), 3–8.
12. *Annual Report of the Board of Railroad Commissioners of the State of New York* (Albany, NY, 1886), 296–297.
13. Reuben Lazarues, a LaGuardia aide who was the city's official representative in Albany.
14. Robert Caro, *The Power Broker: Robert Moses and the Fall of New York* (New York: Vintage Books, 1975), 463.
15. *New York Times*, August 30, 1936.
16. *Ibid.*, July 18, 1939.
17. *Ibid.*, July 25, 1939.
18. Oliver Pilat, and Jo Ranson, *Sodom by the Sea*, 334.
19. Henry B. Liberman, "Nickel Empire," *New York Times*, July 16, 1939, 89.
20. Oliver Pilat, and Jo Ranson, *Sodom by the Sea*, 334.
21. *New York Times*, April 6, 1953, 1.
22. Charles Denson, *Coney Island: Lost and Found* (Berkeley: Ten Speed Press, 2002), 67.
23. Charles Denson, *Wild Ride! A Coney Island Coaster Family*, 77–83.
24. *Ibid.* 67–76.
25. Stephen Weinstein, *The Nickel Empire*, 290–296.
26. Charles Denson, *Coney Island: Lost and Found*, 135.
27. *New York Times*, November 30, 1963.
28. Richard Le Gallienne, "Human Need of Coney Island," *Cosmopolitan* 39 (May–October 1905).

Bibliography

Adams, Judith. *The American Amusement Park Industry: A History of Technology and Thrills*. New York: Twayne, 1991.
Annual Report of the Board of Railroad Commissioners of the State of New York. Albany, New York, 1886.
Ashby, LeRoy. *With Amusement for All: A History of America Popular Culture Since 1830*. Lexington: University Press of Kentucky, 2005.
Baker, Kevin. *Dreamland*. New York: Harper Perennial, 2006.
Barber, Paul. *Vampires, Burial, and Death: Folklore and Reality*. New Haven: Yale University Press, 1988.
Barnes, Djuna. *Nightwood*. New York: New Directions, 1914.
Berman, John S. *Coney Island*. New York: Barnes & Noble, 2003.
Bogart, Michele H. "Barking Architecture, the Sculpture of Coney Island." *Smithsonian Studies in American Art*, Vol. 2, No. 1 (Winter 1988).
Caro, Robert. *The Power Broker: Robert Moses and the Fall of New York*. New York: Vintage Books, 1975.
Carryl, Guy Wetmore, "Marvelous Coney Island." *Munsey's Magazine*, September 1901.
Coney Island and the Jews. New York: G. W. Carlton, 1879.
Creedmoor, Walter. "The Real Coney Island." *Munsey's Magazine*, August 23, 1899.
Cross, Gary S. "Crowds and Leisure: Thinking Comparatively Across the 20th Century." *Journal of Social History*, Vol. 39, No. 3 (Spring 2006).
____, and John K. Walton. *The Playful Crowd: Pleasure Places in the Twentieth Century*. New York: Columbia University Press, 2005.
Cudahy, Brian J. *How We Got to Coney Island: The Development of Mass Transportation in Brooklyn and Kings County*. New York: Fordham University Press, 2002.
Curtis, Henry. *The Play Movement and Its Significance*. New York: Cornell University, 1917.
Davis, Charles Belmont. "The Renaissance of Coney." *The Outing Magazine*, Vol. XLVIII, No. 5 (August 1906).
Denison, Lindsay. "The Biggest Playground in the World," *Munsey's Magazine*, August 1905.
Denson, Charles. *Coney Island: Lost and Found*. Berkeley: Ten Speed Press, 2002.
____. *Wild Ride! A Coney Island Roller Coaster Family*. Berkeley: Dreamland Press.
Ferry, Bart. "The New Popular Resort Architecture, Dreamland, Coney Island." *Architects and Builders Magazine* 36 (August 1904).
Frieman, Christine. *Redefining Respectability: Woman and Coney Island at the Turn of the Century*. M. A. Thesis, Sarah Lawrence College, 2010.

Bibliography

Hardland, Robert O. *The Vice Bondage of a Great City, or the Wickedest City in the World*. Chicago: Young People's Civic League, 1912.

Harper's New Monthly Magazine, Vol. 57, Issue 341 (October, 1878).

Harris, Neil. *The Artist in American Society*. New York: George Braziller, 1966.

Heard, Jason. "Reforming the Sodom by the Sea: Coney Island Prizefighting and Class Stratification." www.columbia.edu/cu/cjas/print/coneyisland_prizefighting.pdf.

Henry, O. "The Greater Coney Island." *Sixes and Sevens*. Garden City: Doubleday, 1919.

Hewitt, William Judkins, "The Amusement Park." *Billboard*, July 25, 1907.

Huneker, James. *New Cosmopolis: A Book of Images: Intimate New York*. New York: Charles Scribner's Sons, 1915.

Immerso, Michael. *Coney Island, The People's Playground*. New Brunswick: Rutgers University Press, 2002.

The Improvement of Coney Island, Rockaway and South Beach, New York. Department of Parks, 1937.

Kasson, John F. *Amusing the Million: Coney Island at the Turn of the Century*. New York: Hill & Wang, 1978.

Kauffman, Reginald Wright. "Why Is Coney?" *Hampton's Magazine*, August 1909.

Koolhaas, Rem. *Delirious New York: A Retroactive Manifesto for Manhattan*. New York: Monacelli Press, 1994.

Le Galliene, Richard. "Human Need of Coney Island." *Cosmopolitan Magazine*, Vol. 30, (May–October 1905).

"The Looker-on." *Brooklyn Life*, June 6, 1903.

Lorca, Federico Garcia. *Poet in New York*. New York: Grove Press, 1955.

Lyon, Peter. "The Master Showman of Coney Island." *American Heritage*, Vol. 9, Issue 4 (June 1958).

Marti, Jose, ed. "Two Views of Coney Island." *Inside the Monster: Writings on the U.S. and American Imperialism*. New York: Monthly Review, 1975.

McCullough, Edo. *Good Old Coney Island*. New York: Charles Scribner's Sons, 1957.

McKennon, Joe. *A Pictorial History of the America Carnival*, Vol. 2. Sarasota, FL: Carnival Publishers of Sarasota, 1972.

Mohun, Arwen P. "Designed for Thrills and Safety: Amusement Parks and the Commodification of Risk, 1880–1928," *Journal of Design History* Vol. 14, No. 4, Technology and the Body (2001).

Nasaw, David. *Going Out: The Rise and Fall of Public Amusements*. New York: Basic Books, 1993.

Neal, Robert Wilson. "New York's City of Play." *The World Today*, June 1–December 1, 1906.

New York City Parks Department: The Improvement of Coney Island. New York: City of New York, 1939.

"New York in Summer." *Harper's New Monthly Magazine*, Vol. 57, Issue 341 (October 1878).

Nickell, Joe. *Secrets of the Sideshow*. Lexington: University Press of Kentucky, 2005.

Onorato, Michael, ed. The Diary of James J. Onorato. Pacific Rim Books, 1997.

Peiss, Kathy. *Cheap Amusements: Working Women and Leisure in Turn of the Century New York*. Philadelphia: Temple University Press, 1986.

Percy, Townsend. *Percy's Pocket Dictionary of Coney Island*. New York: Leypoldt, 1880.

Phelips, Sir Perceval. "Coney Island the Incredible," *London Daily Mail*, August 19, 1929.

Pilat, Oliver, and Jo Ranson. *Sodom by the Sea: An Affectionate History of Coney Island*. Garden City, NY: Doubleday, 1941.

Poe, Edgar Allan. "The Premature Burial." *Collected Works of Edgar Allan Poe.* Cambridge, MA: Harvard University Press, 1988.
Rabinovitz, Lauren. *Electric Dreamland: Amusement Parks, Movies, and American Modernity.* New York: Columbia University Press, 2012.
____. *For the Love of Pleasure: Women, Movies, and Culture in Turn of the Century Chicago.* New Brunswick: Rutgers University Press, 1998.
Ralph, Julian. "Coney Island." *Scribner's Magazine* XX (July 1896).
Register, Woody. *The Kid of Coney Island: Fred Thompson and the Rise of American Amusements.* New York: Oxford University Press, 2001.
Rydell, Robert W, and Bob Kroes. *Buffalo Bill in Bologna: The Americanization of the World, 1869–1922.* University of Chicago Press, 2005.
Shanly, Charles Dawson. "Coney Island." *The Atlantic Monthly*, Vol. 0034, Issue 203 (September 1874).
Slosson, Edwin. "Amusement Business." *The Independent*, July 21, 1904.
Snow, Richard E., and David E. Wright. "Coney Island: A Case Study in Popular Culture and Technical Change." *Journal of Popular Culture* 9 (1976).
Sterngass, Jon. *First Resorts: Pursuing Pleasure at Saratoga Springs, Newport and Coney Island.* Baltimore: Johns Hopkins Press, 2001.
Still, Bayar. *Mirror for Gotham: New York as Seen by Contemporaries From Dutch Days to the Present.* New York University Press, 1956.
Stockwell, Austin Parsons, and William H. Stillwell. "History of the Town of Gravesend, New York." Brooklyn, New York, 1884.
Strong, George Templeton. *Diary.* New York: Macmillan, 1852.
Tarbell, Ida. *New Ideals in Business: An Account of Their Practice and Their Side Effects Upon Men and Profits.* New York: Macmillan, 1916.
Thompson, Frederic. "Amusement Architecture." *Architectural Review*, July 16, 1909.
____. "Amusing the Million." *Everybody's Magazine* 19 (September 1908).
"To Coney Island." *Scribner's Monthly*, Vol. 20, Issue 3 (July 1880).
Waller, James Blaine. *Fifty Years of Rapid Transit.* New York: Law Printing, 1918.
Weinstein, Raymond M. "Dreamland and Coney Island: Reflections on the Evolution of the Modern Amusement Park," *Journal of Popular Culture* 9 (1976).
Weinstein, Stephen F. *The Nickel Empire: Seaside Resorts in the United States.* PhD dissertation, Columbia University, 1984.

Newspapers and Magazines

Architects and Builders Magazine
Architectural Review
The Atlantic Monthly
Brighton Beach Daily Music Programme
Brooklyn Citizen
Brooklyn Daily Eagle
Brooklyn Life
The Brooklyn Union
Catholic Mirror
Century Magazine
Colliers
The Coney Island Sun
Cosmopolitan
Everybody's Magazine
Frank Leslie's Illustrated Newspaper

Bibliography

Hampton's Magazine
Harper's New Monthly Magazine
Illustrated Christian Weekly
The Independent
The Irish-American
Journal of Women's History
Kings County Rural and Brighton Gazette
Kings County Rural Gazette
London Daily Mail
Long Island Star
The Manufacturer and Builder
Metropolitan
Munsey's Magazine
National Police Gazette
New Cosmopolis
New York Commercial Advertiser
New York Evening Mail
New York Evening Post
New York Herald
New York Morning Telegraph
New York Times
New York Tribune
New York World
Philadelphia Ledger
Rockland County Messenger
Scientific American
Scribner's Monthly
Smithsonian Studies in American Art
The Times of London
The World Today

Index

Alcoke, Charles 70
amusement park, history 1
aquariums 68, 174
Astroland 177
automobile 163–164

Bacon Investigating Committee 57
"Bagdad by the Sea" 116
Ball Park Movies 171
Barnum, Phineas T. 8
Bauer, Paul 16, 53–55, 83
Beacon Tower 122
Beame, Abe 173
Behr mono-rail system 27
Beicher, Lena 70
Belmont, August, Jr. 20
Belmont Racetrack 20
Bennett, James Gordon 8
Berlin, Irving 77
Bloomberg, Michael 178
boardwalk 139, 166
Bonsignore, John 173
the Bowery 33–34, 62–63
Boyton, Paul 91
Boyton Bicycle Railroad 26
Brady, "Diamond Jim" 20
Brady, William A. 109
Brighton Beach 37
Brighton Beach Amusement Park 78, 109
Brighton Beach Bathing Pavilion and Ocean Pier 38
Brighton Beach Baths 39
Brighton Beach Hotel 38
Brighton Beach Racing Association 20, 39
Brighton Pier and Navigation Company 49

Brooklyn, Bath, and Coney Island Railroad (Dummy Road) 23, 55
Brooklyn City Railroad Company 22
Brooklyn Elevated Railway Company (Bruff enterprise) 49
Brooklyn, Flatbush, and Coney Island Railroad 25
Brooklyn Rapid Transit Company 78

Cables Hotel 47
Cantor, Eddie 77
Capehart hearings 173
Captive Balloon 90
Caro, Robert 164, 168
Carryl, Guy Wetmore 72–73
Cassatt, A.J. 20
"Caterers to the Millions" 52
Central Amusement International 179
Centrifuge Railway 69
Chase Through the Clouds Coaster 109
children 141–142
City Beautiful 122, 134–135
classes 132–134, 147–148
Clay, Henry 8
Cleveland, Grover 34
Cody, William "Wild Bill" 39
Coler, Bird S. 167
Collier, Barron 148–150
communing 14
Coney Island and Brooklyn Railroad 22
Coney Island: beginning 3; and Blacks 47; by class 41; influence of 82; population 139
Coney Island Development Corporation 178
Coney Island House 8

197

Index

Coney Island Jockey Club 20
Coney Island Plank Road 22
Coney Island Point 30
Coney Island, Sheepshead Bay and Ocean Avenue Railway 27
Corben, Austin 31–32, 41, 50; and the Jews 44–47
Crane, Stephen 86–87
crime 162
Cudahy, Brian, Jr. 168
Culver, Andrew 47–51

De L'Epee, Raymond 19
Denson, Charles 151–152
Dewitt, William C. 41
Doctor Durant 13
Dreamland (novel) 103–104
Dreamland Park 121–127
"dripped" or "drippers" 147–148
Dundy, Skip 110
Durante, Jimmy 77
Dutch settlers 7–8
Duyckinch, Evert 9

East River Bridge and Coney Island Steam Transit Company 49
Eddy and Harts Pavilion 13
Edison, Thomas 88
electricity 87–88
Elephant Hotel 88–89
Engelmann, William 31, 37–43

Falconer, John 9
Feltman, Charles 51–52, 139
ferris wheel 94
fire (Bowery) 103
Flip Flap Roller Coaster 91
freaks 143
Fresh Air Fund 141
Friede, Samuel 102
Furey, Robert 31

Gaites, "Bet-a-Million" 20
gambling 12, 21–22, 68, 83
Germans 80–81
Gignoux, Regis 9
Giuliani, Rudy 177
Glendale and East River Railroad 43
Globe Tower 102
Godfrey, Arthur 160
Gravesend 7, 63
Gravesend and Coney Island Road and Bridge Company 8–9
The Great Boer War Spectacular 109

Gumpertz, Samuel 66–67, 127
the Gut 76–77, 176

Halleck, Fritz-Green 8
Harland, Robert 85
Harrison, Benjamin 35
Herriot, Edward (French prime minister) 139
horse racing 20–22
Hotel Brighton 40
Houston, Sam 8
human roulette wheel 101
Huneker, James 141

Immerso, Michael 140
immigrants 80, 139
insanitarium 103–105
"inside talker" or "lecturer" 66
Iron Pier 29
Iron Steamboat Company 25, 28–29
Irving, Washington 8
Ives Pool Bill 83

Jarvis, Arthur 150
Jim Crow 132

Kaleidoscope Tower 112
Kasson, John 65, 75, 82
Kirby, J. Mason 88

LaGuardia, Fiorello 165, 167
Leap Frog Railway 125
Le Gallienne, Richard 64–65, 179
Lind, Jenny 8
Lindenbaum, Abraham 173
Lindsay Administration 177
Long Island Railroad 43
Loop the Loop 70–71
Lopez, Vincent 77
Lorca, Federico Garcia 140
Luna Park 110–121, 148–151, 158, 169
Luna Park (2009) 179

Macready, William 8
Man, Alrick 60, 83
Manhattan Beach 41–42
Manhattan Beach Hotel 42–43
Marine Railway 26
Matthews, Cornelius 8
Mauch Chunk Railway 69–70
McKane, John Y. 30–37, 48, 51, 53, 55–59, 63, 93
McLaughlin, Hugh 34
Melville, Herman 8–9

Index

Middle Division 37
Moses, Robert 163–172, 174
movies 76
Municipal Bathhouse 137, 143
Mussolini, Benito 169

Nathan's 139
Naushon (steamboat) 14
Neal, Robert Wilson 63–64
New Iron Pier 25
New York and Coney Island Railroad 24
New York and Manhattan Beach Railroad 25
New York and Sea Beach Railroad 25
New York City Housing Authority 174
New York City Planning Commission 171
New York Zoological Society 174
Nickle Empire 137
"Night and Morning" (illusion) 117–118
Norton, "Thunderbolt" Michael 12, 30
Norton's Point 10–12
Norwalk (steamboat) 10, 25, 28

Ocean Parkway 20, 28
Ocean Pavilion 51
Ocean View Walk (The Bowery) 55
Oceanic Hotel 10
Old Mill (boat ride) 91–92
Olmstead, Frederick Law 135
Onorato, James 106, 159–160
Onorato, Michael 107
Oriental Hotel 44
Oriental Scenic Railway 71

Paine, Albert Bigelow 132
Parachute Drop 155–157
Pavilion of Fun 153
Peiss, Kathy 142
Pelham Park and City Island Railroad 27
Philips, Sir Percival 140–141
Pikes Peak Scenic Railway 71–72
Pinkerton Detectives 44
"Pioneer of Coney Island" 40
Poe, Edgar Allan 8–9
The Poe Log 9
Point Comfort Hotel 12
Poverty Zone 175
prizefighting 18–20
Prospect Park and Coney Island Railroad 24, 47

Racing Derby Carousel 152–153
Ralph, Julian 18
Ravenhall, Peter 13
reformers 141, 144
Reigelmann Boardwalk 153
religion 80
Reynolds, William 121
Rogers, Will 109
roller coasters 68–74, 144–147
Roltair, Henry 129
Russian Ice Slide 68–69

Sanger, Adolph L. 45
Saratoga Racetrack 20
Saturday half-holiday 78–79
Sawyer Observatory 51
Sea Lion Park 91
Seagate 60–62
Serpentine Railway 70
Shanley, Charles 17
Shell Road 8
Shoot the Chutes (also Chute the Chutes) 92, 105
Sousa, John Philip 78
spectacles 74–75
"staff" 110
Steeplechase Park 93–108, 137–138, 152–162, 176; court cases 106–108; as example of amusement park 2; fire 102–103, 154–155; floods 159, 161; horse racing rides 95–96; injuries and deaths 105–108; polio 158; rides 97–98; season bathing 158; World War II 157–158
Still, Bayrd 15
Stillwell, William 38, 40
Strong, George Templeton 17
Strong, James H. 155
subway 138, 163
Surf House 13
Surf Theatre 93
Sutherland, Kenneth F. 37
Switchback Railway 70
Sylvan steamboats 28

Tallman, David 7
Talmage, the Rev. T. DeWitt 83–84
ten-in-one 65–66
Terhune, John 7
Thompson, Frederick 110, 135, 148
Thompson, L.A. 70–72
Thor Equities 178
Tilyou, Edward 152
Tilyou, George 35, 56, 93, 131, 152

199

Index

Tilyou, Marie 158, 160–162, 176
Tilyou, Peter 13, 55–57
Tilyou's Real Estate Telephone 93–94
Topsy (elephant) 88
Travers, William R. 20
A Trip to the Moon 96
Trump, Fred 151, 162, 172–174
Tweed "Boss" 30–31

Vanderbilt, Commodore 10
Vanderveer, Lucy 53
Vanderveer, William 53
Van Kannel, Theophilus 118
vice 89–90

visitor's guide to the City of New York, 1899 17–18

Wagner, Robert 173
Webster, Daniel 8
West Brighton Beach (Brighton Beach) Hotel 53
Wheatly, William 12
Whitman, Walt 8
women 98–100
Wyckoff, John 9

Ziz (roller coaster) 52

www.ingramcontent.com/pod-product-compliance
Ingram Content Group UK Ltd.
Pitfield, Milton Keynes, MK11 3LW, UK
UKHW042006140426
5217IPUK00015B/1021